THE NEW FOLGER LIBRARY SHAKESPEARE

Designed to make Shakespeare's great plays available to all readers, the New Folger Library edition of Shakespeare's plays provides accurate texts in modern spelling and punctuation, as well as scene-by-scene action summaries, full explanatory notes, many pictures clarifying Shakespeare's language, and notes recording all significant departures from the early printed versions. Each play is prefaced by a brief introduction, by a guide to reading Shakespeare's language, and by accounts of his life and theater. Each play is followed by an annotated list of further readings and by a "Modern Perspective" written by an expert on that particular play.

Barbara A. Mowat was Director of Research *emerita* at the Folger Shakespeare Library, Consulting Editor of *Shakespeare Quarterly*, and author of *The Dramaturgy of Shakespeare's Romances* and of essays on Shakespeare's plays and their editing.

Paul Werstine is Professor of English at the Graduate School and at King's University College at Western University. He is a general editor of the New Variorum Shakespeare and author of *Early Modern Playhouse Manuscripts and the Editing of Shakespeare* and of many papers and articles on the printing and editing of Shakespeare's plays.

The Folger Shakespeare Library

The Folger Shakespeare Library in Washington, D.C., a privately funded research library dedicated to Shakespeare and the civilization of early modern Europe, was founded in 1932 by Henry Clay and Emily Jordan Folger, and incorporated as part of Amherst College in Amherst, Massachusetts, one of the nation's oldest liberal arts colleges, from which Henry Folger had graduated in 1879. In addition to its role as the world's preeminent Shakespeare collection and its emergence as a leading center for Renaissance studies, the Folger Shakespeare Library offers a wide array of cultural and educational programs and services for the general public.

EDITORS

BARBARA A. MOWAT
Former Director of Research emerita
Folger Shakespeare Library

PAUL WERSTINE
Professor of English
King's University College
at Western University, Canada

Folger SHAKESPEARE LIBRARY

Much Ado About Nothing

By
WILLIAM SHAKESPEARE

An Updated Edition

Edited by Barbara A. Mowat
and Paul Werstine

Simon & Schuster Paperbacks
New York London Toronto Sydney New Delhi

Simon & Schuster Paperbacks
An Imprint of Simon & Schuster, Inc.
1230 Avenue of the Americas
New York, NY 10020

This Simon & Schuster paperback edition November 2018

SIMON & SCHUSTER PAPERBACKS and colophon are registered trademarks of Simon & Schuster, Inc.

For information about special discounts for bulk purchases, please contact Simon & Schuster Special Sales at 1-866-506-1949 or business@simonandschuster.com.

The Simon & Schuster Speakers Bureau can bring authors to your live event. For more information or to book an event, contact the Simon & Schuster Speakers Bureau at 1-866-248-3049 or visit our website at www.simonspeakers.com.

Manufactured in the United States of America

53

ISBN: 978-0-7434-8275-2
ISBN: 978-1-4767-8855-5 (ebook)

From the Director of the Folger Shakespeare Library

It is hard to imagine a world without Shakespeare. Since their composition more than four hundred years ago, Shakespeare's plays and poems have traveled the globe, inviting those who see and read his works to make them their own.

Readers of the New Folger Editions are part of this ongoing process of "taking up Shakespeare," finding our own thoughts and feelings in language that strikes us as old or unusual and, for that very reason, new. We still struggle to keep up with a writer who could think a mile a minute, whose words paint pictures that shift like clouds. These expertly edited texts, presented here with accompanying explanatory notes and up-to-date critical essays, are distinctive because of what they do: they allow readers not simply to keep up, but to engage deeply with a writer whose works invite us to think, and think again.

These New Folger Editions of Shakespeare's plays are also special because of where they come from. The Folger Shakespeare Library in Washington, D.C., where the Editions are produced, is the single greatest documentary source of Shakespeare's works. An unparalleled collection of early modern books, manuscripts, and artwork connected to Shakespeare, the Folger's holdings have been consulted extensively in the preparation of these texts. The Editions also reflect the expertise gained through the regular performance of Shakespeare's works in the Folger's Elizabethan Theater.

I want to express my deep thanks to editors Barbara Mowat and Paul Werstine for creating these indispensable editions of Shakespeare's works, which incorporate the best of textual scholarship with a richness of commentary that is both inspired and engaging. Readers who want to know more about Shakespeare and his plays can follow the paths these distinguished scholars have tread by visiting the Folger itself, where a range of physical and digital resources (available online) exist to supplement the material in these texts. I commend to you these words, and hope that they inspire.

Michael Witmore
Director, Folger Shakespeare Library

Contents

Editors' Preface   *ix*

Shakespeare's *Much Ado About Nothing*   *xiii*

Reading Shakespeare's Language:
    Much Ado About Nothing   *xvii*

Shakespeare's Life   *xxvii*

Shakespeare's Theater   *xxxvii*

The Publication of Shakespeare's Plays   *xlvii*

An Introduction to This Text   *li*

Much Ado About Nothing
    Text of the Play with Commentary   *1*

Longer Notes   *199*

Textual Notes   *205*

Much Ado About Nothing: A Modern
    Perspective by Gail Kern Paster   *213*

Further Reading   *231*

Key to Famous Lines and Phrases   *291*

Editors' Preface

In recent years, ways of dealing with Shakespeare's texts and with the interpretation of his plays have been undergoing significant change. This edition, while retaining many of the features that have always made the Folger Shakespeare so attractive to the general reader, at the same time reflects these current ways of thinking about Shakespeare. For example, modern readers, actors, and teachers have become interested in the differences between, on the one hand, the early forms in which Shakespeare's plays were first published and, on the other hand, the forms in which editors through the centuries have presented them. In response to this interest, we have based our edition on what we consider the best early printed version of a particular play (explaining our rationale in a section called "An Introduction to This Text") and have marked our changes in the text—unobtrusively, we hope, but in such a way that the curious reader can be aware that a change has been made and can consult the "Textual Notes" to discover what appeared in the early printed version.

Current ways of looking at the plays are reflected in our brief prefaces, in many of the commentary notes, in the annotated lists of "Further Reading," and especially in each play's "Modern Perspective," an essay written by an outstanding scholar who brings to the reader his or her fresh assessment of the play in the light of today's interests and concerns.

As in the Folger Library General Reader's Shakespeare, which this edition replaces, we include explanatory notes designed to help make Shakespeare's language clearer to a modern reader, and we place the notes on the page facing the text that they explain. We also follow the earlier edition in including illustrations—of objects, of clothing, of mythological figures—from books and manuscripts in the Folger Library collection. We provide fresh accounts of the life of Shakespeare, of the publishing of his plays, and of the theaters in which his plays were performed, as well as an introduction to the text itself. We also include a section called "Reading Shakespeare's Language," in which we try to help readers learn to "break the code" of Elizabethan poetic language.

For each section of each volume, we are indebted to a host of generous experts and fellow scholars. The "Reading Shakespeare's Language" sections, for example, could not have been written had not Arthur King, of Brigham Young University, and Randal Robinson, author of *Unlocking Shakespeare's Language*, led the way in untangling Shakespearean language puzzles and generously shared their insights and methodologies with us. "Shakespeare's Life" profited by the careful reading given it by S. Schoenbaum, "Shakespeare's Theater" was read and strengthened by Andrew Gurr, John Astington, and William Ingram, and "The Publication of Shakespeare's Plays" is indebted to the comments of Peter W. M. Blayney. We, as editors, take sole responsibility for any errors in our editions.

We are grateful to the authors of the "Modern Perspectives"; to Leeds Barroll and David Bevington for their generous encouragement; to the Huntington and Newberry Libraries for fellowship support; to King's University College for the grants it has provided to Paul Werstine; to the Social Sciences and Humanities Research Council of Canada, which provided him with Research Time Stipends; to Penny Gill and Eva Mary Hooker for insightful conversations about the language of *Much Ado About Nothing*; to Skiles Howard and Scott Reiss for advice on Renaissance music and dance; and to the Folger Institute's Center for Shakespeare Studies for its fortuitous sponsorship of a workshop on "Shakespeare's Texts for Students and Teachers" (funded by the National Endowment for the Humanities and led by Richard Knowles of the University of Wisconsin), a workshop from which we learned an enormous amount about what is wanted by college and high-school teachers of Shakespeare today.

In preparing this preface for the publication of *Much Ado About Nothing* in 1995, we wrote: "Our biggest debt is to the Folger Shakespeare Library—to Werner Gundersheimer, Director of the Library, who made possible our edition; to Jean Miller, the Library's Art Curator, who combs the Library holdings for illustrations, and to Julie Ainsworth, Head of the Photography Department, who carefully photographs them; to Peggy O'Brien, Director of Education, and her assistant, Molly Haws, who continue to give us expert advice about the needs being expressed by Shakespeare teachers and students (and to Martha Christian and other 'master teachers' who used our texts in manuscript in their classrooms); to Jessica Hymowitz, who provides expert computer support; to the staff of the Academic Programs Division, especially Mary Tonkinson, Lena Cowen Orlin, Toni Krieger, Amy Adler, Kathleen Lynch, and Carol Brobeck; and, finally, to the staff of the Library Reading Room, whose patience and support are invaluable."

As we revise the play for publication in 2018, we add to the above our gratitude to Michael Witmore, Director of the Folger Shakespeare Library, who brings to our work a gratifying enthusiasm and vision; to Eric Johnson, the Folger's Director of Digital Access, who expertly manages our editions in both their paper and their many electronic forms; to Gail Kern Paster, Director of the Library from 2002 until July 2011, whose interest and support have been unfailing and whose scholarly expertise continues to be an invaluable resource; to Jonathan Evans and Alysha Bullock, our production editors at Simon & Schuster, whose expertise, attention to detail, and wisdom are essential to this project; to the Folger's Photography Department; to Deborah Curren-Aquino for continuing superb editorial assistance and for her exceptionally fine Further Reading annotations; to Alice Falk for her expert copyediting; to Michael Poston for unfailing computer support; to Sophie Byvik, Gabrielle Linnell, and Stacey Redick; and to Rebecca Niles (whose help is crucial). Among the editions we consulted, we found Claire McEachern's 2015 Arden edition especially useful. Finally, we once again express our thanks to Stephen Llano for twenty-five years of support as our invaluable production editor, to the late Jean Miller for the wonderful images she unearthed, and to the ever-supportive staff of the Library Reading Room.

As we began to revise *Much Ado About Nothing*, Barbara A. Mowat died on Thanksgiving Day 2017. Her knowledge, wisdom, and great care of Shakespeare's texts will be sorely missed.

Paul Werstine
2018

Shakespeare's
Much Ado About Nothing

Much Ado About Nothing is one of Shakespeare's more popular comedies, with a long history of success on the stage. Much of its appeal lies in its two stories of romantic love with their quite different journeys to comedy's happy ending. Hero and Claudio fall in love almost at first sight; their union has the blessing of the older generation (in the persons of Hero's father, Leonato, and Claudio's prince, Don Pedro). All should be well. But from the outside comes the virulent force of Don John, who acts with the kind of malice that strikes out at whatever promises to make someone else happy. For Hero and Claudio to find happiness, they must go beyond Don John's treachery, Claudio's own weak jealousy, Don Pedro's touchy sense of his own honor, and Leonato's too credulous paternal fury. It takes a second (unlikely) outside force in the guise of the bumbling, officious Dogberry to offer any hope of bringing Hero's truth to light.

The story of Beatrice and Benedick is quite other. They are kept apart not by a vicious outsider but by their pride in their own brilliance and by their mutual antagonism and distrust. Both express aversion to marriage; each finds particular pleasure in attacking the other. To outsiders, they seem an ideal pair. So the outsiders decide to play Cupid.

Over the centuries the Beatrice-Benedick plot has most captivated audiences and readers. King Charles I, in his copy of Shakespeare's plays, crossed out the play's title and renamed it "Beatrice and Benedick," and a prefatory poem in a 1640 edition of Shakespeare's son-

Map of Spain, France, and Italy.

From Giovanni Botero, *Le relationi vniuersali . . .* (1618).

nets says, "Let but *Beatrice* / And *Benedick* be seene, lo, in a trice / The Cockpit, Galleries, Boxes all are full." And Berlioz's opera version of *Much Ado* is named *Béatrice et Bénédict*. It is generally agreed that Beatrice and Benedick are the model for the witty lovers in comic drama of later centuries; and it can be argued that they led as well to Jane Austen's Elizabeth and Darcy in *Pride and Prejudice* and to Scarlett and Rhett in *Gone with the Wind*.

It is, however, the conjunction of the Beatrice and Benedick story with the story of Hero and Claudio that makes *Much Ado* so rich and rewarding a play. Beatrice and Benedick, faced with humiliating descriptions of what they had considered their most prized character traits, learn to "suffer love" and to "eat their meat without grudging"; simultaneously, Claudio and Hero are forced into an experience that acquaints them first with life's darkness (with treachery, betrayal, vicious jealousy, public shaming, and abandonment) and then with quite unexpected joy (with the recovery of the irrevocably lost, with discovery at the unlikely hands of the play's "shallow fools"). It can be argued that while the play calls itself "Much Ado About *Nothing*," its stories are actually much ado about life at its most important.

After you have read the play, we invite you to turn to the back of this book and read "*Much Ado About Nothing:* A Modern Perspective," by Gail Kern Paster, Director *Emerita* of the Folger Shakespeare Library.

Reading Shakespeare's Language:
Much Ado About Nothing

For many people today, reading Shakespeare's language can be a problem—but it is a problem that can be solved. Those who have studied Latin (or even French or German or Spanish) and those who are used to reading poetry will have little difficulty understanding the language of Shakespeare's poetic drama. Others, though, need to develop the skills of untangling unusual sentence structures and of recognizing and understanding poetic compressions, omissions, and wordplay. And even those skilled in reading unusual sentence structures may have occasional trouble with Shakespeare's words. More than four hundred years of "static"—caused by changes in language and life—intervene between his speaking and our hearing. Most of his immense vocabulary is still in use, but a few of his words are no longer used, and many of his words now have meanings quite different from those they had in the sixteenth century. In the theater, most of these difficulties are solved for us by actors who study the language and articulate it for us so that the essential meaning is heard—or, when combined with stage action, is at least *felt*. When reading on one's own, one must do what each actor does: go over the lines (often with a dictionary close at hand) until the puzzles are solved and the lines yield up their poetry and the characters speak in words and phrases that are, suddenly, rewarding and wonderfully memorable.

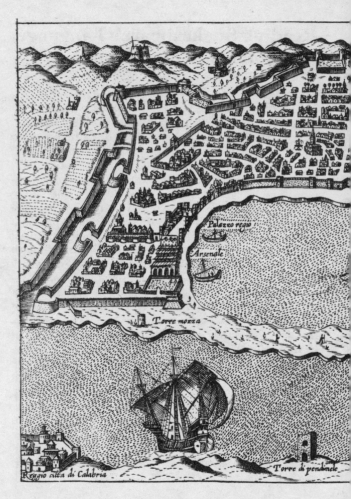

Palazzo regio

Arsenale

Torre mozza

Reggio città di Calabria

Torre di pendinele

Messina.

From Pietro Bertelli, *Theatrum vrbium Italicarum* . . . (1599).

Shakespeare's Words

As you begin to read the opening scenes of a play by
Shakespeare, you may notice occasional unfamiliar
words. Some are unfamiliar simply because we no longer use them. In the opening scenes of *Much Ado About
Nothing,* for example, you will find the words *squarer*
(i.e., fighter, quarreler), *methinks* (it seems to me),
recheat (the notes of a hunting horn), *baldrick* (a belt
for holding bugles, swords, etc.), and *arras* (a hanging
screen of rich tapestry fabric). Words of this kind are
explained in notes to the text and will become familiar
the more of Shakespeare's plays you read.

In *Much Ado About Nothing,* as in all of Shakespeare's
writing, the more problematic are the words that are
still in use but that now have different meanings. In the
opening scenes of *Much Ado,* for example, the word *tax*
has the meaning of "take to task, criticize," *stomach* is
used where we would say "appetite, hunger, or courage," *halting* where we would say "limping," *sad* where
we would say "serious," and *winded* where we would
say "sounded, blown." Such words will be explained in
the notes to the text, but they, too, will become familiar
as you continue to read Shakespeare's language.

Some words are strange not because of the "static"
introduced by changes in language over the past centuries but because these are words that Shakespeare is
using to build a dramatic world that has its own geog-
raphy and history and background mythology. *Much
Ado About Nothing,* for example, through references to
Messina, Venice, and Padua, to "thick-pleached alleys"
and "orchards," creates a location on a wealthy estate in
Italy. Through military language—*action* (i.e., military
engagement), *sort* (i.e., rank, kind), and *sworn brother*
(i.e., brother-in-arms)—it places itself in time, just at

the end of a war. Through complicated references to Cupid and his arrows and to Hercules (a mythological figure prominent both for his massive strength and for his helplessness when trapped by love), it also builds a world in which warfare and romantic love are intricately intertwined. These "local" words and references (each of which will be explained in notes to this text) help to build the world that Beatrice, Benedick, Hero, and Claudio inhabit, and will soon become a familiar part of your reading of the play.

Shakespearean Wordplay

In *Much Ado About Nothing*, Shakespeare plays with language so often and so variously that the entire play can be read and heard as brilliant repartee: witty punning, elaboration of commonplaces, highly figured verbal structures. In the play's opening scene, the Messenger delivers his report of the just-ended war in elaborate verbal figures. He reports that Claudio "hath borne himself beyond the promise of his age, doing in the figure of a lamb the feats of a lion," thus contrasting Claudio's lamblike youth and apparent helplessness with his lionlike ferocity in battle. He then uses figured language to report Claudio's uncle's reception of the news of Claudio's valor: "there appears much joy in him, even so much that joy could not show itself modest enough without a badge of bitterness." (*Badge* here means "sign," and *bitterness* means "anguish of heart, suffering.") These words are such a complicated way of saying "He was so happy he wept" that Leonato is forced to ask for clarification: "Did he break out into tears?" The Messenger's response, "In great measure," leads in turn to Leonato's punning response: "A kind overflow of kindness," where *kind* means both "natural" and "warmhearted" and *kindness* means both "kin-ship" and "affection."

Every major character in *Much Ado About Nothing* has his or her own way of playing with, elaborating, or misusing language. Two of the more intriguing are Beatrice and Benedick, whose linguistic tendencies define them for the other characters. Beatrice, in the prejudice of the time, is seen as "shrewish" or "curst" because of her "sharp tongue." Her first line in the play is to ask whether "Signior Mountanto" (i.e., Benedick) has returned from the war, jabbing at Benedick by naming him with the fencing term *montant* (an upward thrust). More typical of her wordplay is her response to the Messenger's "I see, lady, the gentleman is not in your books." The Messenger is, of course, using the phrase "in your books" figuratively, to mean "in your favor"; she takes the phrase literally and replies "No. An [i.e., if] he were, I would burn my study [i.e., library]." A few lines earlier we find her again taking a figurative phrase and interpreting it literally: when the Messenger describes Benedick as a man "stuffed with all honorable virtues," she responds "It is so indeed. He is no less than a stuffed man, but for the stuffing—well, we are all mortal." In the fourth scene of the play (2.1), when her uncle says to her "Well, niece, I hope to see you one day fitted with a husband," she builds an elaborate response by taking literally the more-or-less figurative biblical passage which reads that "the Lord God also made the man of the dust of the ground" (Genesis 2.7). Combining a literal reading of this verse with the line in the marriage liturgy in which the woman promises to "obey" and "serve" the man she marries, Beatrice responds as follows to Leonato's wish that she find a husband: "Not till God make men of some other metal than earth. Would it not grieve a woman to be overmastered with a piece of valiant dust? To make an account of her life to a clod of wayward marl?" It is to such language that the male characters in the play respond: "By my troth . . . , thou wilt never get thee a husband if thou be so shrewd of thy tongue."

Benedick, too, uses wordplay centered in the double meanings of words (saying, for example, that Hero is "too low for a high praise, too brown for a fair praise, and too little for a great praise"). But his more characteristic wordplay is with metaphor—or, rather, with metaphoric figures. A true metaphor is a play on words in which one object or idea is expressed as if it were something else, something with which it is said to share common features. (Don John uses metaphor when he says "I have decreed not to sing in my cage," picturing his unfree state as that of a caged songbird.) Benedick's metaphoric figures begin as metaphors or similes but spin out into linguistic cartoons: "Prove that ever I lose more blood with love than I will get again with drinking," he boasts, "pick out mine eyes with a ballad-maker's pen and hang me up at the door of a brothel house for the sign of blind Cupid." With a few phrases, he sketches himself as first blinded, then turned into a signboard, and then hung outside a brothel. "If I [fall in love]," he again boasts, "hang me in a bottle like a cat and shoot at me, and he that hits me, let him be clapped on the shoulder and called Adam." Here the wordplay is built on a simile (i.e., he is to be *like* a cat in a bottle), but again the comparison image expands into an entire scenario in which Benedick is to be hung in a bottle, used for archery practice, hit by an arrow, and the winner congratulated. One of his metaphoric overstatements comes back to haunt him. Answering Don Pedro's quoting of the proverb "In time the savage bull doth bear the yoke," Benedick comically dooms himself by saying "The savage bull may, but if ever the sensible Benedick bear it, pluck off the bull's horns and set them in my forehead, and let me be vilely painted, and in such great letters as they write 'Here is good horse to hire' let them signify under my sign 'Here you may see Benedick the married man.' " The image produced here—the sensible Benedick wearing the bull's horns and advertising his married state—seems to be a challenge to Don Pedro that is later picked up in his tricking of Benedick and that is alluded to twice toward the end of the play. One of the play's high comic moments rests on Benedick's turning Claudio's taunts about the savage bull back on Claudio, using metaphoric language to shape a truly elegant riposte:

PRINCE
   Good morrow, Benedick. Why, what's the matter
   That you have such a February face,
   So full of frost, of storm, and cloudiness?
CLAUDIO
   I think he thinks upon the savage bull.
   Tush, fear not, man. We'll tip thy horns with gold,
   And all Europa shall rejoice at thee,
   As once Europa did at lusty Jove
   When he would play the noble beast in love.
BENEDICK
   Bull Jove, sir, had an amiable low,
   And some such strange bull leapt your father's cow
   And got a calf in that same noble feat
   Much like to you, for you have just his bleat.
                           (5.4.41–52)

Benedick's metaphoric conversational style is what leads Don Pedro to characterize Benedick as being "from the crown of his head to the sole of his foot . . . all mirth" (3.2.8–9). This style is also, no doubt, what lies behind Beatrice's taunting characterization of him as "the Prince's jester" (2.1.135).

   Because intricate wordplay—whether the intentional elaborations of Benedick and Beatrice or the unintentional confusions of Dogberry—is so central to the language structure of *Much Ado About Nothing*, one must read the dialogue with special attention to double meanings, elaborated metaphors, verbal confusions, and other forms of linguistic playfulness.

Implied Stage Action

Finally, in reading Shakespeare's plays we should always remember that what we are reading is a performance script. The dialogue is written to be spoken by actors who, at the same time, are moving, gesturing, picking up objects, weeping, shaking their fists. Some stage action is described in what are called "stage directions"; some is suggested within the dialogue itself. We must learn to be alert to such signals as we stage the play in our imaginations. When, in *Much Ado About Nothing* 2.3, Benedick says "I will hide me in the arbor," and a few lines later Don Pedro says "See you where Benedick hath hid himself?" it is clear that the stage action involves Benedick's hiding behind a stage tree (or some structure onstage that represents part of an "arbor"). Again, in 3.1, the stage action is mapped out rather precisely in Hero's line "For look where Beatrice like a lapwing runs / Close by the ground," followed by Ursula's "Beatrice . . . even now / Is couchèd in the woodbine coverture," and Hero's "Then go we near her, that her ear lose nothing / Of the false sweet bait that we lay for it."

At several places in *Much Ado About Nothing*, signals to the reader are not quite so clear. Early in the first wedding scene, Claudio, having been "given" Hero, gives her back again to her father with the lines "There, Leonato, take her back again. / Give not this rotten orange to your friend" (4.1.31–32). It is unclear just what Claudio's actions are as he delivers those lines. In many productions, he throws her toward Leonato, sometimes with such violence that she hits the stage in a bruised heap. One could argue that since this is early in the scene's action, before Claudio's rage truly builds, a less violent gesture is more appropriate, but a range of stage actions offers itself. Again, later in the same scene, Beatrice's question "Why, how now, cousin, wherefore sink you down?" makes it clear that Hero falls to the stage. When she should get back up, however, is left to the imagination of the director, the actor, or us as readers to determine. Learning to read the language of stage action repays one many times over when one reads the play's final scene, with its entrance of masked ladies, its powerful unmasking of the "Hero that is dead," its discovery of the love letters that demonstrate that Beatrice and Benedick do, in fact, love each other, and its final dance. Here, as in so much of *Much Ado About Nothing*, implied stage action vitally affects our response to the play.

It is immensely rewarding to work carefully with Shakespeare's language—with the words, the sentences, the wordplay, and the implied stage action—as readers for the past four centuries have discovered. It may be more pleasurable to attend a good performance of a play—though not everyone has thought so. But the joy of being able to stage one of Shakespeare's plays in one's imagination, to return to passages that continue to yield further meanings (or further questions) the more one reads them—these are pleasures that, for many, rival (or at least augment) those of the performed text, and certainly make it worth considerable effort to "break the code" of Elizabethan poetic drama and let free the remarkable language that makes up a Shakespeare text.

Shakespeare's Life

Surviving documents that give us glimpses into the life of William Shakespeare show us a playwright, poet, and actor who grew up in the market town of Stratford-upon-Avon, spent his professional life in London, and returned to Stratford a wealthy landowner. He was born in April 1564, died in April 1616, and is buried inside the chancel of Holy Trinity Church in Stratford.

We wish we could know more about the life of the world's greatest dramatist. His plays and poems are testaments to his wide reading—especially to his knowledge of Virgil, Ovid, Plutarch, Holinshed's *Chronicles*, and the Bible—and to his mastery of the English language, but we can only speculate about his education. We know that the King's New School in Stratford-upon Avon was considered excellent. The school was one of the English "grammar schools" established to educate young men, primarily in Latin grammar and literature. As in other schools of the time, students began their studies at the age of four or five in the attached "petty school," and there learned to read and write in English, studying primarily the catechism from the Book of Common Prayer. After two years in the petty school, students entered the lower form (grade) of the grammar school, where they began the serious study of Latin grammar and Latin texts that would occupy most of the remainder of their school days. (Several Latin texts that Shakespeare used repeatedly in writing his plays and poems were texts that schoolboys memorized and recited.) Latin comedies were introduced early in the lower form; in the upper form, which the boys entered at age ten or eleven, students wrote their own Latin orations and declamations, studied Latin

Title page of a 1573 Latin and Greek catechism for children.
From Alexander Nowell, *Catechismus paruus pueris
primum Latine . . .* (1573).

historians and rhetoricians, and began the study of Greek using the Greek New Testament.

Since the records of the Stratford "grammar school" do not survive, we cannot prove that William Shakespeare attended the school; however, every indication (his father's position as an alderman and bailiff of Stratford, the playwright's own knowledge of the Latin classics, scenes in the plays that recall grammar-school experiences—for example, *The Merry Wives of Windsor*, 4.1) suggests that he did. We also lack generally accepted documentation about Shakespeare's life after his schooling ended and his professional life in London began. His marriage in 1582 (at age eighteen) to Anne Hathaway and the subsequent births of his daughter Susanna (1583) and the twins Judith and Hamnet (1585) are recorded, but how he supported himself and where he lived are not known. Nor do we know when and why he left Stratford for the London theatrical world, nor how he rose to be the important figure in that world that he had become by the early 1590s.

We do know that by 1592 he had achieved some prominence in London as both an actor and a playwright. In that year was published a book by the playwright Robert Greene attacking an actor who had the audacity to write blank-verse drama and who was "in his own conceit [i.e., opinion] the only Shake-scene in a country." Since Greene's attack includes a parody of a line from one of Shakespeare's early plays, there is little doubt that it is Shakespeare to whom he refers, a "Shake-scene" who had aroused Greene's fury by successfully competing with university-educated dramatists like Greene himself. It was in 1593 that Shakespeare became a published poet. In that year he published his long narrative poem *Venus and Adonis;* in 1594, he followed it with *Lucrece*. Both poems were dedicated to the young earl of Southampton (Henry

Wriothesley), who may have become Shakespeare's patron.

It seems no coincidence that Shakespeare wrote these narrative poems at a time when the theaters were closed because of the plague, a contagious epidemic disease that devastated the population of London. When the theaters reopened in 1594, Shakespeare apparently resumed his double career of actor and playwright and began his long (and seemingly profitable) service as an acting-company shareholder. Records for December of 1594 show him to be a leading member of the Lord Chamberlain's Men. It was this company of actors, later named the King's Men, for whom he would be a principal actor, dramatist, and shareholder for the rest of his career.

So far as we can tell, that career spanned about twenty years. In the 1590s, he wrote his plays on English history as well as several comedies and at least two tragedies (*Titus Andronicus* and *Romeo and Juliet*). These histories, comedies, and tragedies are the plays credited to him in 1598 in a work, *Palladis Tamia*, that in one chapter compares English writers with "Greek, Latin, and Italian Poets." There the author, Francis Meres, claims that Shakespeare is comparable to the Latin dramatists Seneca for tragedy and Plautus for comedy, and calls him "the most excellent in both kinds for the stage." He also names him "Mellifluous and honey-tongued Shakespeare": "I say," writes Meres, "that the Muses would speak with Shakespeare's fine filed phrase, if they would speak English." Since Meres also mentions Shakespeare's "sugared sonnets among his private friends," it is assumed that many of Shakespeare's sonnets (not published until 1609) were also written in the 1590s.

In 1599, Shakespeare's company built a theater for themselves across the river from London, naming it the Globe. The plays that are considered by many to be Shakespeare's major tragedies (*Hamlet, Othello, King Lear,* and *Macbeth*) were written while the company was resident in this theater, as were such comedies as *Twelfth Night* and *Measure for Measure.* Many of Shakespeare's plays were performed at court (both for Queen Elizabeth I and, after her death in 1603, for King James I), some were presented at the Inns of Court (the residences of London's legal societies), and some were doubtless performed in other towns, at the universities, and at great houses when the King's Men went on tour; otherwise, his plays from 1599 to 1608 were, so far as we know, performed only at the Globe. Between 1608 and 1612, Shakespeare wrote several plays—among them *The Winter's Tale* and *The Tempest*—presumably for the company's new indoor Blackfriars theater, though the plays were performed also at the Globe and at court. Surviving documents describe a performance of *The Winter's Tale* in 1611 at the Globe, for example, and performances of *The Tempest* in 1611 and 1613 at the royal palace of Whitehall.

Shakespeare seems to have written very little after 1612, the year in which he probably wrote *King Henry VIII.* (It was at a performance of *Henry VIII* in 1613 that the Globe caught fire and burned to the ground.) Sometime between 1610 and 1613, according to many biographers, he returned to live in Stratford-upon-Avon, where he owned a large house and considerable property, and where his wife and his two daughters lived. (His son Hamnet had died in 1596.) However, other biographers suggest that Shakespeare did not leave London for good until much closer to the time of his death. During his professional years in London, Shakespeare had presumably derived income from the acting company's profits as well as from his own career as an actor, from the sale of his play man-

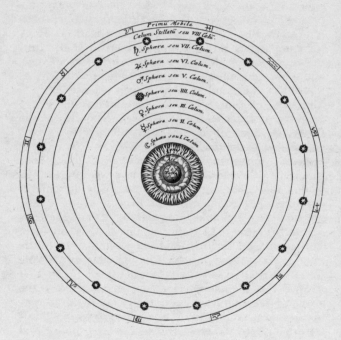

Ptolemaic universe.
From Marcus Manilius, *The sphere of . . .* (1675).

uscripts to the acting company, and, after 1599, from his shares as an owner of the Globe. It was presumably that income, carefully invested in land and other property, that made him the wealthy man that surviving documents show him to have become. It is also assumed that William Shakespeare's growing wealth and reputation played some part in inclining the Crown, in 1596, to grant John Shakespeare, William's father, the coat of arms that he had so long sought. William Shakespeare died in Stratford on April 23, 1616 (according to the epitaph carved under his bust in Holy Trinity Church) and was buried on April 25. Seven years after his death, his collected plays were published as *Mr. William Shakespeares Comedies, Histories, & Tragedies* (the work now known as the First Folio).

The years in which Shakespeare wrote were among the most exciting in English history. Intellectually, the discovery, translation, and printing of Greek and Roman classics were making available a set of works and worldviews that interacted complexly with Christian texts and beliefs. The result was a questioning, a vital intellectual ferment, that provided energy for the period's amazing dramatic and literary output and that fed directly into Shakespeare's plays. The Ghost in *Hamlet*, for example, is wonderfully complicated in part because he is a figure from Roman tragedy— the spirit of the dead returning to seek revenge—who at the same time inhabits a Christian hell (or purgatory); Hamlet's description of humankind reflects at one moment the Neoplatonic wonderment at mankind ("What a piece of work is a man!") and, at the next, the Christian view of the human condition ("And yet, to me, what is this quintessence of dust?").

As intellectual horizons expanded, so also did geographical and cosmological horizons. New worlds—

both North and South America—were explored, and in them were found human beings who lived and worshipped in ways radically different from those of Renaissance Europeans and Englishmen. The universe during these years also seemed to shift and expand. Copernicus had earlier theorized that the Earth was not the center of the cosmos but revolved as a planet around the sun. Galileo's telescope, created in 1609, allowed scientists to see that Copernicus had been correct: the universe was not organized with the Earth at the center, nor was it so nicely circumscribed as people had, until that time, thought. In terms of expanding horizons, the impact of these discoveries on people's beliefs—religious, scientific, and philosophical—cannot be overstated.

London, too, rapidly expanded and changed during the years (from the early 1590s to 1610 or somewhat later) that Shakespeare lived there. London—the center of England's government, its economy, its royal court, its overseas trade—was, during these years, becoming an exciting metropolis, drawing to it thousands of new citizens every year. Troubled by overcrowding, by poverty, by recurring epidemics of the plague, London was also a mecca for the wealthy and the aristocratic, and for those who sought advancement at court, or power in government or finance or trade. One hears in Shakespeare's plays the voices of London—the struggles for power, the fear of venereal disease, the language of buying and selling. One hears as well the voices of Stratford-upon-Avon—references to the nearby Forest of Arden, to sheepherding, to small-town gossip, to village fairs and markets. Part of the richness of Shakespeare's work is the influence felt there of the various worlds in which he lived: the world of metropolitan London, the world of small-town and rural England, the world of the theater, and the worlds of craftsmen and shepherds.

That Shakespeare inhabited such worlds we know from surviving London and Stratford documents, as well as from the evidence of the plays and poems themselves. From such records we can sketch the dramatist's life. We know from his works that he was a voracious reader. We know from legal and business documents that he was a multifaceted theater man who became a wealthy landowner. We know a bit about his family life and a fair amount about his legal and financial dealings. Most scholars today depend upon such evidence as they draw their picture of the world's greatest playwright. Such, however, has not always been the case. Until the late eighteenth century, the William Shakespeare who lived in most biographies was the creation of legend and tradition. This was the Shakespeare who was supposedly caught poaching deer at Charlecote, the estate of Sir Thomas Lucy close by Stratford; this was the Shakespeare who fled from Sir Thomas's vengeance and made his way in London by taking care of horses outside a playhouse; this was the Shakespeare who reportedly could barely read, but whose natural gifts were extraordinary, whose father was a butcher who allowed his gifted son sometimes to help in the butcher shop, where William supposedly killed calves "in a high style," making a speech for the occasion. It was this legendary William Shakespeare whose Falstaff (in *1* and *2 Henry IV*) so pleased Queen Elizabeth that she demanded a play about Falstaff in love, and demanded that it be written in fourteen days (hence the existence of *The Merry Wives of Windsor*). It was this legendary Shakespeare who reached the top of his acting career in the roles of the Ghost in *Hamlet* and old Adam in *As You Like It*—and who died of a fever contracted by drinking too hard at "a merry meeting" with the poets Michael Drayton and Ben Jonson. This legendary Shakespeare is a rambunctious, undisciplined man, as attractively "wild" as his plays were seen by earlier generations to be. Unfortunately, there is no trace of evidence to support these wonderful stories.

Perhaps in response to the disreputable Shakespeare of legend—or perhaps in response to the fragmentary and, for some, all-too-ordinary Shakespeare documented by surviving records—some people since the mid-nineteenth century have argued that William Shakespeare could not have written the plays that bear his name. These persons have put forward some dozen names as more likely authors, among them Queen Elizabeth, Sir Francis Bacon, Edward de Vere (earl of Oxford), and Christopher Marlowe. Such attempts to find what for these people is a more believable author of the plays is a tribute to the regard in which the plays are held. Unfortunately for their claims, the documents that exist that provide evidence for the facts of Shakespeare's life tie him inextricably to the body of plays and poems that bear his name. Unlikely as it seems to those who want the works to have been written by an aristocrat, a university graduate, or an "important" person, the plays and poems seem clearly to have been produced by a man from Stratford-upon-Avon with a very good "grammar-school" education and a life of experience in London and in the world of the London theater. How this particular man produced the works that dominate the cultures of much of the world more than four hundred years after his death is one of life's mysteries—and one that will continue to tease our imaginations as we continue to delight in his plays and poems.

Shakespeare's Theater

The actors of Shakespeare's time are known to have performed plays in a great variety of locations. They played at court (that is, in the great halls of such royal residences as Whitehall, Hampton Court, and Greenwich); they played in halls at the universities of Oxford and Cambridge, and at the Inns of Court (the residences in London of the legal societies); and they also played in the private houses of great lords and civic officials. Sometimes acting companies went on tour from London into the provinces, often (but not only) when outbreaks of bubonic plague in the capital forced the closing of theaters to reduce the possibility of contagion in crowded audiences. In the provinces the actors usually staged their plays in churches (until around 1600), in guildhalls, or in the great houses of individual patrons. While surviving records show only a handful of occasions when actors played at inns while on tour, London inns were important playing places up until the 1590s.

The building of theaters in London had begun only shortly before Shakespeare wrote his first plays in the 1590s. These theaters were of two kinds: outdoor or public playhouses that could accommodate large numbers of playgoers, and indoor or private theaters for much smaller audiences. What is usually regarded as the first London outdoor public playhouse was called simply the Theatre. James Burbage—the father of Richard Burbage, who was perhaps the most famous actor in Shakespeare's company—built it in 1576 in an area north of the city of London called Shoreditch. Among the more famous of the other public playhouses that capitalized on the new fashion were the Curtain and

The Globe

A stylized representation of the Globe theater.
From Claes Jansz Visscher, *Londinum florentissima
Britanniae urbs* . . . [c. 1625].

the Fortune (both also built north of the city), the Rose, the Swan, the Globe, and the Hope (all located on the Bankside, a region just across the Thames south of the city of London). All these playhouses had to be built outside the jurisdiction of the city of London because many civic officials were hostile to the performance of drama and repeatedly petitioned the royal council to abolish it.

The theaters erected on the Bankside (a region under the authority of the Church of England, whose head was the monarch) shared the neighborhood with houses of prostitution and with the Paris Garden, where the blood sports of bearbaiting and bullbaiting were carried on. There may have been no clear distinction between playhouses and buildings for such sports, for we know that the Hope was used for both plays and baiting and that Philip Henslowe, owner of the Rose and, later, partner in the ownership of the Fortune, was also a partner in a monopoly on baiting. All these forms of entertainment were easily accessible to Londoners by boat across the Thames or over London Bridge.

Evidently Shakespeare's company prospered on the Bankside. They moved there in 1599. Threatened by difficulties in renewing the lease on the land where their first theater (the Theatre) had been built, Shakespeare's company took advantage of the Christmas holiday in 1598 to dismantle the Theatre and transport its timbers across the Thames to the Bankside, where, in 1599, these timbers were used in the building of the Globe. The weather in late December 1598 is recorded as having been especially harsh. It was so cold that the Thames was "nigh [nearly] frozen," and there was heavy snow. Perhaps the weather aided Shakespeare's company in eluding their landlord, the snow hiding their activity and the freezing of the Thames allowing them to slide the timbers across to the Bankside with-

out paying tolls for repeated trips over London Bridge.
Attractive as this narrative is, it remains just as likely
that the heavy snow hampered transport of the timbers
in wagons through the London streets to the river. It
also must be remembered that the Thames was, according to report, only "nigh frozen," and therefore did not
necessarily provide solid footing. Whatever the precise
circumstances of this fascinating event in English theater history, Shakespeare's company was able to begin
playing at their new Globe theater on the Bankside in
1599. After this theater burned down in 1613 during
the staging of Shakespeare's *Henry VIII* (its thatch roof
set alight by cannon fire called for in performance),
Shakespeare's company immediately rebuilt on the
same location. The second Globe seems to have been
a grander structure than its predecessor. It remained
in use until 1642, when Parliament officially closed the
theaters. Soon thereafter it was pulled down.

The public theaters of Shakespeare's time were very
different buildings from our theaters today. First of all,
they were open-air playhouses. As recent excavations of
the Rose and the Globe confirm, some were polygonal
or roughly circular in shape; the Fortune, however, was
square. The most recent estimates of their size put the
diameter of these buildings at 72 feet (the Rose) to 100
feet (the Globe), but we know that they held vast audiences of two or three thousand, who must have been
squeezed together quite tightly. Some of these spectators paid extra to sit or stand in the two or three levels
of roofed galleries that extended, on the upper levels,
all the way around the theater and surrounded an open
space. In this space were the stage and, perhaps, the
tiring house (what we would call dressing rooms), as
well as the so-called yard. In the yard stood the spectators who chose to pay less, the ones whom Hamlet
contemptuously called "groundlings." For a roof they

had only the sky, and so they were exposed to all kinds of weather. They stood on a floor that was sometimes made of mortar and sometimes of ash mixed with the shells of hazelnuts, which, it has recently been discovered, were standard flooring material in the period.

Unlike the yard, the stage itself was covered by a roof. Its ceiling, called "the heavens," is thought to have been elaborately painted to depict the sun, moon, stars, and planets. The exact size of the stage remains hard to determine. We have a single sketch of part of the interior of the Swan. A Dutchman named Johannes de Witt visited this theater around 1596 and sent a sketch of it back to his friend, Arend van Buchel. Because van Buchel found de Witt's letter and sketch of interest, he copied both into a book. It is van Buchel's copy, adapted, it seems, to the shape and size of the page in his book, that survives. In this sketch, the stage appears to be a large rectangular platform that thrusts far out into the yard, perhaps even as far as the center of the circle formed by the surrounding galleries. This drawing, combined with the specifications for the size of the stage in the building contract for the Fortune, has led scholars to conjecture that the stage on which Shakespeare's plays were performed must have measured approximately 43 feet in width and 27 feet in depth, a vast acting area. But the digging up of a large part of the Rose by late twentieth-century archaeologists has provided evidence of a quite different stage design. The Rose stage was a platform tapered at the corners and much shallower than what seems to be depicted in the van Buchel sketch. Indeed, its measurements seem to be about 37.5 feet across at its widest point and only 15.5 feet deep. Because the surviving indications of stage size and design differ from each other so much, it is possible that the stages in other theaters, like the Theatre, the Curtain, and the Globe (the outdoor playhouses where we know that Shakespeare's plays were performed), were different from those at both the Swan and the Rose.

After about 1608 Shakespeare's plays were staged not only at the Globe but also at an indoor or private playhouse in Blackfriars. This theater had been constructed in 1596 by James Burbage in an upper hall of a former Dominican priory or monastic house. Although Henry VIII had dissolved all English monasteries in the 1530s (shortly after he had founded the Church of England), the area remained under church, rather than hostile civic, control. The hall that Burbage had purchased and renovated was a large one in which Parliament had once met. In the private theater that he constructed, the stage, lit by candles, was built across the narrow end of the hall, with boxes flanking it. The rest of the hall offered seating room only. Because there was no provision for standing room, the largest audience it could hold was less than a thousand, or about a quarter of what the Globe could accommodate. Admission to Blackfriars was correspondingly more expensive. Instead of a penny to stand in the yard at the Globe, it cost a minimum of sixpence to get into Blackfriars. The best seats at the Globe (in the Lords' Room in the gallery above and behind the stage) cost sixpence; but the boxes flanking the stage at Blackfriars were half a crown, or five times sixpence. Some spectators who were particularly interested in displaying themselves paid even more to sit on stools on the Blackfriars stage.

Whether in the outdoor or indoor playhouses, the stages of Shakespeare's time were different from ours. They were not separated from the audience by the dropping of a curtain between acts and scenes. Therefore the playwrights of the time had to find other ways of signaling to the audience that one scene (to be imagined as occurring in one location at a given time) had ended and the next (to be imagined at perhaps a different location at a later time) had begun. The customary way used by Shakespeare and many of his contemporaries was to have everyone on stage exit at the end of one scene and have one or more different characters enter to begin the next. In a few cases, where characters remain onstage from one scene to another, the dialogue or stage action makes the change of location clear, and the characters are generally to be imagined as having moved from one place to another. For example, in *Romeo and Juliet,* Romeo and his friends remain onstage in Act 1 from scene 4 to scene 5, but they are represented as having moved between scenes from the street that leads to Capulet's house into Capulet's house itself. The new location is signaled in part by the appearance onstage of Capulet's servingmen carrying table napkins, something they would not take into the streets. Playwrights had to be quite resourceful in the use of hand properties, like the napkin, or in the use of dialogue to specify where the action was taking place in their plays because, in contrast to most of today's theaters, the playhouses of Shakespeare's time did not fill the stage with scenery to make the setting precise. A consequence of this difference was that the playwrights of Shakespeare's time did not have to specify exactly where the action of their plays was set when they did not choose to do so, and much of the action of their plays is tied to no specific place.

Usually Shakespeare's stage is referred to as a "bare stage," to distinguish it from the stages of the last two or three centuries with their elaborate sets. But the stage in Shakespeare's time was not completely bare. Philip Henslowe, owner of the Rose, lists in his inventory of stage properties a rock, three tombs, and two mossy banks. Stage directions in plays of the time also call for such things as thrones (or "states"), banquets (presumably tables with plaster replicas of food on them), and beds and tombs to be pushed onto the stage. Thus the stage often held more than the actors.

The actors did not limit their performing to the stage alone. Occasionally they went beneath the stage, as the Ghost appears to do in the first act of *Hamlet*. From there they could emerge onto the stage through a trapdoor. They could retire behind the hanging across the back of the stage, as, for example, the actor playing Polonius does when he hides behind the arras. Sometimes the hangings could be drawn back during a performance to "discover" one or more actors behind them. When performance required that an actor appear "above," as when Juliet is imagined to stand at the window of her chamber in the famous and misnamed "balcony scene," then the actor probably climbed the stairs to the gallery over the back of the stage and temporarily shared it with some of the spectators. The stage was also provided with ropes and winches so that actors could descend from, and reascend to, the "heavens."

Perhaps the greatest difference between dramatic performances in Shakespeare's time and ours was that in Shakespeare's England the roles of women were played by boys. (Some of these boys grew up to take male roles in their maturity.) There were no women in the acting companies. It was not so in Europe, and it had not always been so in the history of the English stage. There are records of women on English stages in the thirteenth and fourteenth centuries, two hundred years before Shakespeare's plays were performed. After the accession of James I in 1603, the queen of England and her ladies took part in entertainments at court called masques, and with the reopening of the theaters in 1660 at the restoration of Charles II, women again took their place on the public stage.

The chief competitors of such acting companies as the one to which Shakespeare belonged and for which he wrote were companies of exclusively boy actors. The competition was most intense in the early 1600s. There were then two principal children's companies: the Children of Paul's (the choirboys from St. Paul's Cathedral, whose private playhouse was near the cathedral), and the Children of the Chapel Royal (the choirboys from the monarch's private chapel, who performed at the Blackfriars theater built by Burbage in 1596). In *Hamlet* Shakespeare writes of "an aeric [nest] of children, little eyases [hawks], that cry out on the top of question and are most tyrannically clapped for 't. These are now the fashion and . . . berattle the common stages [attack the public theaters]." In the long run, the adult actors prevailed. The Children of Paul's dissolved around 1606. By about 1608 the Children of the Chapel Royal had been forced to stop playing at the Blackfriars theater, which was then taken over by the King's Men, Shakespeare's own troupe.

Acting companies and theaters of Shakespeare's time seem to have been organized in various ways. For example, with the building of the Globe, Shakespeare's company apparently managed itself, with the principal actors, Shakespeare among them, having the status of "sharers" and the right to a share in the takings, as well as the responsibility for a part of the expenses. Five of the sharers, including Shakespeare, owned the Globe. As actor, as sharer in an acting company and in ownership of theaters, and as playwright, Shakespeare was about as involved in the theatrical industry as one could imagine. Although Shakespeare and his fellows prospered, their status under the law was conditional upon the protection of powerful patrons. "Common players"—those who did not have patrons or masters—were classed in the language of the law with "vagabonds and sturdy beggars." So the actors had to secure for themselves the official rank of servants of patrons. Among the patrons under whose protection Shakespeare's company worked were the lord chamberlain and, after the accession of King James in 1603, the king himself.

In the early 1990s we began to learn a great deal more about the theaters in which Shakespeare and his contemporaries performed—or, at least, began to open up new questions about them. At that time about 70 percent of the Rose had been excavated, as had about 10 percent of the second Globe, the one built in 1614. Excavation was halted at that point, but London has come to value the sites of its early playhouses, and takes what opportunities it can to explore them more deeply, both on the Bankside and in Shoreditch. Information about the playhouses of Shakespeare's London is therefore a constantly changing resource.

The Publication of Shakespeare's Plays

Eighteen of Shakespeare's plays found their way into print during the playwright's lifetime, but there is nothing to suggest that he took any interest in their publication. These eighteen appeared separately in editions in quarto or, in the case of *Henry VI, Part 3,* octavo format. The quarto pages are not much larger than a modern mass-market paperback book, and the octavo pages are even smaller; these little books were sold unbound for a few pence. The earliest of the quartos that still survive were printed in 1594, the year that both *Titus Andronicus* and a version of the play now called *Henry VI, Part 2* became available. While almost every one of these early quartos displays on its title page the name of the acting company that performed the play, only about half provide the name of the playwright, Shakespeare. The first quarto edition to bear the name Shakespeare on its title page is *Love's Labor's Lost* of 1598. A few of the quartos were popular with the book-buying public of Shakespeare's lifetime; for example, quarto *Richard II* went through five editions between 1597 and 1615. But most of the quartos were far from best sellers; *Love's Labor's Lost* (1598), for instance, was not reprinted in quarto until 1631. After Shakespeare's death, two more of his plays appeared in quarto format: *Othello* in 1622 and *The Two Noble Kinsmen,* coauthored with John Fletcher, in 1634.

In 1623, seven years after Shakespeare's death, *Mr. William Shakespeares Comedies, Histories, & Tragedies* was published. This printing offered readers in a single book thirty-six of the thirty-eight plays now thought to have been written by Shakespeare, including eighteen that had never been printed before. And it offered them in a style that was then reserved for serious literature and scholarship. The plays were arranged in double columns on pages nearly a foot high. This large page size is called "folio," as opposed to the smaller "quarto," and the 1623 volume is usually called the Shakespeare First Folio. It is reputed to have sold for the lordly price of a pound. (One copy at the Folger Shakespeare Library is marked fifteen shillings—that is, three-quarters of a pound.)

In a preface to the First Folio titled "To the great Variety of Readers," two of Shakespeare's former fellow actors in the King's Men, John Heminge and Henry Condell, wrote that they themselves had collected their dead companion's plays. They suggested that they had seen his own papers: "we have scarce received from him a blot in his papers." The title page of the Folio declared that the plays within it had been printed "according to the True Original Copies." Comparing the Folio to the quartos, Heminge and Condell disparaged the quartos, advising their readers that "before you were abused with divers stolen and surreptitious copies, maimed, and deformed by the frauds and stealths of injurious impostors." Many Shakespeareans of the eighteenth and nineteenth centuries believed Heminge and Condell and regarded the Folio plays as superior to anything in the quartos.

Once we begin to examine the Folio plays in detail, it becomes less easy to take at face value the word of Heminge and Condell about the superiority of the Folio texts. For example, of the first nine plays in the Folio (one-quarter of the entire collection), four were essentially reprinted from earlier quarto printings that Heminge and Condell had disparaged, and four have now been identified as printed from copies written in the hand of a professional scribe of the 1620s named Ralph Crane; the ninth, *The Comedy of Errors*, was apparently also printed from a manuscript, but one whose origin cannot be readily identified. Evidently, then, eight of the first nine plays in the First Folio were not printed, in spite of what the Folio title page announces, "according to the True Original Copies," or Shakespeare's own papers, and the source of the ninth is unknown. Since today's editors have been forced to treat Heminge and Condell's pronouncements with skepticism, they must choose whether to base their own editions upon quartos or the Folio on grounds other than Heminge and Condell's story of where the quarto and Folio versions originated.

Editors have often fashioned their own narratives to explain what lies behind the quartos and Folio. They have said that Heminge and Condell meant to criticize only a few of the early quartos, the ones that offer much shorter and sometimes quite different, often garbled, versions of plays. Among the examples of these are the 1600 quarto of *Henry V* (the Folio offers a much fuller version) or the 1603 *Hamlet* quarto. (In 1604 a different, much longer form of the play got into print as a quarto.) Early twentieth-century editors and some scholars in the present century have speculated that these questionable texts were produced when someone in the audience took notes from the plays' dialogue during performances and then employed "hack poets" to fill out the notes. The poor results were then sold to a publisher and presented in print as Shakespeare's plays. For much of the twentieth century this story gave way to another in which the shorter versions are said to be re-creations from memory of Shakespeare's plays by actors who wanted to stage them in the provinces but lacked manuscript copies. Most of the quartos offer much better texts than these so-called bad quartos. Indeed, in most of the quartos we find texts that are at least equal to or better than what is printed in the Folio. Many Shakespeare enthusiasts persuaded themselves that most of the quartos were set into type directly from Shakespeare's own papers, although there is nothing on which to base this conclusion except the desire for it to be true. Thus speculation continues about how the Shakespeare plays got to be printed. All that we have are the printed texts.

The book collector who was most successful in bringing together copies of the quartos and the First Folio was Henry Clay Folger, founder of the Folger Shakespeare Library in Washington, D.C. While it is estimated that there survive around the world only about 230 copies of the First Folio, Mr. Folger was able to acquire more than seventy-five copies, as well as a large number of fragments, for the library that bears his name. He also amassed a substantial number of quartos. For example, only fourteen copies of the First Quarto of *Love's Labor's Lost* are known to exist, and three are at the Folger Shakespeare Library. As a consequence of Mr. Folger's labors, scholars visiting the Folger Shakespeare Library have been able to learn a great deal about sixteenth- and seventeenth-century printing and, particularly, about the printing of Shakespeare's plays. And Mr. Folger did not stop at the First Folio, but collected many copies of later editions of Shakespeare, beginning with the Second Folio (1632), the Third (1663–64), and the Fourth (1685). Each of these later folios was based on its immediate predecessor and was edited anonymously. The first editor of Shakespeare whose name we know was Nicholas Rowe, whose first edition came out in 1709. Mr. Folger collected this edition and many, many more by Rowe's successors, and the collecting and scholarship continue.

An Introduction to This Text

Much Ado About Nothing was first printed in 1600 as a quarto. This quarto is remarkable among early printed texts of Shakespeare's plays for the contrast it presents between the superb correctness of its dialogue and the many obvious errors and ambiguities in its stage directions and speech prefixes. Editors have found very little to require correction in the dialogue but are hard pressed to impose order on the stage directions and speech prefixes.

In 1623 the play was printed again, this time as part of the collection of Shakespeare's plays now known as the First Folio. The First Folio text is generally thought to be based on a lightly annotated copy of the First Quarto of 1600. Some scholars believe that this very copy of the quarto was employed by Shakespeare's company in their theaters to regulate performance of the play. Other scholars argue that whoever annotated the copy of the 1600 quarto used by the printers of the First Folio *Ado* must have referred to a manuscript of the play that had been used in the theater. To support this opinion, these scholars point to the substitution of what may be an actor's name (*"Iacke Wilson"*) for the name of the character Balthasar in one Folio stage direction, as well as to the Folio correction of one of the several errors in the quarto's stage directions and the addition of some stage directions for music. (It should be noted that the Folio also adds to the errors in the quarto's stage directions.) On the basis of this evidence, these scholars assert that the Folio *Ado* thus must be (indirectly) based on *the* manuscript that was used in the theater, and that the quarto must have been printed from Shakespeare's own manuscript—his so-called "foul papers." While these scholars are probably right about the Folio, there is no reason to believe that there existed only these two play manuscripts, since many different kinds of manuscripts of (non-Shakespearean) plays are still extant from the period. And there are just as good grounds for asserting that the quarto (rather than, or as well as, the Folio) may be based on a theatrical manuscript; the quarto speech prefixes, after all, contain the names of two quite well-known actors from Shakespeare's company—the clowns Will Kemp and Richard Cowley (see the textual notes to 4.2). To sum up: as today's scholars reexamine earlier accounts of the origins of the printed texts, we discover that some of these narratives are based on questionable evidence.

The present edition is based directly on the earliest quarto of 1600.* (After surveying the Folio changes, we have chosen largely to ignore them in preparing this edition of the quarto.) For the convenience of the reader, we have generally modernized the punctuation and the spelling of the quarto. Sometimes we go so far as to modernize certain old forms of words; for example, when *a* means "he," we change it to *he;* we change *mo* to *more,* and *ye* to *you.* But it is not our practice in editing any of the plays to modernize words that sound distinctly different from modern forms. For example, when the early printed texts read *sith* or *apricocks* or *porpentine,* we have not modernized to *since, apricots, porcupine.* When the forms *an, and,* or *and if* appear instead of the modern form *if,* we have reduced *and* to *an* but have not changed any of these forms to their modern equivalent, *if.* We also modernize and, where

---

*We have also consulted the computerized text of the First Quarto provided by the Text Archive of the Oxford University Computing Centre, to which we are grateful.

necessary, correct passages in foreign languages, unless an error in the early printed text can be reasonably explained as a joke.

Although in general we have reduced the punctuation of the First Quarto to modern standards, we have left untouched in many cases one feature of its punctuation that arises from its use of the comma for many of the purposes nowadays filled by the semicolon, colon, and period. Take, for example, the First Quarto's punctuation of these words of the Friar in the play's last scene:

> All this amazement can I qualify,
> When after that the holy rites are ended,
> I'll tell you largely of fair Hero's death.

As punctuated, the speech may be read in two ways because the "when" clause in the second line may be attached either to the first line or to the third. Depending on the attachment the reader makes, the speech may say either "after the rites I can mitigate all this amazement" or "after the rites I'll tell you all about Hero's death." There are no grounds for preferring one of these meanings to the other, and so, in such cases, we have not altered the First Quarto's punctuation, but instead we have presented the reader with the First Quarto's ambiguity.

Whenever we change the wording of the First Quarto or add anything to its stage directions, we mark the change by enclosing it in superior half-brackets (⌐⌐). We want our readers to be immediately aware when we have intervened. (Only when we correct an obvious typographical error in the First Quarto does the change not get marked.) Whenever we change either the First Quarto's wording or its punctuation so that meaning changes, we list the change in the textual notes at the back of the book, even if all we have done is fix an obvious error.

We correct or regularize a number of the proper names, as is the usual practice in editions of the play. For example, when the Prince, usually called "Don Pedro," is twice referred to as "Peter," we change "Peter" to "Pedro." Or when Hero's waiting gentlewoman Ursula appears twice as "Ursley" in the First Quarto, we substitute "Ursula" on these occasions.

This edition differs from many earlier ones in its efforts to aid the reader in imagining the play as a performance. Thus stage directions are written with reference to the stage. For example, in 4.1, after the character Hero has been accused of gross immorality, in the fiction of the play she faints (line 114). Thus traditional editions read *"Hero swoons."* But in performance the actor playing Hero does not, of course, swoon; she merely slips down onto the stage. Since the stage directions in this edition are written with a view to performance, here our edition reads *"Hero falls."* Whenever it is reasonably certain, in our view, that a speech is accompanied by a particular action, we provide a stage direction describing the action. (Occasional exceptions to this rule occur when the action is so obvious that to add a stage direction would insult the reader.) Stage directions for the entrance of characters in mid-scene are, with rare exceptions, placed so that they immediately precede the characters' participation in the scene, even though these entrances may appear somewhat earlier in the early printed texts. Whenever we move a stage direction, we record this change in the textual notes. Latin stage directions (e.g., *Exeunt*) are translated into English (e.g., *They exit*).

We expand the often severely abbreviated forms of

names used as speech prefixes in early printed texts into the full names of the characters. We also regularize the speakers' names in speech prefixes, using only a single designation for each character, even though the early printed texts sometimes use a variety of designations. This task is a particularly challenging one for *Much Ado* because of the high incidence of inconsistency in the use of speech prefixes. The problem is particularly vexing, for example, in 3.3, where the Watchmen first appear. The quarto sometimes makes distinctions among these figures, using the speech prefixes *"Watch 1"* and *"Watch 2"*; but often it employs the thoroughly ambiguous speech prefix *"Watch."* Some recent editors have despaired of reducing these speech prefixes to any order and have simply used "A WATCHMAN" as the speech prefix throughout. While we sympathize with this practice, we have tried to help the reader by searching out patterns in the speeches that might be used to distinguish among the different Watchmen. We distinguish among three Watchmen. For one we use as his speech prefix the proper name given him in dialogue—Seacoal. He is chosen leader of the Watch, and we assign him speeches appropriate to a leader, mainly orders. To a second, whom we identify as "FIRST WATCHMAN" in speech prefixes, we give the speeches in which the word "deformed" is mistaken for the name of a criminal. The third we call "SECOND WATCHMAN." While the distinctions we observe among these three characters are not entirely consistent, we hope the attempt to sort out the quarto's ambiguity may be of some use to readers. Variations in the speech prefixes of the early printed text are recorded in the textual notes.

In the present edition, as well, we mark with a dash any change of address within a speech, unless a stage direction intervenes. When the *-ed* ending of a word is to be pronounced, we mark it with an accent. Like editors for the last two centuries, we print metrically linked lines in the following way:

BENEDICK
  Do not you love me?
BEATRICE   Why no, no more than reason.

However, when there are a number of short verse lines that can be linked in more than one way, we do not, with rare exceptions, indent any of them.

The Explanatory Notes

The notes that appear on the pages facing the text are designed to provide readers with the help they may need to enjoy the play. Whenever the meaning of a word in the text is not readily accessible in a good contemporary dictionary, we offer the meaning in a note. Sometimes we provide a note even when the relevant meaning is to be found in the dictionary but when the word has acquired since Shakespeare's time other potentially confusing meanings. In our notes, we try to offer modern synonyms for Shakespeare's words. We also try to indicate to the reader the connection between the word in the play and the modern synonym. For example, Shakespeare sometimes uses the word *head* to mean "source," but, for modern readers, there may be no connection evident between these two words. We provide the connection by explaining Shakespeare's usage as follows: "**head:** fountainhead, source." On some occasions, a whole phrase or clause needs explanation. Then, if space allows, we rephrase in our own words the difficult passage, and add at the end synonyms for individual words in the passage. When scholars have been unable to determine the meaning of a word or phrase, we acknowledge the uncertainty. Unless otherwise noted, biblical quotations are from the Geneva Bible (1560), with spelling modernized.

MUCH ADO
ABOUT NOTHING

Characters in the Play

LEONATO, Governor of Messina
HERO, his daughter
BEATRICE, his niece
LEONATO'S BROTHER
MARGARET
URSULA } *waiting gentlewomen to Hero*

DON PEDRO, Prince of Aragon
COUNT CLAUDIO, a young lord from Florence
SIGNIOR BENEDICK, a gentleman from Padua
BALTHASAR
SIGNIOR ANTONIO

DON JOHN, Don Pedro's brother
BORACHIO
CONRADE } *Don John's followers*

DOGBERRY, Master Constable in Messina
VERGES, Dogberry's partner
GEORGE SEACOAL, leader of the Watch
FIRST WATCHMAN
SECOND WATCHMAN
SEXTON
FRIAR FRANCIS

MESSENGER to Leonato
MESSENGER to Don Pedro
BOY

Musicians, Lords, Attendants, Leonato's nephew

3

MUCH ADO
ABOUT NOTHING

ACT 1

1.1 The army of Don Pedro of Aragon arrives in Messina and is welcomed by Leonato, Messina's governor. Benedick of Padua, a soldier in Don Pedro's army, proclaims his enmity to love and engages in a skirmish of wits with Leonato's niece, Beatrice. Count Claudio, the hero of Don Pedro's just-ended war, falls in love with Leonato's daughter Hero and confesses his love to Don Pedro, who decides to woo Hero for Claudio.

────────────

0 SD. **Enter Leonato:** Early editions of the play include an entrance for a character named "Innogen," Leonato's "wife," who plays no part in the dialogue or action. See longer note, page 199.

2. **Aragon:** a region in northeast Spain; **Messina:** a port city in Sicily (See pages xiv–xv and xviii–xix.)

3. **this:** i.e., **this** time

6. **action:** battle

7. **sort:** rank; or, kind; **name:** fame, reputation

8. **achiever:** victor

13. **remembered:** rewarded

14–15. **in . . . lamb:** i.e., while seeming young and weak **figure:** appearance

15–16. **better bettered:** i.e., more greatly exceeded

18. **will:** i.e., who **will**

23. **badge:** sign; **bitterness:** i.e., suffering, anguish of heart

⌜ACT 1⌝

Enter Leonato, Governor of Messina, Hero his daughter,
and Beatrice his niece, with a Messenger.

LEONATO, ⌜*with a letter*⌝ I learn in this letter that Don
Pedro of Aragon comes this night to Messina.

MESSENGER   He is very near by this. He was not three
leagues off when I left him.

LEONATO   How many gentlemen have you lost in this   5
action?

MESSENGER   But few of any sort, and none of name.

LEONATO   A victory is twice itself when the achiever
brings home full numbers. I find here that Don
Pedro hath bestowed much honor on a young   10
Florentine called Claudio.

MESSENGER   Much deserved on his part, and equally
remembered by Don Pedro. He hath borne himself
beyond the promise of his age, doing in the figure
of a lamb the feats of a lion. He hath indeed better   15
bettered expectation than you must expect of me to
tell you how.

LEONATO   He hath an uncle here in Messina will be
very much glad of it.

MESSENGER   I have already delivered him letters, and   20
there appears much joy in him, even so much that
joy could not show itself modest enough without a
badge of bitterness.

7

25. **In great measure:** abundantly

26. **kind:** (1) natural; (2) warmhearted; **kindness:** (1) kinship; (2) affection

27. **truer:** more honorable; more sincere

30. **Mountanto:** a fencing term (A *montant* is an upward thrust.)

36. **pleasant:** merry

38. **bills:** handbills, posters

39. **Cupid:** the god of love, whose arrows cause people to fall in love (See pictures, pages 16 and 76.) **at the flight:** i.e., to an archery contest (perhaps to show that he could make women fall in love better than Cupid can) See picture, page 12. **Fool:** a servant who makes his living by amusing his aristocratic patron

40. **subscribed for Cupid:** i.e., signed on Cupid's behalf

41. **bird-bolt:** a blunt-headed arrow used to shoot birds

42. **he:** i.e., Benedick

43–44. **promised . . . killing:** proverbial, with the implication that he has killed no one

45. **Faith:** by my faith (a mild oath); **tax:** i.e., take to task, criticize

46. **meet:** even

49. **hath holp:** i.e., has helped

50. **trencherman:** eater (also, insultingly, "parasitical dependent")

51. **stomach:** Beatrice plays on **stomach** as meaning both "appetite" and "courage."

55. **stuffed:** provided

57–58. **stuffed man:** perhaps, a figure **stuffed** with cotton to resemble a human

LEONATO   Did he break out into tears?

MESSENGER   In great measure.   25

LEONATO   A kind overflow of kindness. There are no
faces truer than those that are so washed. How
much better is it to weep at joy than to joy at
weeping!

BEATRICE   I pray you, is Signior Mountanto returned   30
from the wars or no?

MESSENGER   I know none of that name, lady. There
was none such in the army of any sort.

LEONATO   What is he that you ask for, niece?

HERO   My cousin means Signior Benedick of Padua.   35

MESSENGER   O, he's returned, and as pleasant as ever
he was.

BEATRICE   He set up his bills here in Messina and
challenged Cupid at the flight, and my uncle's Fool,
reading the challenge, subscribed for Cupid and   40
challenged him at the bird-bolt. I pray you, how
many hath he killed and eaten in these wars? But
how many hath he killed? For indeed I promised to
eat all of his killing.

LEONATO   Faith, niece, you tax Signior Benedick too   45
much, but he'll be meet with you, I doubt it not.

MESSENGER   He hath done good service, lady, in these
wars.

BEATRICE   You had musty victual, and he hath holp to
eat it. He is a very valiant trencherman; he hath an   50
excellent stomach.

MESSENGER   And a good soldier too, lady.

BEATRICE   And a good soldier to a lady, but what is he
to a lord?

MESSENGER   A lord to a lord, a man to a man, stuffed   55
with all honorable virtues.

BEATRICE   It is so indeed. He is no less than a stuffed
man, but for the stuffing—well, we are all mortal.

61. **skirmish of wit:** i.e., exchange of verbal thrusts

64. **five wits:** i.e., the mental faculties of human beings; **halting:** limping

65. **with:** i.e., by

67. **a difference:** i.e., a mark on a coat of arms that indicates one's rank within a family (See picture, below.)

70–71. **sworn brother:** i.e., brother-in-arms, friend **sworn** to support one as if one's **brother**

75. **block:** fashion (literally: a mold for shaping a felt hat)

76–77. **in your books:** i.e., **in your** favor

78. **An:** if; **study:** i.e., library

80. **squarer:** fighter, quarreler

84. **he:** i.e., Benedick

86. **taker:** i.e., victim; **presently:** immediately

89. **hold:** i.e., remain

93. **is approached:** i.e., has come near, has arrived

Coat of arms showing a mark of "difference." (1.1.67)
From Ralph Brooke, *A catalogue . . . of the kings . . .* (1622).

LEONATO   You must not, sir, mistake my niece. There is
a kind of merry war betwixt Signior Benedick and   60
her. They never meet but there's a skirmish of wit
between them.

BEATRICE   Alas, he gets nothing by that. In our last
conflict, four of his five wits went halting off, and
now is the whole man governed with one, so that if   65
he have wit enough to keep himself warm, let him
bear it for a difference between himself and his
horse, for it is all the wealth that he hath left to
be known a reasonable creature. Who is his companion now? He hath every month a new sworn   70
brother.

MESSENGER   Is 't possible?

BEATRICE   Very easily possible. He wears his faith but
as the fashion of his hat; it ever changes with the
next block.   75

MESSENGER   I see, lady, the gentleman is not in your
books.

BEATRICE   No. An he were, I would burn my study. But
I pray you, who is his companion? Is there no
young squarer now that will make a voyage with   80
him to the devil?

MESSENGER   He is most in the company of the right
noble Claudio.

BEATRICE   O Lord, he will hang upon him like a
disease! He is sooner caught than the pestilence,   85
and the taker runs presently mad. God help the
noble Claudio! If he have caught the Benedick, it
will cost him a thousand pound ere he be cured.

MESSENGER   I will hold friends with you, lady.

BEATRICE   Do, good friend.   90

LEONATO   You will never run mad, niece.

BEATRICE   No, not till a hot January.

MESSENGER   Don Pedro is approached.

96. **cost:** expense (here, the expense of the army's visit, which Leonato, as the Prince's host, must bear); **encounter:** come to meet

101. **charge:** (1) duty; (2) expense

107. **have it full:** perhaps, are well answered **full:** completely

109. **fathers herself:** i.e., proclaims in her looks who her father is

119. **meet:** suitable, appropriate

120. **convert to:** turn into

124. **would:** wish

"At the flight." (1.1.39)
From Gilles Corrozet, *Hecatongraphie . . .* (1543).

Enter Don Pedro, ⌜*Prince of Aragon, with*⌝ *Claudio,*
   Benedick, Balthasar, and John the Bastard.

PRINCE   Good Signior Leonato, are you come to meet
   your trouble? The fashion of the world is to avoid   95
   cost, and you encounter it.

LEONATO   Never came trouble to my house in the
   likeness of your Grace, for trouble being gone,
   comfort should remain, but when you depart from
   me, sorrow abides and happiness takes his leave.   100

PRINCE   You embrace your charge too willingly. ⌜*Turning to Hero.*⌝ I think this is your daughter.

LEONATO   Her mother hath many times told me so.

BENEDICK   Were you in doubt, sir, that you asked her?

LEONATO   Signior Benedick, no, for then were you a   105
   child.

PRINCE   You have it full, Benedick. We may guess by
   this what you are, being a man. Truly the lady
   fathers herself.—Be happy, lady, for you are like
   an honorable father.   110

              ⌜*Leonato and the Prince move aside.*⌝

BENEDICK   If Signior Leonato be her father, she would
   not have his head on her shoulders for all Messina,
   as like him as she is.

BEATRICE   I wonder that you will still be talking, Signior Benedick, nobody marks you.   115

BENEDICK   What, my dear Lady Disdain! Are you yet
   living?

BEATRICE   Is it possible disdain should die while she
   hath such meet food to feed it as Signior Benedick?
   Courtesy itself must convert to disdain if you come   120
   in her presence.

BENEDICK   Then is courtesy a turncoat. But it is certain I am loved of all ladies, only you excepted; and
   I would I could find in my heart that I had not a
   hard heart, for truly I love none.   125

127. **else:** otherwise

128. **cold blood:** i.e., **blood** not warmed by passion

128–29. **I am . . . that:** i.e., in that (i.e., loving no one) you and I agree

131. **still:** always

132–33. **predestinate:** i.e., predestined, fated

134–35. **an 'twere:** if it were

135. **were:** i.e., is

136. **you . . . parrot-teacher:** i.e., you jabber (or, repeat yourself) expertly, as if teaching a parrot to talk

137. **of my tongue:** perhaps, who speaks like me; or, perhaps, who is able to speak

137–38. **a beast of yours:** perhaps, who speaks like you; or, perhaps, who cannot speak (i.e., is a dumb **beast**); or, perhaps, who speaks hypocritically (i.e., with a "forked tongue")

140. **so good a continuer:** i.e., was so tireless in running

142. **a jade's trick:** i.e., an unfair or foolish conclusion (An untrustworthy horse [a **jade**] might trick its rider by pulling its neck out of the halter or by stopping suddenly, as Benedick has just done.)

143. **of old:** i.e., from the past

150–51. **shall . . . forsworn:** i.e., will not have sworn falsely, perjured yourself

152. **being:** now you are

156. **Please it . . . lead:** i.e., will you **please lead**

158. **note:** notice, pay attention to

BEATRICE   A dear happiness to women. They would else have been troubled with a pernicious suitor. I thank God and my cold blood I am of your humor for that. I had rather hear my dog bark at a crow than a man swear he loves me.   130

BENEDICK   God keep your Ladyship still in that mind, so some gentleman or other shall 'scape a predestinate scratched face.

BEATRICE   Scratching could not make it worse an 'twere such a face as yours were.   135

BENEDICK   Well, you are a rare parrot-teacher.

BEATRICE   A bird of my tongue is better than a beast of yours.

BENEDICK   I would my horse had the speed of your tongue and so good a continuer, but keep your   140 way, i' God's name, I have done.

BEATRICE   You always end with a jade's trick. I know you of old.

⌈*Leonato and the Prince come forward.*⌉

PRINCE   That is the sum of all, Leonato.—Signior Claudio and Signior Benedick, my dear friend   145 Leonato hath invited you all. I tell him we shall stay here at the least a month, and he heartily prays some occasion may detain us longer. I dare swear he is no hypocrite, but prays from his heart.

LEONATO   If you swear, my lord, you shall not be   150 forsworn. ⌈*To Don John.*⌉ Let me bid you welcome, my lord, being reconciled to the Prince your brother, I owe you all duty.

DON JOHN   I thank you. I am not of many words, but I thank you.   155

LEONATO   Please it your Grace lead on?

PRINCE   Your hand, Leonato. We will go together.

⌈*All*⌉ *exit except Benedick and Claudio.*

CLAUDIO   Benedick, didst thou note the daughter of Signior Leonato?

161. **modest:** well-mannered

167. **methinks:** it seems to me; **low:** i.e., short

168. **fair:** beautiful

173. **in sport:** joking

179. **sad:** serious

179–80. **flouting jack:** mocking fellow

180. **Cupid . . . hare-finder:** Since Cupid is blind, he would not be a good finder of hares. (See picture, below.)

181. **Vulcan . . . carpenter:** Vulcan is blacksmith of the gods, not a carpenter. (See picture, page 132.)

182. **go . . . song:** i.e., join with you in singing

187. **possessed with a fury:** i.e., as if under the control of one of the Furies, dread goddesses sent from hell to avenge crimes (See picture, page 18.)

194–95. **but . . . suspicion:** i.e., who will refuse to marry because of the fear that his wife will prove unfaithful and make him a cuckold (A cuckold is imaged as growing horns, which his cap may hide. See picture, page 32, and longer note, page 199.)

"Cupid is a good hare-finder." (1.1.180)
From Francesco Petrarca, *Opera . . .* (1508).

BENEDICK   I noted her not, but I looked on her.   160

CLAUDIO   Is she not a modest young lady?

BENEDICK   Do you question me as an honest man
should do, for my simple true judgment? Or would
you have me speak after my custom, as being a
professed tyrant to their sex?   165

CLAUDIO   No, I pray thee, speak in sober judgment.

BENEDICK   Why, i' faith, methinks she's too low for a
high praise, too brown for a fair praise, and too
little for a great praise. Only this commendation I
can afford her, that were she other than she is, she   170
were unhandsome, and being no other but as she is,
I do not like her.

CLAUDIO   Thou thinkest I am in sport. I pray thee tell
me truly how thou lik'st her.

BENEDICK   Would you buy her that you enquire after   175
her?

CLAUDIO   Can the world buy such a jewel?

BENEDICK   Yea, and a case to put it into. But speak you
this with a sad brow? Or do you play the flouting
Jack, to tell us Cupid is a good hare-finder and   180
Vulcan a rare carpenter? Come, in what key shall a
man take you to go in the song?

CLAUDIO   In mine eye she is the sweetest lady that ever
I looked on.

BENEDICK   I can see yet without spectacles, and I see   185
no such matter. There's her cousin, an she were not
possessed with a fury, exceeds her as much in
beauty as the first of May doth the last of December.
But I hope you have no intent to turn husband, have
you?   190

CLAUDIO   I would scarce trust myself, though I had
sworn the contrary, if Hero would be my wife.

BENEDICK   Is 't come to this? In faith, hath not the
world one man but he will wear his cap with
suspicion? Shall I never see a bachelor of three-   195

196. **Go to:** an expression of impatience

196–98. **wilt needs . . . Sundays:** Benedick attacks marriage with the image of the **yoke** of marriage (see picture, page 221), the yoke's **print** (i.e., imprint, impression), and its depressing impact on one's leisure time (**sigh away Sundays**). See picture, page 174.

206. **dumb:** mute, speechless

211. **If . . . uttered:** i.e., **if this were** true, **it** would be told to you this way

212. **old tale:** Benedick refers to a fairy tale in which the formula he quotes plays a key role.

215. **passion:** feeling, desire

219. **fetch me in:** trick me

220. **By my troth:** a mild oath by one's faith

227–50. **opinion . . . faith:** Benedick's references to **fire** (l. 228) and **the stake** (l. 229) introduce the idea of religious heresy and its punishments, picked up with such words as **obstinate heretic** (l. 230) and **fall from this faith** (l. 250).

The Furies. (1.1.187)
From Vincenzo Cartari, *Le vere e noue imagini . . .* (1615).

score again? Go to, i' faith, an thou wilt needs thrust
thy neck into a yoke, wear the print of it, and sigh
away Sundays. Look, Don Pedro is returned to seek
you.

Enter Don Pedro, ⌈Prince of Aragon.⌉

PRINCE   What secret hath held you here that you fol-   200
lowed not to Leonato's?

BENEDICK   I would your Grace would constrain me to
tell.

PRINCE   I charge thee on thy allegiance.

BENEDICK   You hear, Count Claudio, I can be secret as   205
a dumb man, I would have you think so, but on my
allegiance—mark you this, on my allegiance—he
is in love. With who? Now, that is your Grace's part.
Mark how short his answer is: with Hero, Leonato's
short daughter.   210

CLAUDIO   If this were so, so were it uttered.

BENEDICK   Like the old tale, my lord: "It is not so, nor
'twas not so, but, indeed, God forbid it should be
so."

CLAUDIO   If my passion change not shortly, God forbid   215
it should be otherwise.

PRINCE   Amen, if you love her, for the lady is very well
worthy.

CLAUDIO   You speak this to fetch me in, my lord.

PRINCE   By my troth, I speak my thought.   220

CLAUDIO   And in faith, my lord, I spoke mine.

BENEDICK   And by my two faiths and troths, my lord, I
spoke mine.

CLAUDIO   That I love her, I feel.

PRINCE   That she is worthy, I know.   225

BENEDICK   That I neither feel how she should be loved
nor know how she should be worthy is the opinion
that fire cannot melt out of me. I will die in it at the
stake.

230–31. **in the despite of:** i.e., in disdaining

232. **but in:** i.e., except through

236–38. **have a recheat . . . baldrick:** i.e., wear the horns of a cuckold **recheat:** notes of a hunting horn **winded:** sounded, blown (See picture, page 46.) **baldrick:** belt for holding bugles, swords, etc. Here the baldrick is **invisible** because the bugle is the purely imaginary horn of the cuckold. (See longer note to 1.1.194–95, page 199, and picture, page 32.)

241. **fine:** conclusion; **the finer:** i.e., better dressed

245–46. **lose . . . drinking:** In Elizabethan thinking, sighs of **love** draw **blood** from the heart while wine restores it.

248–49. **for . . . Cupid:** i.e., in place of a signboard with a picture **of blind Cupid**

251. **argument:** theme of discussion

252. **do:** i.e., **fall from this faith; hang . . . cat: A cat** hung in a wicker or leather basket was sometimes used as a target.

254. **Adam:** The archer Adam Bell was the hero of an old ballad.

255. **try:** test (Proverb: "**Time** tries [i.e., tests] all things.")

256. **In . . . yoke:** proverbial (See picture, page 68.)

259. **let . . . painted:** i.e., have a picture made of me (with my horns)

261. **sign:** i.e., picture (on the signboard)

264. **horn-mad:** i.e., raving mad (with a pun on his cuckold's horns)

PRINCE   Thou wast ever an obstinate heretic in the   230
despite of beauty.

CLAUDIO   And never could maintain his part but in the
force of his will.

BENEDICK   That a woman conceived me, I thank her;
that she brought me up, I likewise give her most   235
humble thanks. But that I will have a recheat
winded in my forehead or hang my bugle in an
invisible baldrick, all women shall pardon me.
Because I will not do them the wrong to mistrust
any, I will do myself the right to trust none. And the   240
fine is, for the which I may go the finer, I will live a
bachelor.

PRINCE   I shall see thee, ere I die, look pale with love.

BENEDICK   With anger, with sickness, or with hunger,
my lord, not with love. Prove that ever I lose more   245
blood with love than I will get again with drinking,
pick out mine eyes with a ballad-maker's pen and
hang me up at the door of a brothel house for the
sign of blind Cupid.

PRINCE   Well, if ever thou dost fall from this faith, thou   250
wilt prove a notable argument.

BENEDICK   If I do, hang me in a bottle like a cat and
shoot at me, and he that hits me, let him be clapped
on the shoulder and called Adam.

PRINCE   Well, as time shall try.   255
In time the savage bull doth bear the yoke.

BENEDICK   The savage bull may, but if ever the sensible
Benedick bear it, pluck off the bull's horns and set
them in my forehead, and let me be vilely painted,
and in such great letters as they write "Here is good   260
horse to hire" let them signify under my sign "Here
you may see Benedick the married man."

CLAUDIO   If this should ever happen, thou wouldst be
horn-mad.

265. **spent . . . quiver:** used up his quiverful of arrows

266. **Venice:** a city famous at the time for its courtesans; **quake:** tremble with love

267. **earthquake:** i.e., extraordinary event

268. **temporize:** adapt yourself, change

269. **repair:** go

270. **Commend me:** offer my respects

271. **fail him:** i.e., **fail** (to appear)

273. **matter:** sense

274. **embassage:** embassy, mission; **commit you:** a polite phrase at parting, which the Prince and Claudio treat as if it were the complimentary close of a letter

275. **tuition:** protection

280. **guarded:** trimmed

281. **guards:** ornaments, trimmings; **but . . . neither:** i.e., only loosely sewn on or connected

282. **flout old ends:** banter with bits and pieces of conventional language

286. **apt:** inclined; ready

290. **affect:** like or love

292. **onward:** forward; **action:** military engagement

296. **now:** i.e., **now** that; **that:** now **that**

PRINCE   Nay, if Cupid have not spent all his quiver in   265
    Venice, thou wilt quake for this shortly.

BENEDICK   I look for an earthquake too, then.

PRINCE   Well, you will temporize with the hours. In the
    meantime, good Signior Benedick, repair to Leona-
    to's. Commend me to him, and tell him I will not   270
    fail him at supper, for indeed he hath made great
    preparation.

BENEDICK   I have almost matter enough in me for such
    an embassage, and so I commit you—

CLAUDIO   To the tuition of God. From my house, if I had   275
    it—

PRINCE   The sixth of July. Your loving friend, Bene-
    dick.

BENEDICK   Nay, mock not, mock not. The body of your
    discourse is sometimes guarded with fragments,   280
    and the guards are but slightly basted on neither.
    Ere you flout old ends any further, examine your
    conscience. And so I leave you.   *He exits.*

CLAUDIO
My liege, your Highness now may do me good.

PRINCE
My love is thine to teach. Teach it but how,   285
And thou shalt see how apt it is to learn
Any hard lesson that may do thee good.

CLAUDIO
Hath Leonato any son, my lord?

PRINCE
No child but Hero; she's his only heir.
Dost thou affect her, Claudio?   290

CLAUDIO   O, my lord,
When you went onward on this ended action,
I looked upon her with a soldier's eye,
That liked, but had a rougher task in hand
Than to drive liking to the name of love.   295
But now I am returned and that war thoughts

299. **fair:** beautiful

301. **presently:** soon

304. **break with:** reveal (the matter) to

306. **twist:** i.e., spin (literally, to form a thread by combining fibers)

308. **his complexion:** its outward signs (its pallor)

310. **salved it:** i.e., explained it; or, smoothed it over; **treatise:** story

311. **What . . . bridge:** i.e., why should **the bridge** be; **flood:** river

312. **fairest grant:** best gift: **the necessity:** i.e., that which is needed

313. **Look what:** whatever

315. **reveling:** i.e., masked dancing

318. **in her bosom:** i.e., privately; **unclasp:** i.e., open (as if the heart were a book fastened with metal clasps) See picture, below.

321. **after:** i.e., afterward; **break:** i.e., speak, reveal (my mind)

323. **presently:** immediately

A book with clasps. (1.1.318)
From *Notitia vtraque cum Orientis . . .* (1552).

Have left their places vacant, in their rooms
Come thronging soft and delicate desires,
All prompting me how fair young Hero is,
Saying I liked her ere I went to wars.   300

PRINCE
Thou wilt be like a lover presently
And tire the hearer with a book of words.
If thou dost love fair Hero, cherish it,
And I will break with her and with her father,
And thou shalt have her. Was 't not to this end   305
That thou began'st to twist so fine a story?

CLAUDIO
How sweetly you do minister to love,
That know love's grief by his complexion!
But lest my liking might too sudden seem,
I would have salved it with a longer treatise.   310

PRINCE
What need the bridge much broader than the flood?
The fairest grant is the necessity.
Look what will serve is fit. 'Tis once, thou lovest,
And I will fit thee with the remedy.
I know we shall have reveling tonight.   315
I will assume thy part in some disguise
And tell fair Hero I am Claudio,
And in her bosom I'll unclasp my heart
And take her hearing prisoner with the force
And strong encounter of my amorous tale.   320
Then after to her father will I break,
And the conclusion is, she shall be thine.
In practice let us put it presently.

They exit.

1.2 Leonato is given a garbled account of the conversation between Don Pedro and Claudio, and is led to believe that Don Pedro wishes to marry Hero.

---

0 SD. brother to Leonato: Most editors assume that the **old man** is the same character as the Signior Antonio who appears with the maskers in 2.1. Our reasons for questioning this assumption are explained in the longer note on page 199.

1. cousin: i.e., kinsman, nephew (This character is mentioned only in this scene.)

6. they: i.e., the **news** (originally a plural noun)

7. stamps them: i.e., shows or proves them to be (literally, impresses or prints them)

8. cover: outer binding (as on a book)

9–10. a thick-pleached alley: a walkway bordered with intertwined boughs (See picture, page 223.)

10. orchard: formal garden (See picture, page 74.)

11. man: servant; **discovered:** revealed

14. accordant: in agreement

14–15. take . . . top: a proverb meaning "seize the moment" (**Present time,** or Occasion, was often pictured as having a single lock of hair growing from the top of his or her head.)

15–16. break . . . it: reveal (the matter) to you

17. wit: intelligence

20. hold: consider

22. withal: i.e., with it

23. peradventure: perhaps

25–26. I cry you mercy: a polite phrase of apology

27. have a care: take **care**

⌜Scene 2⌝
Enter Leonato, ⌜*meeting*⌝ *an old man, brother to*
Leonato.

LEONATO   How now, brother, where is my cousin, your
    son? Hath he provided this music?

LEONATO'S BROTHER   He is very busy about it. But,
    brother, I can tell you strange news that you yet
    dreamt not of.   5

LEONATO   Are they good?

LEONATO'S BROTHER   As the events stamps them, but
    they have a good cover; they show well outward.
    The Prince and Count Claudio, walking in a thick-
    pleached alley in mine orchard, were thus much   10
    overheard by a man of mine: the Prince discovered
    to Claudio that he loved my niece your daughter and
    meant to acknowledge it this night in a dance, and if
    he found her accordant, he meant to take the
    present time by the top and instantly break with you   15
    of it.

LEONATO   Hath the fellow any wit that told you this?

LEONATO'S BROTHER   A good sharp fellow. I will send
    for him, and question him yourself.

LEONATO   No, no, we will hold it as a dream till it   20
    appear itself. But I will acquaint my daughter
    withal, that she may be the better prepared for an
    answer, if peradventure this be true. Go you and tell
    her of it.

⌜*Enter Leonato's nephew, with a Musician*
and Attendants.⌝

Cousins, you know what you have to do.—O, I cry   25
you mercy, friend. Go you with me and I will use
your skill.—Good cousin, have a care this busy
time.

They exit.

1.3 Don John, Don Pedro's brother, receives a true account of Don Pedro's plan to woo Hero for Claudio. Resentful of both Don Pedro and Claudio, who have defeated him in the just-ended war, Don John hopes to find a way to block the marriage.

———————

1. **goodyear:** euphemism for "devil"
2. **out of measure:** beyond all limits, excessively
3. **measure:** limit
4. **breeds:** causes (it)
9. **sufferance:** endurance
11. **born under Saturn:** i.e., **born** when the planet **Saturn** was in the ascendant, and thus "saturnine" or gloomy
11–12. **apply . . . mischief:** i.e., use sayings from **moral** philosophy to cure a deadly disease
14. **stomach:** appetite, hunger
16. **tend on:** take care of, serve
17. **claw . . . humor:** flatter or fawn upon any man **humor:** mood, whim
19. **controlment:** restraint
20. **of late:** lately; **stood out against:** opposed
21. **grace:** favor
24. **frame:** fashion; **season:** time
25. **canker:** prickly wild rose (*Rosa canina*)
26. **blood: Blood** was considered the seat of emotions and passions.
27. **of:** i.e., by; **fashion a carriage:** i.e., assume a manner
31. **enfranchised:** freed; **with a clog:** i.e., weighted down as if by a heavy block (See picture, page 158.)
32. **decreed:** resolved

⌜Scene 3⌝

Enter Sir John the Bastard, and Conrade, his
companion.

CONRADE   What the goodyear, my lord, why are you
thus out of measure sad?

DON JOHN   There is no measure in the occasion that
breeds. Therefore the sadness is without limit.

CONRADE   You should hear reason.   5

DON JOHN   And when I have heard it, what blessing
brings it?

CONRADE   If not a present remedy, at least a patient
sufferance.

DON JOHN   I wonder that thou, being, as thou sayst thou   10
art, born under Saturn, goest about to apply a moral
medicine to a mortifying mischief. I cannot hide
what I am. I must be sad when I have cause, and
smile at no man's jests; eat when I have stomach,
and wait for no man's leisure; sleep when I am   15
drowsy, and tend on no man's business; laugh when
I am merry, and claw no man in his humor.

CONRADE   Yea, but you must not make the full show of
this till you may do it without controlment. You
have of late stood out against your brother, and he   20
hath ta'en you newly into his grace, where it is
impossible you should take true root but by the fair
weather that you make yourself. It is needful that
you frame the season for your own harvest.

DON JOHN   I had rather be a canker in a hedge than a   25
rose in his grace, and it better fits my blood to be
disdained of all than to fashion a carriage to rob
love from any. In this, though I cannot be said to be
a flattering honest man, it must not be denied but I
am a plain-dealing villain. I am trusted with a   30
muzzle and enfranchised with a clog; therefore I
have decreed not to sing in my cage. If I had my

37. **I make . . . only:** i.e., **I make** every **use of it, for it** is all that I use

42. **intelligence:** information

44. **model:** groundplan

45. **What . . . fool:** i.e., what kind of **fool is he**

47. **Marry:** i.e., indeed (originally an oath "by the Virgin Mary")

50. **proper squire:** here, a term of contempt **proper:** fine, handsome

54. **forward:** precocious; **March chick:** i.e., young one

56. **entertained for:** employed as; **perfumer:** i.e., fumigator

57. **smoking:** i.e., using smoke to fumigate (See picture, below.) **comes me:** i.e., come

58. **sad conference:** serious conversation

59. **whipped me:** i.e., **whipped; arras:** a hanging screen of rich tapestry fabric

64. **start-up:** upstart, parvenu

65. **cross:** impede, thwart (An additional meaning, "to make the sign of the cross," is suggested with the words **bless myself** in the next line.)

A censer "smoking a musty room." (1.3.57)
From Giovanni Ferro, *Teatro d'imprese* . . . (1623).

mouth, I would bite; if I had my liberty, I would do
my liking. In the meantime, let me be that I am, and
seek not to alter me.   35

CONRADE   Can you make no use of your discontent?

DON JOHN   I make all use of it, for I use it only. Who
comes here?

Enter Borachio.

What news, Borachio?

BORACHIO   I came yonder from a great supper. The   40
Prince your brother is royally entertained by
Leonato, and I can give you intelligence of an
intended marriage.

DON JOHN   Will it serve for any model to build mischief
on? What is he for a fool that betroths himself to   45
unquietness?

BORACHIO   Marry, it is your brother's right hand.

DON JOHN   Who, the most exquisite Claudio?

BORACHIO   Even he.

DON JOHN   A proper squire. And who, and who? Which   50
way looks he?

BORACHIO   Marry, on Hero, the daughter and heir of
Leonato.

DON JOHN   A very forward March chick! How came you
to this?   55

BORACHIO   Being entertained for a perfumer, as I was
smoking a musty room, comes me the Prince and
Claudio, hand in hand, in sad conference. I
whipped me behind the arras, and there heard it
agreed upon that the Prince should woo Hero for   60
himself, and having obtained her, give her to Count
Claudio.

DON JOHN   Come, come, let us thither. This may prove
food to my displeasure. That young start-up hath
all the glory of my overthrow. If I can cross him any   65

66. **sure:** i.e., secure, loyal
69. **cheer:** gladness
70. **subdued:** overpowered
71. **prove:** test, check out
72. **wait:** attend

A cuckold. (1.1.194–95; 2.1.44)
From *Bagford Ballads* (printed in 1878).

way, I bless myself every way. You are both sure, and
will assist me?

CONRADE   To the death, my lord.

DON JOHN   Let us to the great supper. Their cheer is the
greater that I am subdued. Would the cook were o'   70
my mind! Shall we go prove what's to be done?

BORACHIO   We'll wait upon your Lordship.

⌜*They*⌝ *exit.*

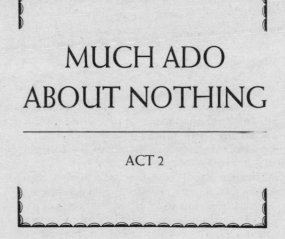

MUCH ADO
ABOUT NOTHING

ACT 2

2.1 Don Pedro and his soldiers, disguised in masks, dance with the ladies of Leonato's household. While Don Pedro woos Hero, Beatrice mocks Benedick. After the dance, Don John distresses Claudio by telling him that Don Pedro has won Hero's love. When Claudio learns that Hero has been won in his name, he wants to marry her immediately. Leonato insists that at least a week is needed to prepare for the wedding. Don Pedro proposes that the intervening time be used to trick Benedick and Beatrice into falling in love.

———————

3. **tartly:** sour
6. **He . . . man:** i.e., **an excellent man** would be one
8. **image:** i.e., statue, picture
9. **my lady's eldest son:** i.e., a pampered boy
10. **tattling:** chattering, talking aimlessly
18. **By my troth:** a mild oath by one's faith
19. **shrewd:** malicious, harsh; **of thy tongue:** i.e., with what you say
20. **curst:** a word used to describe women considered quarrelsome, talkative, or sharp-tongued
22. **sending that way:** gift in that respect
22–23. **God . . . horns:** a proverb that supposedly illustrates God's providence (In the proverb, **curst** means ill-tempered, vicious.)

⌜ACT 2⌝

⌜Scene 1⌝

Enter Leonato, his brother, Hero his daughter, and
Beatrice his niece, ⌜with Ursula and Margaret.⌝

LEONATO   Was not Count John here at supper?

LEONATO'S BROTHER   I saw him not.

BEATRICE   How tartly that gentleman looks! I never
can see him but I am heartburned an hour after.

HERO   He is of a very melancholy disposition.   5

BEATRICE   He were an excellent man that were made
just in the midway between him and Benedick. The
one is too like an image and says nothing, and the
other too like my lady's eldest son, evermore
tattling.   10

LEONATO   Then half Signior Benedick's tongue in
Count John's mouth, and half Count John's melancholy in Signior Benedick's face—

BEATRICE   With a good leg and a good foot, uncle, and
money enough in his purse, such a man would win   15
any woman in the world if he could get her goodwill.

LEONATO   By my troth, niece, thou wilt never get thee a
husband if thou be so shrewd of thy tongue.

LEONATO'S BROTHER   In faith, she's too curst.   20

BEATRICE   Too curst is more than curst. I shall lessen
God's sending that way, for it is said "God sends a

37

27. **Just:** i.e., exactly; **send . . . husband:** The man whose wife is unfaithful supposedly grows horns. Beatrice jokes that the only horns God might send her would grow on her husband's forehead.

30–31. **lie in the woolen:** i.e., sleep with a wool blanket next to my skin

32. **light on:** come upon unexpectedly

35. **waiting gentlewoman:** a **gentlewoman** who serves a lady of higher rank

40. **earnest:** a small payment to seal a bargain; **of:** i.e., from; **bearherd:** keeper of a performing bear (See picture, below.)

40–41. **lead his apes into hell:** Proverbial: "Those who die maids do **lead apes** in hell," meaning that women who do not marry are punished in the afterlife. **his apes:** Bearherds often had performing apes as well as bears.

47–48. **Saint Peter . . . sit:** These puzzling lines have the general sense that **Saint Peter,** in Beatrice's fantasy, will direct her to the bachelors' part of heaven.

A bearherd. (2.1.40)
From Jacobus a. Bruck, *Emblemata moralia . . .* (1615).

curst cow short horns," but to a cow too curst, he
sends none.

LEONATO   So, by being too curst, God will send you no   25
horns.

BEATRICE   Just, if He send me no husband, for the
which blessing I am at Him upon my knees every
morning and evening. Lord, I could not endure a
husband with a beard on his face. I had rather lie in   30
the woolen!

LEONATO   You may light on a husband that hath no
beard.

BEATRICE   What should I do with him? Dress him in my
apparel and make him my waiting gentlewoman?   35
He that hath a beard is more than a youth, and he
that hath no beard is less than a man; and he that is
more than a youth is not for me, and he that is less
than a man, I am not for him. Therefore I will even
take sixpence in earnest of the bearherd, and lead   40
his apes into hell.

LEONATO   Well then, go you into hell?

BEATRICE   No, but to the gate, and there will the devil
meet me like an old cuckold with horns on his
head, and say "Get you to heaven, Beatrice, get you   45
to heaven; here's no place for you maids." So deliver
I up my apes and away to Saint Peter; for the
heavens, he shows me where the bachelors sit, and
there live we as merry as the day is long.

LEONATO'S BROTHER, ⌜to Hero⌝   Well, niece, I trust you   50
will be ruled by your father.

BEATRICE   Yes, faith, it is my cousin's duty to make
curtsy and say "Father, as it please you." But yet for
all that, cousin, let him be a handsome fellow, or
else make another curtsy and say "Father, as it   55
please me."

LEONATO   Well, niece, I hope to see you one day fitted
with a husband.

59. **metal:** i.e., the "stuff" of which a person is made (with wordplay on *mettle* as referring to a person's character and on *metal* as referring to the physical body)

61. **dust:** See Genesis 2.7: "the Lord God also made the man of the dust of the ground."

62. **wayward:** perverse; **marl:** soil

63. **I'll none:** i.e., I'll have no husband

64. **match in:** i.e., marry

66. **in that kind:** i.e., **in that** regard (i.e., with reference to marriage)

69. **in good time:** (1) at the proper **time;** (2) with the proper rhythm

70. **important:** importunate; **measure:** moderation; rhythm

72. **repenting:** regretting; **jig:** lively dance

73. **measure:** grave or stately dance, such as a pavan; **cinquepace:** i.e., galliard, a popular lively dance (pronounced "sink-a-pace"); **first suit:** i.e., wooing

74. **fantastical:** impulsive, fanciful

75. **mannerly modest:** politely decorous

76. **state:** i.e., stateliness; **ancientry:** old-fashioned style; **repentance:** regret

79. **passing:** surpassingly, extremely

82–83. **Make good room:** i.e., step aside

83 SD. **Drum:** i.e., a person with a small drum or tabor (See longer note, page 200.); **Signior Antonio:** See longer note to 1.2.0 SD, page 199.

84. **walk a bout:** i.e., dance a round

BEATRICE   Not till God make men of some other metal
    than earth. Would it not grieve a woman to be   60
    overmastered with a piece of valiant dust? To make
    an account of her life to a clod of wayward marl?
    No, uncle, I'll none. Adam's sons are my brethren,
    and truly I hold it a sin to match in my kindred.

LEONATO, ⌜to Hero⌝   Daughter, remember what I told   65
    you. If the Prince do solicit you in that kind, you
    know your answer.

BEATRICE   The fault will be in the music, cousin, if you
    be not wooed in good time. If the Prince be too
    important, tell him there is measure in everything,   70
    and so dance out the answer. For hear me, Hero,
    wooing, wedding, and repenting is as a Scotch jig, a
    measure, and a cinquepace. The first suit is hot and
    hasty like a Scotch jig, and full as fantastical; the
    wedding, mannerly modest as a measure, full of   75
    state and ancientry; and then comes repentance,
    and with his bad legs falls into the cinquepace faster
    and faster till he sink into his grave.

LEONATO   Cousin, you apprehend passing shrewdly.

BEATRICE   I have a good eye, uncle; I can see a church   80
    by daylight.

LEONATO   The revelers are entering, brother. Make
    good room.   ⌜*Leonato and his brother step aside.*⌝

*Enter, ⌜with a Drum,⌝ Prince Pedro, Claudio, and
Benedick, ⌜Signior Antonio,⌝ and Balthasar, ⌜all in
masks, with Borachio and Don⌝ John.*

PRINCE, ⌜to Hero⌝   Lady, will you walk a bout with your
    friend?   ⌜*They begin to dance.*⌝   85

HERO   So you walk softly, and look sweetly, and say
    nothing, I am yours for the walk, and especially
    when I walk away.

PRINCE   With me in your company?

HERO   I may say so when I please.   90

92. **favor:** face; **defend:** forbid

92–93. **the lute . . . case:** i.e., your face should resemble your mask (See picture, page 122.)

94–95. **My . . . Jove:** In classical mythology, **Jove,** king of the Roman gods, was entertained by a poor man, Philemon, in his thatched hut.   **visor:** mask

98 SP. **Benedick:** See longer note, page 201.

98. **would:** wish

100. **ill:** bad

108. **clerk:** i.e., parish **clerk,** who led the responses during church services

112. **At a word:** i.e., in short, briefly

113. **waggling:** wobbling; tremor

114. **counterfeit:** impersonate

116. **dry hand:** supposedly a sign of age or sickness

120. **Go to:** expression of impatience

Dancers.
From Fabritio Caroso, *Il ballarino* . . . (1581).

PRINCE   And when please you to say so?

HERO   When I like your favor, for God defend the lute
should be like the case.

PRINCE   My visor is Philemon's roof; within the house
is Jove.   95

HERO   Why, then, your visor should be thatched.

PRINCE   Speak low if you speak love.

⌐*They move aside;*
Benedick and Margaret move forward.⌐

BENEDICK, ⌐*to Margaret*⌐   Well, I would you did like me.

MARGARET   So would not I for your own sake, for I have
many ill qualities.   100

BENEDICK   Which is one?

MARGARET   I say my prayers aloud.

BENEDICK   I love you the better; the hearers may cry
"Amen."

MARGARET   God match me with a good dancer.   105

⌐*They separate; Benedick moves aside;*
Balthasar moves forward.⌐

BALTHASAR   Amen.

MARGARET   And God keep him out of my sight when the
dance is done. Answer, clerk.

BALTHASAR   No more words. The clerk is answered.

⌐*They move aside;*
Ursula and Antonio move forward.⌐

URSULA   I know you well enough. You are Signior   110
Antonio.

ANTONIO   At a word, I am not.

URSULA   I know you by the waggling of your head.

ANTONIO   To tell you true, I counterfeit him.

URSULA   You could never do him so ill-well unless you   115
were the very man. Here's his dry hand up and
down. You are he, you are he.

ANTONIO   At a word, I am not.

URSULA   Come, come, do you think I do not know you
by your excellent wit? Can virtue hide itself? Go to,   120

121. **mum:** i.e., hush; **Graces:** virtues

121–22. **there's an end:** i.e., that's all there is to it

128. **The Hundred Merry Tales:** a popular joke book (See picture, below.)

135. **jester:** i.e., professional fool

136. **only his gift:** i.e., his only talent

137. **libertines:** dissolute men

137–38. **commendation:** recommendation

141. **fleet:** i.e., company of maskers; **boarded:** i.e., accosted, spoken to (literally, come aboard)

144. **break a comparison:** i.e., hit me with figures of speech as if they were lances in a joust

145. **peradventure not marked:** if perhaps not noted

151. **ill:** bad (thing)

From *A hundred merry tales* (1526; 1887 facs.).

mum, you are he. Graces will appear, and there's an
end.

⌈They move aside;
Benedick and Beatrice move forward.⌉

BEATRICE   Will you not tell me who told you so?

BENEDICK   No, you shall pardon me.

BEATRICE   Nor will you not tell me who you are?   125

BENEDICK   Not now.

BEATRICE   That I was disdainful, and that I had my
good wit out of *The Hundred Merry Tales*! Well, this
was Signior Benedick that said so.

BENEDICK   What's he?   130

BEATRICE   I am sure you know him well enough.

BENEDICK   Not I, believe me.

BEATRICE   Did he never make you laugh?

BENEDICK   I pray you, what is he?

BEATRICE   Why, he is the Prince's jester, a very dull   135
fool; only his gift is in devising impossible slanders.
None but libertines delight in him, and the commendation is not in his wit but in his villainy, for he
both pleases men and angers them, and then they
laugh at him and beat him. I am sure he is in the   140
fleet. I would he had boarded me.

BENEDICK   When I know the gentleman, I'll tell him
what you say.

BEATRICE   Do, do. He'll but break a comparison or two
on me, which peradventure not marked or not   145
laughed at strikes him into melancholy, and then
there's a partridge wing saved, for the fool will eat
no supper that night. *⌈Music for the dance.⌉* We must
follow the leaders.

BENEDICK   In every good thing.   150

BEATRICE   Nay, if they lead to any ill, I will leave them
at the next turning.

Dance. ⌈Then⌉ exit ⌈all except
Don John, Borachio, and Claudio.⌉

153. **Sure:** i.e., surely

154–55. **break with:** i.e., speak to

156. **visor:** i.e., masker

163. **birth:** inherited social rank

169. **the banquet:** i.e., dessert and wine

171. **these ill news:** i.e., this bad **news**

174. **Save:** except; **office:** duties, functions; **affairs:** pursuits

175. **Therefore all:** i.e., **therefore,** let **all**

178. **faith:** faithfulness, loyalty; **blood:** i.e., sensual appetite, passion

179. **accident:** occurrence, happening; **of hourly proof:** i.e., demonstrated every hour

180. **mistrusted not:** did not suspect or anticipate

Winding a recheat. (1.1.236–37)
From T[homas] F[ella],
A book of diverse devices . . . (1585–1622).

DON JOHN, ⌜*to Borachio*⌝ Sure my brother is amorous
    on Hero, and hath withdrawn her father to break
    with him about it. The ladies follow her, and but one   155
    visor remains.
BORACHIO And that is Claudio. I know him by his
    bearing.
DON JOHN, ⌜*to Claudio*⌝ Are not you Signior Benedick?
CLAUDIO You know me well. I am he.   160
DON JOHN Signior, you are very near my brother in his
    love. He is enamored on Hero. I pray you dissuade
    him from her. She is no equal for his birth. You
    may do the part of an honest man in it.
CLAUDIO How know you he loves her?   165
DON JOHN I heard him swear his affection.
BORACHIO So did I too, and he swore he would marry
    her tonight.
DON JOHN Come, let us to the banquet.
                            They exit. Claudio remains.
CLAUDIO, ⌜*unmasking*⌝
    Thus answer I in name of Benedick,   170
    But hear these ill news with the ears of Claudio.
    'Tis certain so, the Prince woos for himself.
    Friendship is constant in all other things
    Save in the office and affairs of love.
    Therefore all hearts in love use their own tongues.   175
    Let every eye negotiate for itself
    And trust no agent, for beauty is a witch
    Against whose charms faith melteth into blood.
    This is an accident of hourly proof,
    Which I mistrusted not. Farewell therefore, Hero.   180

Enter Benedick.

BENEDICK Count Claudio?
CLAUDIO Yea, the same.
BENEDICK Come, will you go with me?
CLAUDIO Whither?

185. **willow:** Willow garlands signified the grief of unrequited or lost love. (See picture, page 70.)

186. **county:** i.e., count

187. **of:** in

189. **one way:** i.e., **one way** or the other

192–93. **so ... bullocks:** i.e., cattle drivers (**drovers**) use such language when selling their oxen (See picture, page 150.)

194. **served:** treated

196–98. **now ... post:** i.e., you are hitting out blindly, striking the messenger (**post**) rather than the thief (See longer note, page 201.)

199. **If ... be:** i.e., if you will not leave me

203. **merry:** cheerful

203–4. **but so:** perhaps, but in being merry; or, perhaps, in allowing myself to believe that "I go under that title"

205. **base:** unworthy, despicable; **bitter:** stinging, cutting

206. **puts ... person:** i.e., thinks the whole world sees me as she does

206–7. **so gives me out:** describes me that way

210. **Troth:** i.e., in **troth,** in faith (a mild oath)

211. **Lady Fame: Fame** (or Rumor) was sometimes personified as a woman. (See picture, page 78.)

212. **lodge:** perhaps, a solitary house; **warren:** an enclosed game preserve (There is disagreement about what this phrase might mean.)

213. **goodwill:** agreement

216. **rod:** i.e., a bundle of willow switches

BENEDICK   Even to the next willow, about your own 185
   business, county. What fashion will you wear the
   garland of? About your neck like an usurer's chain?
   Or under your arm like a lieutenant's scarf? You
   must wear it one way, for the Prince hath got your
   Hero.   190
CLAUDIO   I wish him joy of her.
BENEDICK   Why that's spoken like an honest drover; so
   they sell bullocks. But did you think the Prince
   would have served you thus?
CLAUDIO   I pray you, leave me.   195
BENEDICK   Ho, now you strike like the blind man.
   'Twas the boy that stole your meat, and you'll beat
   the post.
CLAUDIO   If it will not be, I'll leave you.   *He exits.*
BENEDICK   Alas, poor hurt fowl, now will he creep into 200
   sedges. But that my Lady Beatrice should know
   me, and not know me! The Prince's fool! Ha, it may
   be I go under that title because I am merry. Yea, but
   so I am apt to do myself wrong. I am not so reputed!
   It is the base, though bitter, disposition of Beatrice 205
   that puts the world into her person and so gives me
   out. Well, I'll be revenged as I may.

   Enter the Prince, Hero, ⌈and⌉ Leonato.

PRINCE   Now, signior, where's the Count? Did you see
   him?
BENEDICK   Troth, my lord, I have played the part of 210
   Lady Fame. I found him here as melancholy as a
   lodge in a warren. I told him, and I think I told him
   true, that your Grace had got the goodwill of this
   young lady, and I offered him my company to a
   willow tree, either to make him a garland, as being 215
   forsaken, or to bind him up a rod, as being worthy to
   be whipped.
PRINCE   To be whipped? What's his fault?

219. **flat:** downright

220. **shows it:** i.e., **shows it** to

222. **a trust:** i.e., trusting someone

229. **them:** i.e., the birds in the nest

231. **If . . . saying:** i.e., if Hero's "song" is in accord with what you say

233. **to:** i.e., with

241. **a great thaw:** perhaps, a time when muddy roads would make travel impossible and life therefore dull; **huddling:** piling up

242. **conveyance:** dexterity

243. **mark:** archery or musket target

244. **poniards:** daggers (See picture, page 64.)

246. **terminations:** perhaps, terms or expressions (literally, the grammatical endings of words)

247. **to . . . Star:** i.e., everything as far as **the North Star**

248. **though . . . endowed with:** i.e., even if she possessed

250. **Hercules:** in classical mythology, a hero of extraordinary strength and courage; **turned spit:** i.e., turn the roasting spit (See longer note, page 201.)

251. **his club:** Hercules is generally pictured wielding or leaning on a mighty **club,** which he uses as a weapon. (See picture, page 146.)

252. **Ate:** Greek goddess of discord (pronounced Ah-tay)

252–56. **I would . . . thither:** i.e., I devoutly wish she would be conjured back into hell, since her presence on earth makes hell, where she belongs, a place of tranquillity and makes earth a place of discord **scholar:** i.e., someone who knows how to address evil spirits **conjure:** i.e., exorcise **thither:** i.e., to hell (See picture, page 170.)

BENEDICK The flat transgression of a schoolboy who,
 being overjoyed with finding a bird's nest, shows it 220
 his companion, and he steals it.
PRINCE Wilt thou make a trust a transgression? The
 transgression is in the stealer.
BENEDICK Yet it had not been amiss the rod had been
 made, and the garland too, for the garland he 225
 might have worn himself, and the rod he might
 have bestowed on you, who, as I take it, have stolen
 his bird's nest.
PRINCE I will but teach them to sing and restore them
 to the owner. 230
BENEDICK If their singing answer your saying, by my
 faith, you say honestly.
PRINCE The Lady Beatrice hath a quarrel to you. The
 gentleman that danced with her told her she is
 much wronged by you. 235
BENEDICK O, she misused me past the endurance of a
 block! An oak but with one green leaf on it would
 have answered her. My very visor began to assume
 life and scold with her. She told me, not thinking I
 had been myself, that I was the Prince's jester, that I 240
 was duller than a great thaw, huddling jest upon jest
 with such impossible conveyance upon me that I
 stood like a man at a mark with a whole army
 shooting at me. She speaks poniards, and every
 word stabs. If her breath were as terrible as her 245
 terminations, there were no living near her; she
 would infect to the North Star. I would not marry
 her though she were endowed with all that Adam
 had left him before he transgressed. She would have
 made Hercules have turned spit, yea, and have cleft 250
 his club to make the fire, too. Come, talk not of her.
 You shall find her the infernal Ate in good apparel. I
 would to God some scholar would conjure her, for
 certainly, while she is here, a man may live as quiet

261. **Antipodes:** the region on the opposite side of the globe (See picture, page 162.)

262. **toothpicker:** i.e., toothpick (usually a pointed quill, but sometimes made of gold or silver)

263–64. **Prester John:** in legend, a priest and monarch of a vast empire in Asia or Africa

264. **great Cham:** emperor of China

265. **Pygmies:** in legend, a race of very small people living in Ethiopia or India

266. **harpy:** sharp-tongued woman; monstrous mythological creature with the face and breasts of a woman and the wings and talons of a bird (See picture, below.)

273–77. **Indeed . . . lost it:** These enigmatic lines suggest a past love relationship between Benedick and Beatrice. **gave him use:** i.e., paid him interest

278. **put . . . down:** humiliated; defeated (Beatrice, in her reply, gives the words a literal, sexual, meaning.)

283. **wherefore:** why

A harpy. (2.1.266)
From Conrad Lycosthenes, *Prodigiorum . . .* (1557).

in hell as in a sanctuary, and people sin upon 255
purpose because they would go thither. So indeed
all disquiet, horror, and perturbation follows her.

Enter Claudio and Beatrice.

PRINCE   Look, here she comes.
BENEDICK   Will your Grace command me any service
to the world's end? I will go on the slightest errand 260
now to the Antipodes that you can devise to send
me on. I will fetch you a toothpicker now from the
furthest inch of Asia, bring you the length of Prester
John's foot, fetch you a hair off the great Cham's
beard, do you any embassage to the Pygmies, rather 265
than hold three words' conference with this harpy.
You have no employment for me?
PRINCE   None but to desire your good company.
BENEDICK   O God, sir, here's a dish I love not! I cannot
endure my Lady Tongue.   *He exits.* 270
PRINCE, ⌜*to Beatrice*⌝ Come, lady, come, you have lost
the heart of Signior Benedick.
BEATRICE   Indeed, my lord, he lent it me awhile, and I
gave him use for it, a double heart for his single
one. Marry, once before he won it of me with false 275
dice. Therefore your Grace may well say I have lost
it.
PRINCE   You have put him down, lady, you have put
him down.
BEATRICE   So I would not he should do me, my lord, 280
lest I should prove the mother of fools. I have
brought Count Claudio, whom you sent me to seek.
PRINCE   Why, how now, count, wherefore are you sad?
CLAUDIO   Not sad, my lord.
PRINCE   How then, sick?   285
CLAUDIO   Neither, my lord.
BEATRICE   The Count is neither sad, nor sick, nor mer-

288. **civil as an orange:** i.e., like a Seville **orange,** described as "between sweet and sour"

289. **something . . . complexion:** i.e., he is jealous (The **complexion** of the orange is close to yellow, a color associated with jealousy.)

290. **blazon . . . true:** description . . . accurate

291. **conceit:** notion, idea

293. **broke with:** i.e., broached (the subject) with

298. **all grace:** perhaps, may God himself

300. **herald:** announcer

307–8. **on the windy side of:** i.e., out of reach of **windy:** windward

311. **alliance:** marriage

311–12. **goes everyone to the world:** i.e., everyone gets married (a common idiom)

312. **sunburnt:** perhaps, dark-skinned (and hence unattractive, in Elizabethan eyes); or, perhaps, unprotected by marriage and thus open to the rough effects of wind and sun

313. **Heigh-ho for a husband:** proverbial (and also the title of a ballad)

316. **getting:** begetting

317. **got:** begot; **maid:** young unmarried woman

318. **come by:** acquire

321. **costly:** valuable

323. **no matter:** i.e., nothing of significance or substance

ry, nor well, but civil count, civil as an orange, and
something of that jealous complexion.

PRINCE   I' faith, lady, I think your blazon to be true, 290
though I'll be sworn, if he be so, his conceit is
false.—Here, Claudio, I have wooed in thy name,
and fair Hero is won. I have broke with her father
and his goodwill obtained. Name the day of marriage, and God give thee joy.   295

LEONATO   Count, take of me my daughter, and with her
my fortunes. His Grace hath made the match, and
all grace say "Amen" to it.

BEATRICE   Speak, count, 'tis your cue.

CLAUDIO   Silence is the perfectest herald of joy. I were 300
but little happy if I could say how much.—Lady, as
you are mine, I am yours. I give away myself for you
and dote upon the exchange.

BEATRICE   Speak, cousin, or, if you cannot, stop his
mouth with a kiss and let not him speak neither.   305

PRINCE   In faith, lady, you have a merry heart.

BEATRICE   Yea, my lord. I thank it, poor fool, it keeps on
the windy side of care. My cousin tells him in his ear
that he is in her heart.

CLAUDIO   And so she doth, cousin.   310

BEATRICE   Good Lord for alliance! Thus goes everyone
to the world but I, and I am sunburnt. I may sit in a
corner and cry "Heigh-ho for a husband!"

PRINCE   Lady Beatrice, I will get you one.

BEATRICE   I would rather have one of your father's 315
getting. Hath your Grace ne'er a brother like you?
Your father got excellent husbands, if a maid could
come by them.

PRINCE   Will you have me, lady?

BEATRICE   No, my lord, unless I might have another for 320
working days. Your Grace is too costly to wear
every day. But I beseech your Grace pardon me. I
was born to speak all mirth and no matter.

325. **out o' question:** i.e., beyond dispute

332–33. **I cry . . . pardon:** Beatrice apologizes to Leonato and excuses herself from Don Pedro's presence.

342. **out of suit:** i.e., **out of** wooing her

343. **were:** i.e., would be

346–47. **go to church:** i.e., get married

349. **his:** i.e., its

351. **a just sevennight:** i.e., exactly a week

352. **answer my mind:** i.e., correspond to my wishes

354. **breathing:** i.e., pause (literally, a time to breathe or rest); **warrant:** promise

356. **Hercules' labors:** Hercules was forced to perform twelve impossible tasks. (See note to line 250.)

359. **fain:** gladly

"Time goes on crutches." (2.1.348)
From Francesco Petrarca, *Opera . . .* (1508).

PRINCE   Your silence most offends me, and to be merry
best becomes you, for out o' question you were   325
born in a merry hour.

BEATRICE   No, sure, my lord, my mother cried, but then
there was a star danced, and under that was I
born.—Cousins, God give you joy!

LEONATO   Niece, will you look to those things I told   330
you of?

BEATRICE   I cry you mercy, uncle.—By your Grace's
pardon.   *Beatrice exits.*

PRINCE   By my troth, a pleasant-spirited lady.

LEONATO   There's little of the melancholy element in   335
her, my lord. She is never sad but when she sleeps,
and not ever sad then, for I have heard my daughter
say she hath often dreamt of unhappiness and
waked herself with laughing.

PRINCE   She cannot endure to hear tell of a husband.   340

LEONATO   O, by no means. She mocks all her wooers
out of suit.

PRINCE   She were an excellent wife for Benedick.

LEONATO   O Lord, my lord, if they were but a week
married, they would talk themselves mad.   345

PRINCE   County Claudio, when mean you to go to
church?

CLAUDIO   Tomorrow, my lord. Time goes on crutches
till love have all his rites.

LEONATO   Not till Monday, my dear son, which is hence   350
a just sevennight, and a time too brief, too, to have
all things answer my mind.

PRINCE, ⌈*to Claudio*⌉   Come, you shake the head at so
long a breathing, but I warrant thee, Claudio, the
time shall not go dully by us. I will in the interim   355
undertake one of Hercules' labors, which is to bring
Signior Benedick and the Lady Beatrice into a
mountain of affection, th' one with th' other. I
would fain have it a match, and I doubt not but to

360. **fashion:** contrive, manage; **minister:** provide

362. **I am for you:** i.e., **I** support **you**

362–63. **ten nights' watchings:** i.e., **ten** nights without sleep

366. **do . . . office:** play any small (or, perhaps, tasteful, suitable) part

368. **unhopefullest:** most unpromising

370. **strain:** birth; **approved:** demonstrated

372. **that:** i.e., so **that**

373. **practice on:** play a trick on, deceive

375. **queasy stomach:** i.e., distaste (for marriage)

376. **Cupid . . . archer:** See note to 1.1.39.

378. **drift:** scheme, plan

2.2 Don John and his henchman Borachio agree on a plan to disrupt the coming marriage: Borachio will convince Claudio that Hero is unfaithful by staging a meeting with Margaret, Hero's waiting gentlewoman. Margaret will be dressed in Hero's clothes, and Claudio will think that Borachio is Hero's lover.

_____

3. **cross:** impede, block

4. **bar:** barrier; **cross:** trouble, misfortune, annoyance

5. **med'cinable:** medicinal, healing

6. **comes athwart:** opposes the progress of

6–7. **ranges evenly with:** i.e., goes in the same direction as

fashion it, if you three will but minister such 360
assistance as I shall give you direction.

LEONATO   My lord, I am for you, though it cost me ten
nights' watchings.

CLAUDIO   And I, my lord.

PRINCE   And you too, gentle Hero? 365

HERO   I will do any modest office, my lord, to help my
cousin to a good husband.

PRINCE   And Benedick is not the unhopefullest husband that I know. Thus far can I praise him: he is of
a noble strain, of approved valor, and confirmed 370
honesty. I will teach you how to humor your
cousin that she shall fall in love with Benedick.—
And I, with your two helps, will so practice on
Benedick that, in despite of his quick wit and his
queasy stomach, he shall fall in love with Beatrice. 375
If we can do this, Cupid is no longer an archer; his
glory shall be ours, for we are the only love gods. Go
in with me, and I will tell you my drift.

⌜*They*⌝ *exit.*

⌜Scene 2⌝
Enter ⌜*Don*⌝ *John and Borachio.*

DON JOHN   It is so. The Count Claudio shall marry the
daughter of Leonato.

BORACHIO   Yea, my lord, but I can cross it.

DON JOHN   Any bar, any cross, any impediment will be
med'cinable to me. I am sick in displeasure to him, 5
and whatsoever comes athwart his affection ranges
evenly with mine. How canst thou cross this marriage?

BORACHIO   Not honestly, my lord, but so covertly that
no dishonesty shall appear in me. 10

DON JOHN   Show me briefly how.

12. **since:** ago

13. **in the favor of:** i.e., **in favor** with, in the good graces of

14. **waiting gentlewoman:** See note to 2.1.35.

16. **unseasonable:** unsuitable, unseemly

17. **appoint her:** make an appointment with her

17–18. **her lady's chamber window:** i.e., the window of Hero's private quarters, perhaps her bedroom

21. **temper:** compound, produce by mixing ingredients

22. **spare not to tell:** i.e., go so far as **to tell spare:** refrain

24. **estimation:** i.e., reputation

25. **hold up:** support; **stale:** low-class harlot or prostitute

27. **What . . . that:** i.e., how will **I** prove **that?**

28. **misuse:** deceive; **vex:** distress

29. **undo:** destroy

30. **issue:** result

31. **despite:** spite, torment

33. **meet:** suitable

35. **intend:** pretend, claim

36. **as in love of:** i.e., as if because of your concern for

38. **like:** likely; **cozened:** tricked, cheated

39. **the semblance:** only the appearance

41. **trial:** i.e., putting it to the test; **instances:** evidence

43. **term:** call

44. **Claudio:** Some editors substitute the word "Borachio" here. See longer note, page 202.

46. **fashion:** contrive, cleverly plan

BORACHIO   I think I told your Lordship a year since,
   how much I am in the favor of Margaret, the
   waiting gentlewoman to Hero.

DON JOHN   I remember.   15

BORACHIO   I can, at any unseasonable instant of the
   night, appoint her to look out at her lady's chamber window.

DON JOHN   What life is in that to be the death of this
   marriage?   20

BORACHIO   The poison of that lies in you to temper. Go
   you to the Prince your brother; spare not to tell
   him that he hath wronged his honor in marrying
   the renowned Claudio, whose estimation do you
   mightily hold up, to a contaminated stale, such a   25
   one as Hero.

DON JOHN   What proof shall I make of that?

BORACHIO   Proof enough to misuse the Prince, to vex
   Claudio, to undo Hero, and kill Leonato. Look you
   for any other issue?   30

DON JOHN   Only to despite them I will endeavor anything.

BORACHIO   Go then, find me a meet hour to draw Don
   Pedro and the Count Claudio alone. Tell them that
   you know that Hero loves me; intend a kind of zeal   35
   both to the Prince and Claudio, as in love of your
   brother's honor, who hath made this match, and his
   friend's reputation, who is thus like to be cozened
   with the semblance of a maid, that you have discovered thus. They will scarcely believe this without   40
   trial. Utter them instances, which shall bear no less
   likelihood than to see me at her chamber window,
   hear me call Margaret "Hero," hear Margaret term
   me "Claudio," and bring them to see this the very
   night before the intended wedding, for in the mean- 45
   time I will so fashion the matter that Hero shall be
   absent, and there shall appear such seeming truth

48. **disloyalty:** unfaithfulness; **jealousy:** suspicion, distrust

49. **assurance:** certainty; **preparation:** i.e., for the wedding

50. **issue:** result

51. **this:** i.e., of **this**

52. **ducats:** gold coins

53. **constant:** steadfast, firm

55. **presently:** at once

2.3 Leonato, Claudio, and Don Pedro stage a conversation for Benedick to overhear. They talk about Beatrice's desperate love for Benedick, about their fears that her suffering will destroy her, and about how Benedick would mock Beatrice if he knew of her love. Benedick decides that he must love Beatrice in return.

———————

4. **orchard:** formal garden (See picture, page 74.)

5. **I am here already:** i.e., I will return immediately (Benedick pretends that the words have their literal meaning.)

11. **argument:** subject, theme

14. **drum, fife:** i.e., military music (See picture, page 215.)

15. **tabor:** small drum, used with a **tabor-pipe** to accompany dancing (See picture, page 102.)

17. **armor:** i.e., suit of **armor**

18. **carving:** i.e., planning; **doublet:** close-fitting jacket (See picture, page 144.)

18–19. **was wont to:** i.e., used to

19. **plain:** i.e., simply, straightforwardly

of Hero's disloyalty that jealousy shall be called
assurance and all the preparation overthrown.

DON JOHN Grow this to what adverse issue it can, I will　50
put it in practice. Be cunning in the working this,
and thy fee is a thousand ducats.

BORACHIO Be you constant in the accusation, and my
cunning shall not shame me.

DON JOHN I will presently go learn their day of mar-　55
riage.

⌜*They*⌝ *exit.*

⌜Scene 3⌝
Enter Benedick alone.

BENEDICK Boy!

⌜*Enter Boy.*⌝

BOY Signior?

BENEDICK In my chamber window lies a book. Bring it
hither to me in the orchard.

BOY I am here already, sir.　5

BENEDICK I know that, but I would have thee hence
and here again.　　　　　　　　　⌜*Boy*⌝ *exits.*
I do much wonder that one man, seeing how much
another man is a fool when he dedicates his behaviors to love, will, after he hath laughed at such　10
shallow follies in others, become the argument of
his own scorn by falling in love and such a man is
Claudio. I have known when there was no music
with him but the drum and the fife, and now had he
rather hear the tabor and the pipe; I have known　15
when he would have walked ten mile afoot to see a
good armor, and now will he lie ten nights awake
carving the fashion of a new doublet. He was wont
to speak plain and to the purpose, like an honest

20–21. **turned orthography:** i.e., become a fancy speaker (**Orthography** is, literally, the study of proper spelling.)

27. **fair:** beautiful; **well:** i.e., healthy (not "sick" with love)

29. **graces:** pleasing qualities

30. **grace:** favor

31. **I'll none:** i.e., **I'll** not have her; **cheapen:** bid for

32. **look on:** observe

33. **noble, angel:** In addition to their usual meanings, these words were also the names of coins.

34. **discourse:** i.e., ability to converse

39. **harmony:** music, pleasing sounds

41. **The music ended:** i.e., when **the music** has **ended**

42. **fit . . . pennyworth:** This much-debated phrase links Benedick to the **kid-fox** (perhaps, a young fox) and to some form of punishment. "To get one's **pennyworth** on" is "to take revenge on"; **pennyworth** also meant "a reward" or "a bargain." (Some editors print "hid-fox," since Benedick is hiding.)

44. **tax:** order, challenge

The Ponyard.

A poniard. (2.1.244)
From Louis de Gaya,
A treatise of the arms . . . (1678).

man and a soldier, and now is he turned orthogra-   20
phy; his words are a very fantastical banquet, just so
many strange dishes. May I be so converted and see
with these eyes? I cannot tell; I think not. I will not
be sworn but love may transform me to an oyster,
but I'll take my oath on it, till he have made an   25
oyster of me, he shall never make me such a fool.
One woman is fair, yet I am well; another is wise, yet
I am well; another virtuous, yet I am well; but till all
graces be in one woman, one woman shall not
come in my grace. Rich she shall be, that's certain;   30
wise, or I'll none; virtuous, or I'll never cheapen
her; fair, or I'll never look on her; mild, or come not
near me; noble, or not I for an angel; of good
discourse, an excellent musician, and her hair shall
be of what color it please God. Ha! The Prince and   35
Monsieur Love! I will hide me in the arbor.
                                             ⌜*He hides.*⌝

Enter Prince, Leonato, Claudio, and Balthasar
with music.

PRINCE   Come, shall we hear this music?
CLAUDIO
    Yea, my good lord. How still the evening is,
    As hushed on purpose to grace harmony!
PRINCE, ⌜*aside to Claudio*⌝
    See you where Benedick hath hid himself?   40
CLAUDIO, ⌜*aside to Prince*⌝
    O, very well, my lord. The music ended,
    We'll fit the kid-fox with a pennyworth.
PRINCE
    Come, Balthasar, we'll hear that song again.
BALTHASAR
    O, good my lord, tax not so bad a voice
    To slander music any more than once.   45

46. **witness:** sign, token; **still:** always

47. **put a strange face:** perhaps, pretend not to know; **his:** its

48. **let me woo:** i.e., make me entreat

50–52. **Since . . . loves:** Balthasar compares Don Pedro, who has flattered his music, to a man who courts a woman whom he knows is unworthy.

55. **notes:** i.e., music

56. **Note:** take notice of

58. **crotchets:** (1) peculiar ideas; (2) quarter notes in music

59. **nothing:** There is some evidence that "nothing" and "noting" were pronounced alike in Shakespeare's day. If so, this word is yet another pun on "noting," and the title of the play itself could be heard as "Much Ado about Noting."

60. **air:** melody

61. **sheeps' guts:** used to make strings for lutes and other musical instruments (See picture, page 122.)

62. **hale:** pull, draw

67. **constant:** faithful

69. **blithe:** merry; **bonny:** smiling, bright

71. **nonny nonny:** a meaningless refrain

72. **mo:** i.e., more

73. **dumps:** (1) fits of melancholy or depression; (2) mournful songs; **dull:** gloomy; **heavy:** sad

75. **leavy:** filled with leaves

PRINCE
　It is the witness still of excellency
　To put a strange face on his own perfection.
　I pray thee, sing, and let me woo no more.

BALTHASAR
　Because you talk of wooing, I will sing,
　Since many a wooer doth commence his suit   50
　To her he thinks not worthy, yet he woos,
　Yet will he swear he loves.

PRINCE   Nay, pray thee, come,
　Or if thou wilt hold longer argument,
　Do it in notes.   55

BALTHASAR   Note this before my notes:
　There's not a note of mine that's worth the noting.

PRINCE
　Why, these are very crotchets that he speaks!
　Note notes, forsooth, and nothing.   「*Music plays.*」

BENEDICK, 「*aside*」 Now, divine air! Now is his soul   60
　　ravished. Is it not strange that sheeps' guts should
　　hale souls out of men's bodies? Well, a horn for my
　　money, when all's done.

「BALTHASAR *sings*」
　　　Sigh no more, ladies, sigh no more,
　　　　Men were deceivers ever,   65
　　　One foot in sea and one on shore,
　　　　To one thing constant never.
　　　Then sigh not so, but let them go,
　　　　And be you blithe and bonny,
　　　Converting all your sounds of woe   70
　　　　Into Hey, nonny nonny.

　　　Sing no more ditties, sing no mo,
　　　　Of dumps so dull and heavy.
　　　The fraud of men was ever so,
　　　　Since summer first was leavy.   75

81. **an ill:** i.e., a bad

82–83. **for a shift:** i.e., as a makeshift, for lack of something better

86. **bode no mischief:** i.e., does not prophesy misfortune

86–87. **had as lief:** i.e., would just as gladly

87. **night raven:** Proverbial: "The croaking **raven** bodes disaster."

98. **Stalk on:** i.e., pursue our prey stealthily

99. **sits:** i.e., is roosting (thus easily caught)

105–6. **Sits . . . corner?:** i.e., does **the wind** blow from **that** direction?

108. **enraged:** inflamed

109. **the infinite of:** i.e., the range of

110. **counterfeit:** pretend

111. **like enough:** i.e., that is likely

"In time the savage bull
doth bear the yoke." (1.1.256)
From Philip Ayres, *Emblemata amatoria* . . . (1683).

> *Then sigh not so, but let them go,*
> *And be you blithe and bonny,*
> *Converting all your sounds of woe*
> *Into Hey, nonny nonny.*

PRINCE   By my troth, a good song.   80

BALTHASAR   And an ill singer, my lord.

PRINCE   Ha, no, no, faith, thou sing'st well enough for a
shift.

BENEDICK, ⌈*aside*⌉ An he had been a dog that should
have howled thus, they would have hanged him. And   85
I pray God his bad voice bode no mischief. I had as
lief have heard the night raven, come what plague
could have come after it.

PRINCE   Yea, marry, dost thou hear, Balthasar? I pray
thee get us some excellent music, for tomorrow   90
night we would have it at the Lady Hero's chamber
window.

BALTHASAR   The best I can, my lord.

PRINCE   Do so. Farewell.   *Balthasar exits.*
Come hither, Leonato. What was it you told me of   95
today, that your niece Beatrice was in love with
Signior Benedick?

CLAUDIO   O, ay. ⌈*Aside to Prince.*⌉ Stalk on, stalk on; the
fowl sits.—I did never think that lady would have
loved any man.   100

LEONATO   No, nor I neither, but most wonderful that
she should so dote on Signior Benedick, whom she
hath in all outward behaviors seemed ever to
abhor.

BENEDICK, ⌈*aside*⌉ Is 't possible? Sits the wind in that   105
corner?

LEONATO   By my troth, my lord, I cannot tell what to
think of it, but that she loves him with an enraged
affection, it is past the infinite of thought.

PRINCE   Maybe she doth but counterfeit.   110

CLAUDIO   Faith, like enough.

114. **discovers:** reveals, shows
115. **effects:** signs
118. **sit you:** i.e., **sit** (ethical dative)
126. **gull:** trick; **but:** except
127. **Knavery:** a trick
128. **himself:** i.e., itself; **reverence:** a reverend or venerable person
129. **ta'en th' infection:** i.e., caught the disease (we are spreading) **ta'en:** taken
130. **Hold it up:** i.e., keep **it up**
136. **says she:** i.e., **says** Beatrice
140. **smock:** slip, chemise
144. **she:** Beatrice; **it . . . it:** the **sheet of paper**

A willow. (2.1.185)
From Henry Peacham, *Minerua Britanna* . . . (1612).

LEONATO   O God! Counterfeit? There was never counterfeit of passion came so near the life of passion as
she discovers it.

PRINCE   Why, what effects of passion shows she?   115

CLAUDIO, ⌜*aside to Leonato*⌝   Bait the hook well; this fish
will bite.

LEONATO   What effects, my lord? She will sit you—you
heard my daughter tell you how.

CLAUDIO   She did indeed.   120

PRINCE   How, how I pray you? You amaze me. I would
have thought her spirit had been invincible against
all assaults of affection.

LEONATO   I would have sworn it had, my lord, especially against Benedick.   125

BENEDICK, ⌜*aside*⌝   I should think this a gull but that the
white-bearded fellow speaks it. Knavery cannot,
sure, hide himself in such reverence.

CLAUDIO, ⌜*aside to Prince*⌝   He hath ta'en th' infection.
Hold it up.   130

PRINCE   Hath she made her affection known to Benedick?

LEONATO   No, and swears she never will. That's her
torment.

CLAUDIO   'Tis true indeed, so your daughter says. "Shall   135
I," says she, "that have so oft encountered him with
scorn, write to him that I love him?"

LEONATO   This says she now when she is beginning to
write to him, for she'll be up twenty times a night,
and there will she sit in her smock till she have writ   140
a sheet of paper. My daughter tells us all.

CLAUDIO   Now you talk of a sheet of paper, I remember
a pretty jest your daughter told ⌜us of.⌝

LEONATO   O, when she had writ it and was reading it
over, she found "Benedick" and "Beatrice" be-   145
tween the sheet?

CLAUDIO   That.

148–49. **halfpence:** i.e., little pieces

149. **railed at:** berated

150. **immodest:** forward, impudent; **flout:** mock, scoff at

158. **ecstasy:** frenzy, madness; **overborne her:** overcome her

159–60. **do . . . herself:** harm herself dangerously

162. **discover:** reveal

163. **sport:** joke, jest

165. **an alms:** a good deed

166. **out of:** i.e., beyond

170. **blood:** passion

174. **dotage:** excessive love

175. **daffed:** put aside; **respects:** considerations

175–76. **made . . . myself:** i.e., married her

179. **she says:** i.e., Beatrice **says**

182. **rather than she will bate:** i.e., before she will leave off

183. **crossness:** contrariness

LEONATO   O, she tore the letter into a thousand halfpence, railed at herself that she should be so
immodest to write to one that she knew would flout   150
her. "I measure him," says she, "by my own spirit,
for I should flout him if he writ to me, yea, though I
love him, I should."

CLAUDIO   Then down upon her knees she falls, weeps,
sobs, beats her heart, tears her hair, prays, curses: 155
"O sweet Benedick, God give me patience!"

LEONATO   She doth indeed, my daughter says so, and
the ecstasy hath so much overborne her that my
daughter is sometimes afeared she will do a desperate outrage to herself. It is very true.   160

PRINCE   It were good that Benedick knew of it by some
other, if she will not discover it.

CLAUDIO   To what end? He would make but a sport of it
and torment the poor lady worse.

PRINCE   An he should, it were an alms to hang him.   165
She's an excellent sweet lady, and, out of all suspicion, she is virtuous.

CLAUDIO   And she is exceeding wise.

PRINCE   In everything but in loving Benedick.

LEONATO   O, my lord, wisdom and blood combating in   170
so tender a body, we have ten proofs to one that
blood hath the victory. I am sorry for her, as I have
just cause, being her uncle and her guardian.

PRINCE   I would she had bestowed this dotage on me. I
would have daffed all other respects and made her   175
half myself. I pray you tell Benedick of it, and hear
what he will say.

LEONATO   Were it good, think you?

CLAUDIO   Hero thinks surely she will die, for she says
she will die if he love her not, and she will die ere   180
she make her love known, and she will die if he woo
her rather than she will bate one breath of her
accustomed crossness.

184. **make tender of:** i.e., offer
186. **contemptible:** contemptuous, scornful
187. **proper:** handsome; or, fine, respectable
188. **good outward happiness:** perhaps, an attractive appearance
191. **wit:** intelligence
193. **Hector:** a Trojan warrior noted for courage (See picture, page 90.)
194. **quarrels:** hostilities, violent altercations
201. **by:** i.e., to judge by; **large:** improper, licentious
205. **counsel:** advice
209. **the while:** in the meanwhile
214–15. **expectation:** ability to predict
218. **carry:** manage; **sport:** amusement, fun

An orchard. (1.2.10; 2.3.4; 3.1.5)
From Octavio Boldoni, *Theatrum temporaneum* . . . (1636).

PRINCE   She doth well. If she should make tender of
her love, 'tis very possible he'll scorn it, for the man,   185
as you know all, hath a contemptible spirit.

CLAUDIO   He is a very proper man.

PRINCE   He hath indeed a good outward happiness.

CLAUDIO   Before God, and in my mind, very wise.

PRINCE   He doth indeed show some sparks that are like   190
wit.

CLAUDIO   And I take him to be valiant.

PRINCE   As Hector, I assure you, and in the managing
of quarrels you may say he is wise, for either he
avoids them with great discretion or undertakes   195
them with a most Christianlike fear.

LEONATO   If he do fear God, he must necessarily keep
peace. If he break the peace, he ought to enter into
a quarrel with fear and trembling.

PRINCE   And so will he do, for the man doth fear God,   200
howsoever it seems not in him by some large jests
he will make. Well, I am sorry for your niece. Shall
we go seek Benedick and tell him of her love?

CLAUDIO   Never tell him, my lord, let her wear it out
with good counsel.   205

LEONATO   Nay, that's impossible; she may wear her
heart out first.

PRINCE   Well, we will hear further of it by your daughter. Let it cool the while. I love Benedick well, and I
could wish he would modestly examine himself to   210
see how much he is unworthy so good a lady.

LEONATO   My lord, will you walk? Dinner is ready.
⌜*Leonato, Prince, and Claudio begin to exit.*⌝

CLAUDIO, ⌜*aside to Prince and Leonato*⌝ If he do not
dote on her upon this, I will never trust my expectation.   215

PRINCE, ⌜*aside to Leonato*⌝ Let there be the same net
spread for her, and that must your daughter and her
gentlewomen carry. The sport will be when they

219. hold one an opinion of another's dotage: i.e., each holds the **opinion** that the other is in love

221. dumb show: literally, a theatrical scene without speech

224. conference: conversation; **sadly borne:** seriously conducted

226. have their full bent: This phrase suggests a bow, in archery, bent to its limit. (See picture, below.)

232. their detractions: i.e., words pointing out their faults

232–33. put . . . mending: i.e., mend the faults

235. reprove: reject

238. some odd quirks: i.e., a few quibbles

241. meat: i.e., food

242. sentences: maxims, sayings

243. awe: restrain through fear

244. career: course; **humor:** inclination

Cupid with a bow at "full bent." (2.3.226)
From August Casimir Redel,
Apophtegmata symbolica . . . (n.d.).

hold one an opinion of another's dotage, and no
such matter. That's the scene that I would see,   220
which will be merely a dumb show. Let us send her
to call him in to dinner.

⌜*Prince, Leonato, and Claudio exit.*⌝

BENEDICK, ⌜*coming forward*⌝   This can be no trick. The
conference was sadly borne; they have the truth of
this from Hero; they seem to pity the lady. It seems   225
her affections have their full bent. Love me? Why, it
must be requited! I hear how I am censured. They
say I will bear myself proudly if I perceive the love
come from her. They say, too, that she will rather
die than give any sign of affection. I did never think   230
to marry. I must not seem proud. Happy are they
that hear their detractions and can put them to
mending. They say the lady is fair; 'tis a truth, I can
bear them witness. And virtuous; 'tis so, I cannot
reprove it. And wise, but for loving me; by my troth,   235
it is no addition to her wit, nor no great argument of
her folly, for I will be horribly in love with her! I
may chance have some odd quirks and remnants of
wit broken on me because I have railed so long
against marriage, but doth not the appetite alter? A   240
man loves the meat in his youth that he cannot
endure in his age. Shall quips and sentences and
these paper bullets of the brain awe a man from the
career of his humor? No! The world must be peopled. When I said I would die a bachelor, I did not   245
think I should live till I were married. Here comes
Beatrice. By this day, she's a fair lady. I do spy some
marks of love in her.

Enter Beatrice.

BEATRICE   Against my will, I am sent to bid you come
in to dinner.   250

BENEDICK   Fair Beatrice, I thank you for your pains.

257. **daw:** jackdaw, a small kind of crow; **withal:** with it

258. **stomach:** appetite

264. **pity of:** i.e., **pity** on

265. **Jew:** From the Middle Ages, when Jews were kept from almost all occupations except moneylending, the word "Jew" was sometimes used as a term of contempt for anyone who (like the stereotypical moneylender) was ungenerous or cruel.

"Lady Fame." (2.1.211)
From August Casimir Redel,
Apophtegmata symbolica . . . (n.d.).

BEATRICE I took no more pains for those thanks than
you take pains to thank me. If it had been painful, I
would not have come.

BENEDICK You take pleasure then in the message? 255

BEATRICE Yea, just so much as you may take upon a
knife's point and choke a daw withal. You have no
stomach, signior. Fare you well. *She exits.*

BENEDICK Ha! "Against my will I am sent to bid you
come in to dinner." There's a double meaning in 260
that. "I took no more pains for those thanks than
you took pains to thank me." That's as much as to
say "Any pains that I take for you is as easy as
thanks." If I do not take pity of her, I am a villain; if I
do not love her, I am a Jew. I will go get her picture. 265
He exits.

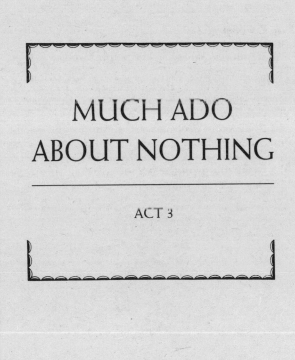

MUCH ADO
ABOUT NOTHING

ACT 3

3.1 Beatrice is lured into overhearing a staged conversation between Hero and Ursula, a waiting gentlewoman, who talk about Benedick's desperate love for Beatrice and about Beatrice's arrogance. Beatrice decides that she must return Benedick's love.

---

3. **Proposing:** talking
4. **Whisper her:** i.e., **whisper** in **her**
7. **pleachèd:** bordered with intertwined boughs (See picture, page 223.)
9–10. **favorites . . . that advance:** i.e., especially indulged courtiers . . . who display or raise up
11. **bred it:** brought it forth
13. **listen our propose:** i.e., **listen** to **our** discussion; **office:** assigned part
14. **Bear thee:** i.e., conduct yourself
15. **warrant:** promise; **presently:** at once
17. **trace:** tread; **alley:** garden path

Honeysuckle or woodbine. (3.1.8, 31)
From John Gerard, *The herball . . .* (1597).

⌜ACT 3⌝

⌜Scene 1⌝

Enter Hero and two gentlewomen, Margaret and Ursula.

HERO
  Good Margaret, run thee to the parlor.
  There shalt thou find my cousin Beatrice
  Proposing with the Prince and Claudio.
  Whisper her ear and tell her I and Ursula
  Walk in the orchard, and our whole discourse   5
  Is all of her. Say that thou overheardst us,
  And bid her steal into the pleachèd bower
  Where honeysuckles ripened by the sun
  Forbid the sun to enter, like favorites,
  Made proud by princes, that advance their pride   10
  Against that power that bred it. There will she hide
    her
  To listen our propose. This is thy office.
  Bear thee well in it, and leave us alone.

MARGARET
  I'll make her come, I warrant you, presently.   15
                                    ⌜*She exits.*⌝

HERO
  Now, Ursula, when Beatrice doth come,
  As we do trace this alley up and down,
  Our talk must only be of Benedick.
  When I do name him, let it be thy part
  To praise him more than ever man did merit.   20

83

22. **matter:** i.e., material
23. **Cupid's . . . arrow:** See note to 1.1.39.
24. **only wounds by:** i.e., **wounds by** mere
25. **lapwing:** plover, a ground-nesting bird
26. **conference:** conversation
27–29. **The pleasant'st . . . bait:** i.e., the most pleasant moment in fishing is when **the fish** rushes to take the **bait   her . . . oars:** i.e., its fins
31. **couchèd:** hidden; **woodbine coverture:** i.e., screen of honeysuckle (See picture, page 82.)
32. **Fear you not:** i.e., don't worry about
36. **coy:** distant, disdainful; **wild:** rebellious
37. **haggards:** wild female hawks (See picture, below.) **rock:** cliff
40. **new-trothèd:** newly betrothed
44. **with affection:** i.e., with his emotions

A haggard falcon. (3.1.37)
From George Turberville, *The booke of faulconrie . . .* (1575).

My talk to thee must be how Benedick
Is sick in love with Beatrice. Of this matter
Is little Cupid's crafty arrow made,
That only wounds by hearsay. Now begin,
For look where Beatrice like a lapwing runs   25
Close by the ground, to hear our conference.

Enter Beatrice, ⌜who hides in the bower.⌝

URSULA, ⌜*aside to Hero*⌝
The pleasant'st angling is to see the fish
Cut with her golden oars the silver stream
And greedily devour the treacherous bait.
So angle we for Beatrice, who even now   30
Is couchèd in the woodbine coverture.
Fear you not my part of the dialogue.

HERO, ⌜*aside to Ursula*⌝
Then go we near her, that her ear lose nothing
Of the false sweet bait that we lay for it.—
⌜*They walk near the bower.*⌝
No, truly, Ursula, she is too disdainful.   35
I know her spirits are as coy and wild
As haggards of the rock.

URSULA   But are you sure
That Benedick loves Beatrice so entirely?

HERO
So says the Prince and my new-trothèd lord.   40

URSULA
And did they bid you tell her of it, madam?

HERO
They did entreat me to acquaint her of it,
But I persuaded them, if they loved Benedick,
To wish him wrestle with affection
And never to let Beatrice know of it.   45

URSULA
Why did you so? Doth not the gentleman

47. **as full:** i.e., fully
48. **couch:** lie down
50. **yielded:** allowed, granted
53. **sparkling:** flashing
54. **Misprizing:** despising; **wit:** cleverness
56. **All matter else seems weak:** i.e., **all** other conversation **seems** worthless
57. **project:** idea, notion
58. **self-endeared:** in love with herself
61. **make sport at:** i.e., mock, **make** fun of
63. **How:** i.e., no matter **how; rarely:** beautifully; **featured:** formed
64. **spell him backward:** i.e., describe him perversely; **fair-faced:** of a fair complexion; or, beautifully featured
67. **black:** i.e., dark-skinned; **of an antic:** i.e., a grotesque or fantastic figure
68. **lance ill-headed:** dull spear
69. **low:** short; **an agate:** i.e., like a tiny figure carved on an agate-stone ring
70. **vane:** i.e., weather **vane**
71. **moved . . . none:** i.e., that cannot be **moved** by any wind, no matter how strong
74. **simpleness:** sincerity, integrity; **purchaseth:** earns
75. **commendable:** pronounced **còmmendable**
76. **from all fashions:** unlike customary or accepted ways of behaving

Deserve as full as fortunate a bed
As ever Beatrice shall couch upon?

HERO
O god of love! I know he doth deserve
As much as may be yielded to a man,   50
But Nature never framed a woman's heart
Of prouder stuff than that of Beatrice.
Disdain and scorn ride sparkling in her eyes,
Misprizing what they look on, and her wit
Values itself so highly that to her   55
All matter else seems weak. She cannot love,
Nor take no shape nor project of affection,
She is so self-endeared.

URSULA   Sure, I think so,
And therefore certainly it were not good   60
She knew his love, lest she'll make sport at it.

HERO
Why, you speak truth. I never yet saw man,
How wise, how noble, young, how rarely featured,
But she would spell him backward. If fair-faced,
She would swear the gentleman should be her   65
    sister;
If black, why, Nature, drawing of an antic,
Made a foul blot; if tall, a lance ill-headed;
If low, an agate very vilely cut;
If speaking, why, a vane blown with all winds;   70
If silent, why, a block moved with none.
So turns she every man the wrong side out,
And never gives to truth and virtue that
Which simpleness and merit purchaseth.

URSULA
Sure, sure, such carping is not commendable.   75

HERO
No, not to be so odd and from all fashions
As Beatrice is cannot be commendable.
But who dare tell her so? If I should speak,

81. **press me to death:** an allusion to the torture of a prisoner by loading heavy weights on his chest until he dies

82. **covered fire:** Proverbial: "**Fire** that's closest kept burns most of all."

83. **Consume away, waste:** i.e., be destroyed (**Sighs** were thought to draw blood from the heart.)

89. **honest slanders:** perhaps, malicious statements that do not, however, attack her chastity (**Honest,** when applied to a woman, standardly meant "chaste.")

95. **prized to have:** esteemed as having; or, credited with having

96. **rare:** splendid

97. **the only:** i.e., the very best

100. **Speaking my fancy:** i.e., for expressing my own preference

101. **bearing:** demeanor; **argument:** ability to converse

103. **name:** reputation

105. **are you married:** i.e., will **you** be **married**

106. **every day, tomorrow:** i.e., after **tomorrow** (I'll be married) all the time

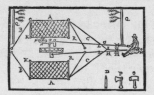

Woodcock. (5.1.170)
From Henry Parrot, *Laquei ridiculosi* . . . (1613).

She would mock me into air. O, she would laugh
  me 80
Out of myself, press me to death with wit.
Therefore let Benedick, like covered fire,
Consume away in sighs, waste inwardly.
It were a better death than die with mocks,
Which is as bad as die with tickling. 85

URSULA
Yet tell her of it. Hear what she will say.

HERO
No, rather I will go to Benedick
And counsel him to fight against his passion;
And truly I'll devise some honest slanders
To stain my cousin with. One doth not know 90
How much an ill word may empoison liking.

URSULA
O, do not do your cousin such a wrong!
She cannot be so much without true judgment,
Having so swift and excellent a wit
As she is prized to have, as to refuse 95
So rare a gentleman as Signior Benedick.

HERO
He is the only man of Italy,
Always excepted my dear Claudio.

URSULA
I pray you be not angry with me, madam,
Speaking my fancy: Signior Benedick, 100
For shape, for bearing, argument, and valor,
Goes foremost in report through Italy.

HERO
Indeed, he hath an excellent good name.

URSULA
His excellence did earn it ere he had it.
When are you married, madam? 105

HERO
Why, every day, tomorrow. Come, go in.

107. **attires:** headdresses; clothes
109. **limed:** i.e., trapped like a bird in birdlime
111. **haps:** chance, accident
116. **such:** i.e., contemptuous and proud maidens
120. **band:** i.e., bond
122. **reportingly:** i.e., by report or hearsay

3.2 Benedick appears with his beard shaved off and showing other signs of having fallen in love. When he exits with Leonato, Don John tells Don Pedro and Claudio that Hero is unfaithful and that he will show them a man entering her chamber window that very night, the night before the wedding.

1–2. **consummate:** i.e., consummated, completed
3. **bring you thither:** i.e., go with you to Aragon
3–4. **vouchsafe:** allow
5. **soil in:** i.e., stain on
7–8. **be bold with:** i.e., take the liberty of asking

Hector. (2.3.193)
From [Guillaume Rouillé,] . . .
Promptuarii iconum . . . (1553).

I'll show thee some attires and have thy counsel
Which is the best to furnish me tomorrow.
               ⌜*They move away from the bower.*⌝

URSULA, ⌜*aside to Hero*⌝
  She's limed, I warrant you. We have caught her,
    madam.   110

HERO, ⌜*aside to Ursula*⌝
  If it prove so, then loving goes by haps;
  Some Cupid kills with arrows, some with traps.
                 ⌜*Hero and Ursula exit.*⌝

BEATRICE, ⌜*coming forward*⌝
  What fire is in mine ears? Can this be true?
    Stand I condemned for pride and scorn so much?
  Contempt, farewell, and maiden pride, adieu!   115
    No glory lives behind the back of such.
  And Benedick, love on; I will requite thee,
    Taming my wild heart to thy loving hand.
  If thou dost love, my kindness shall incite thee
    To bind our loves up in a holy band.   120
  For others say thou dost deserve, and I
  Believe it better than reportingly.
                               She exits.

⌜Scene 2⌝
Enter Prince, Claudio, Benedick, and Leonato.

PRINCE   I do but stay till your marriage be consum-
    mate, and then go I toward Aragon.
CLAUDIO   I'll bring you thither, my lord, if you'll vouch-
    safe me.
PRINCE   Nay, that would be as great a soil in the new   5
    gloss of your marriage as to show a child his new
    coat and forbid him to wear it. I will only be bold
    with Benedick for his company, for from the crown
    of his head to the sole of his foot he is all mirth. He

11. **hangman:** i.e., executioner, torturer (Cupid)

16. **Methinks:** it seems to me; **sadder:** more serious

18. **truant:** rogue; **true:** honest, sincere

20. **wants:** lacks

22. **Draw it:** i.e., pull (the tooth)

23. **Hang it:** an exclamation of impatience

24. **hang, draw:** Traitors were first hanged, then drawn (disemboweled).

26. **Where is but a humor or a worm:** In Elizabethan thinking, **toothache** was caused by humors (morbid secretions) descending from the head or rising from the stomach, or by worms invading the tooth.

27. **grief:** hurt, injury, suffering

30. **fancy:** love

31. **fancy:** whim, sudden liking (as also in line 36); **strange:** foreign

34. **slops:** wide baggy breeches or hose

37. **fool for fancy:** i.e., victim of love

40. **bode:** indicate

42. **man:** i.e., servant

43. **the old ornament of his cheek:** i.e., his beard

hath twice or thrice cut Cupid's bowstring, and the 10
little hangman dare not shoot at him. He hath a
heart as sound as a bell, and his tongue is the
clapper, for what his heart thinks, his tongue
speaks.

BENEDICK   Gallants, I am not as I have been. 15

LEONATO   So say I. Methinks you are sadder.

CLAUDIO   I hope he be in love.

PRINCE   Hang him, truant! There's no true drop of
blood in him to be truly touched with love. If he be
sad, he wants money. 20

BENEDICK   I have the toothache.

PRINCE   Draw it.

BENEDICK   Hang it!

CLAUDIO   You must hang it first, and draw it afterwards.

PRINCE   What, sigh for the toothache? 25

LEONATO   Where is but a humor or a worm.

BENEDICK   Well, everyone ⌜can⌝ master a grief but he
that has it.

CLAUDIO   Yet say I, he is in love.

PRINCE   There is no appearance of fancy in him, unless 30
it be a fancy that he hath to strange disguises, as to
be a Dutchman today, a Frenchman tomorrow, or
in the shape of two countries at once, as a German
from the waist downward, all slops, and a Spaniard
from the hip upward, no doublet. Unless he have a 35
fancy to this foolery, as it appears he hath, he is no
fool for fancy, as you would have it appear he is.

CLAUDIO   If he be not in love with some woman, there
is no believing old signs. He brushes his hat o'
mornings. What should that bode? 40

PRINCE   Hath any man seen him at the barber's?

CLAUDIO   No, but the barber's man hath been seen
with him, and the old ornament of his cheek hath
already stuffed tennis balls.

47. **civet:** i.e., perfume (from the scent glands of a **civet** cat; see picture, below)

47–48. **smell him out:** i.e., discover his secret (with a pun on **smell**)

51. **note:** indication

53. **paint himself:** i.e., use cosmetics (**Wash his face,** line 52, may also have this meaning.) **the which:** i.e., his use of cosmetics

55–56. **crept . . . stops:** i.e., converted to love songs   **stops:** the positions on the lute where the fingers are pressed to make particular sounds (with a pun on the **stops** or silences in his speech)

57. **heavy:** distressing

62. **ill conditions:** i.e., bad qualities

63. **dies:** wastes away (The Prince's response in line 64 plays on the Elizabethan use of the word *die* to allude to sexual orgasm.)

65. **charm for:** i.e., magic spell to cure

68. **hobby-horses:** i.e., jesters, buffoons

69. **For my life:** i.e., upon **my life**

70. **by this:** i.e., **by this** time

74. **e'en:** afternoon (literally, evening)

75. **If . . . served:** i.e., if you have the time

Civet. (3.2.47)
From Edward Topsell, *The historie of foure-footed beastes . . .* (1607).

LEONATO   Indeed he looks younger than he did, by the   45
loss of a beard.

PRINCE   Nay, he rubs himself with civet. Can you smell
him out by that?

CLAUDIO   That's as much as to say, the sweet youth's in
love.   50

⌜PRINCE⌝   The greatest note of it is his melancholy.

CLAUDIO   And when was he wont to wash his face?

PRINCE   Yea, or to paint himself? For the which I hear
what they say of him.

CLAUDIO   Nay, but his jesting spirit, which is now crept   55
into a lute string and now governed by stops—

PRINCE   Indeed, that tells a heavy tale for him. Conclude, conclude, he is in love.

CLAUDIO   Nay, but I know who loves him.

PRINCE   That would I know, too. I warrant, one that   60
knows him not.

CLAUDIO   Yes, and his ill conditions; and, in despite of
all, dies for him.

PRINCE   She shall be buried with her face upwards.

BENEDICK   Yet is this no charm for the toothache.—   65
Old signior, walk aside with me. I have studied eight
or nine wise words to speak to you, which these
hobby-horses must not hear.
⌜*Benedick and Leonato exit.*⌝

PRINCE   For my life, to break with him about Beatrice!

CLAUDIO   'Tis even so. Hero and Margaret have by this   70
played their parts with Beatrice, and then the two
bears will not bite one another when they meet.

Enter John the Bastard.

DON JOHN   My lord and brother, God save you.

PRINCE   Good e'en, brother.

DON JOHN   If your leisure served, I would speak with   75
you.

PRINCE   In private?

80. **matter:** i.e., subject **matter**

86–87. **discover:** reveal

89. **hereafter:** later; **aim better at me:** judge me more highly or more accurately; **by that:** i.e., in the light of that which

90. **For:** i.e., as for

90–91. **holds you well:** i.e., thinks **well** of **you**

91. **dearness of heart:** i.e., affection; **holp:** i.e., helped; **effect:** bring about

92. **suit:** courtship

95–96. **circumstances shortened:** i.e., to cut out the details

97. **a-talking of:** i.e., in our talking; **disloyal:** unfaithful, unchaste

102. **paint out:** i.e., depict, describe

105. **till . . . warrant:** i.e., until you have conclusive proof

112. **that you see:** i.e., **that** which **you** will **see**

113. **that you know:** i.e., **that** which **you know**

DON JOHN If it please you. Yet Count Claudio may
  hear, for what I would speak of concerns him.

PRINCE What's the matter? 80

DON JOHN, ⌈*to Claudio*⌉ Means your Lordship to be
  married tomorrow?

PRINCE You know he does.

DON JOHN I know not that, when he knows what I
  know. 85

CLAUDIO If there be any impediment, I pray you discover it.

DON JOHN You may think I love you not. Let that
  appear hereafter, and aim better at me by that I
  now will manifest. For my brother, I think he holds 90
  you well, and in dearness of heart hath holp to effect
  your ensuing marriage—surely suit ill spent and
  labor ill bestowed.

PRINCE Why, what's the matter?

DON JOHN I came hither to tell you; and, circum- 95
  stances shortened, for she has been too long
  a talking of, the lady is disloyal.

CLAUDIO Who, Hero?

DON JOHN Even she: Leonato's Hero, your Hero, every
  man's Hero. 100

CLAUDIO Disloyal?

DON JOHN The word is too good to paint out her
  wickedness. I could say she were worse. Think you
  of a worse title, and I will fit her to it. Wonder not
  till further warrant. Go but with me tonight, you 105
  shall see her chamber window entered, even the
  night before her wedding day. If you love her then,
  tomorrow wed her. But it would better fit your
  honor to change your mind.

CLAUDIO, ⌈*to Prince*⌉ May this be so? 110

PRINCE I will not think it.

DON JOHN If you dare not trust that you see, confess
  not that you know. If you will follow me, I will

119. **as:** i.e., since; or, in the same way that
122. **coldly:** coolly, calmly
123. **issue:** result (of what you see); **show:** reveal
124. **untowardly:** unluckily
125. **mischief:** evil, wickedness
126. **plague:** i.e., calamity
127. **the sequel:** that which follows

3.3 That night, Messina's master constable, Dogberry, and his assistant, Verges, set the night watch, telling the watchmen to pay particular attention to any activity around Leonato's house. Borachio enters, telling his companion, Conrade, about the charade that made Claudio and Don Pedro think that Hero had just allowed him to enter her chamber. Borachio and Conrade are arrested by the watch.

---

0 SD. **compartner:** copartner, associate; **Watch:** watchmen (citizens chosen to act as a night patrol)
2. **it were pity but they:** i.e., it would be regrettable if they did not
3. **salvation:** a mistake for "damnation"
5. **allegiance:** Dogberry seems to mean "lack of allegiance."
7. **charge:** i.e., orders
9. **most desartless:** i.e., least deserving (his mistake for "**most** deserving")
10. **constable:** perhaps, chief watchman (Dogberry himself is identified as "master constable"— officer of the peace—at line 17 and as *the Constable* in the opening stage direction of 3.5.)

show you enough, and when you have seen more
and heard more, proceed accordingly.   115

CLAUDIO   If I see anything tonight why I should not
marry her, tomorrow in the congregation, where I
should wed, there will I shame her.

PRINCE   And as I wooed for thee to obtain her, I will
join with thee to disgrace her.   120

DON JOHN   I will disparage her no farther till you are
my witnesses. Bear it coldly but till midnight, and
let the issue show itself.

PRINCE   O day untowardly turned!

CLAUDIO   O mischief strangely thwarting!   125

DON JOHN   O plague right well prevented! So will you
say when you have seen the sequel.
                                    ⌜*They exit.*⌝

⌜Scene 3⌝
Enter Dogberry and his compartner ⌜Verges⌝
with the Watch.

DOGBERRY   Are you good men and true?

VERGES   Yea, or else it were pity but they should suffer
salvation, body and soul.

DOGBERRY   Nay, that were a punishment too good for
them if they should have any allegiance in them,   5
being chosen for the Prince's watch.

VERGES   Well, give them their charge, neighbor Dogberry.

DOGBERRY   First, who think you the most desartless
man to be constable?   10

FIRST WATCHMAN   Hugh Oatcake, sir, or George Seacoal, for they can write and read.

DOGBERRY   Come hither, neighbor Seacoal. ⌜*Seacoal*
steps forward.⌝ God hath blessed you with a good

15. **well-favored:** i.e., handsome

19. **favor:** appearance

22. **vanity:** perhaps, foolishness or worthlessness; or, perhaps, self-conceit; or, perhaps, a mistake for "talent"

23. **senseless:** a mistake for, perhaps, "sensible"

25. **comprehend:** a mistake for "apprehend," arrest; **vagrom:** i.e., vagrant, vagabond

26. **bid . . . stand:** i.e., order . . . to come to a halt

28. **take no note of:** i.e., pay no attention to

32. **none:** i.e., not one

36. **tolerable:** a mistake for "intolerable"

38. **belongs to:** i.e., is appropriate for

41. **bills:** long-handled pointed weapons carried by watchmen

50. **true:** honest; **for:** i.e., as **for**

A watchman.
From Thomas Dekker, *The belman of London . . .* (1616).

name. To be a well-favored man is the gift of   15
fortune, but to write and read comes by nature.

⌜SEACOAL⌝   Both which, master constable—

DOGBERRY   You have. I knew it would be your answer.
Well, for your favor, sir, why, give God thanks, and
make no boast of it, and for your writing and   20
reading, let that appear when there is no need of
such vanity. You are thought here to be the most
senseless and fit man for the constable of the watch;
therefore bear you the lantern. This is your charge:
you shall comprehend all vagrom men; you are to   25
bid any man stand, in the Prince's name.

⌜SEACOAL⌝   How if he will not stand?

DOGBERRY   Why, then, take no note of him, but let him
go, and presently call the rest of the watch together
and thank God you are rid of a knave.   30

VERGES   If he will not stand when he is bidden, he is
none of the Prince's subjects.

DOGBERRY   True, and they are to meddle with none but
the Prince's subjects.—You shall also make no
noise in the streets; for, for the watch to babble and   35
to talk is most tolerable and not to be endured.

⌜SECOND⌝ WATCHMAN   We will rather sleep than talk.
We know what belongs to a watch.

DOGBERRY   Why, you speak like an ancient and most
quiet watchman, for I cannot see how sleeping   40
should offend; only have a care that your bills be not
stolen. Well, you are to call at all the alehouses and
bid those that are drunk get them to bed.

⌜SEACOAL⌝   How if they will not?

DOGBERRY   Why then, let them alone till they are sober.   45
If they make you not then the better answer, you
may say they are not the men you took them for.

⌜SEACOAL⌝   Well, sir.

DOGBERRY   If you meet a thief, you may suspect him, by
virtue of your office, to be no true man, and for such   50

51. **meddle or make with:** have to do with (a proverbial expression)

52. **the more is:** i.e., the better it is

54. **lay hands on:** i.e., seize

56. **they . . . defiled:** proverbial

62. **by my will:** i.e., willingly

63. **more:** a mistake for "less"

65. **still:** i.e., quiet

74. **present:** represent

75. **stay:** stop

76. **by 'r Lady:** "by our **Lady**" (the Virgin Mary)

83. **An:** if

84. **there be . . . chances:** i.e., anything important happens

85. **counsels:** secrets

Playing a tabor and pipe. (2.3.15)
From William Kemp,
Kempes nine daies wonder (1600; 1884 facs.).

kind of men, the less you meddle or make with
them, why, the more is for your honesty.

⌈SEACOAL⌉ If we know him to be a thief, shall we not
lay hands on him?

DOGBERRY Truly, by your office you may, but I think   55
they that touch pitch will be defiled. The most
peaceable way for you, if you do take a thief, is to
let him show himself what he is and steal out of
your company.

VERGES You have been always called a merciful man,   60
partner.

DOGBERRY Truly, I would not hang a dog by my will,
much more a man who hath any honesty in him.

VERGES, ⌈to the Watch⌉ If you hear a child cry in the
night, you must call to the nurse and bid her still it.   65

⌈SECOND⌉ WATCHMAN How if the nurse be asleep and
will not hear us?

DOGBERRY Why, then depart in peace, and let the
child wake her with crying, for the ewe that will
not hear her lamb when it baas will never answer a   70
calf when he bleats.

VERGES 'Tis very true.

DOGBERRY This is the end of the charge. You, constable, are to present the Prince's own person. If you
meet the Prince in the night, you may stay him.   75

VERGES Nay, by 'r Lady, that I think he cannot.

DOGBERRY Five shillings to one on 't, with any man that
knows the statutes, he may stay him—marry, not
without the Prince be willing, for indeed the watch
ought to offend no man, and it is an offense to stay a   80
man against his will.

VERGES By 'r Lady, I think it be so.

DOGBERRY Ha, ah ha!—Well, masters, goodnight. An
there be any matter of weight chances, call up me.
Keep your fellows' counsels and your own, and   85
goodnight.—Come, neighbor.

                    ⌈*Dogberry and Verges begin to exit.*⌉

92. **coil:** fuss, turmoil

93. **vigitant:** a mistake for "vigilant"

98. **Mass:** an oath "by the Mass"; **my elbow itched:** a proverbial warning against bad company

99. **scab:** (1) crust over a wound; (2) scoundrel

100. **answer:** return thrust (a fencing term)

102–3. **penthouse:** canopy; or, overhanging eaves

105. **treason:** treachery

105–6. **Yet stand close:** i.e., remain hidden

108. **ducats:** gold coins

110. **dear:** expensive, costly

112. **villainy:** perhaps, person who instigates wickedness

114. **make . . . will:** i.e., charge **what they** wish

116. **unconfirmed:** ignorant, uninformed

117–18. **the fashion . . . man:** See longer note, page 202. **fashion:** style or cut **doublet:** short, close-fitting jacket (See picture, page 144.)

⌜SEACOAL⌝ Well, masters, we hear our charge. Let us go
sit here upon the church bench till two, and then all
to bed.

DOGBERRY One word more, honest neighbors. I pray   90
you watch about Signior Leonato's door, for the
wedding being there tomorrow, there is a great coil
tonight. Adieu, be vigitant, I beseech you.

⌜*Dogberry and Verges*⌝ *exit.*

Enter Borachio and Conrade.

BORACHIO What, Conrade!

⌜SEACOAL, *aside*⌝ Peace, stir not.   95

BORACHIO Conrade, I say!

CONRADE Here, man, I am at thy elbow.

BORACHIO Mass, and my elbow itched, I thought there
would a scab follow.

CONRADE I will owe thee an answer for that. And now   100
forward with thy tale.

BORACHIO Stand thee close, then, under this penthouse, for it drizzles rain, and I will, like a true
drunkard, utter all to thee.

⌜SEACOAL, *aside*⌝ Some treason, masters. Yet stand   105
close.

BORACHIO Therefore know, I have earned of ⌜Don⌝
John a thousand ducats.

CONRADE Is it possible that any villainy should be so
dear?   110

BORACHIO Thou shouldst rather ask if it were possible
any villainy should be so rich. For when rich
villains have need of poor ones, poor ones may
make what price they will.

CONRADE I wonder at it.   115

BORACHIO That shows thou art unconfirmed. Thou
knowest that the fashion of a doublet, or a hat, or a
cloak, is nothing to a man.

126–27. **up and down:** i.e., here and there

129. **vane:** weather **vane**

132. **hot bloods:** i.e., hot-blooded young men

133. **fashioning:** dressing; **Pharaoh:** in the Bible, the king of Egypt from whom the Israelites fled

134. **reechy:** smoky, dirty

134–35. **Bel's priests:** i.e., the priests of Baal in the Apocrypha in the Bible

135. **old . . . window:** i.e., stained-glass **church window**

136. **Hercules:** See notes to 2.1.250 and 251, and picture, page 146. The reference to **Hercules** as shaven has not been satisfactorily explained. **smirched:** besmirched, soiled

137. **codpiece:** a showy attachment to the front of a man's breeches; **massy:** massive, huge

139–40. **fashion . . . man:** i.e., changes in **fashion** cause clothes to be discarded **more than** do wear and tear

146. **by the name of Hero:** i.e., calling her "Hero"; **leans me:** i.e., **leans** (ethical dative)

150. **possessed:** given information

151. **amiable:** amorous

CONRADE Yes, it is apparel.

BORACHIO I mean the fashion. 120

CONRADE Yes, the fashion is the fashion.

BORACHIO Tush, I may as well say the fool's the fool. But seest thou not what a deformed thief this fashion is?

⌜FIRST⌝ WATCHMAN, ⌜*aside*⌝ I know that Deformed. He 125 has been a vile thief this seven year. He goes up and down like a gentleman. I remember his name.

BORACHIO Didst thou not hear somebody?

CONRADE No, 'twas the vane on the house.

BORACHIO Seest thou not, I say, what a deformed thief 130 this fashion is, how giddily he turns about all the hot bloods between fourteen and five-and-thirty, sometimes fashioning them like Pharaoh's soldiers in the reechy painting, sometimes like god Bel's priests in the old church window, sometimes like 135 the shaven Hercules in the smirched worm-eaten tapestry, where his codpiece seems as massy as his club?

CONRADE All this I see, and I see that the fashion wears out more apparel than the man. But art not thou 140 thyself giddy with the fashion too, that thou hast shifted out of thy tale into telling me of the fashion?

BORACHIO Not so, neither. But know that I have to-night wooed Margaret, the Lady Hero's gentle- 145 woman, by the name of Hero. She leans me out at her mistress' chamber window, bids me a thousand times goodnight. I tell this tale vilely. I should first tell thee how the Prince, Claudio, and my master, planted and placed and possessed by my master 150 Don John, saw afar off in the orchard this amiable encounter.

CONRADE And thought they Margaret was Hero?

BORACHIO Two of them did, the Prince and Claudio,

156. **possessed:** influenced (but with a sense of demonic possession)

160–61. **as he was appointed:** i.e., as had been arranged (literally, as he had an appointment to do)

161. **temple:** church

163. **o'ernight:** the preceding evening

166. **stand:** halt

167. **right:** perhaps, as in the formula "**right** honorable"

168. **recovered:** a mistake for "discovered"

169. **lechery:** perhaps he means "villainy" or, perhaps, "treachery"

172. **a lock: a** long **lock** of hair

172 SD. **Enter Dogberry:** See longer note, page 202.

173. **Masters:** a title of respect

174. **made bring:** i.e., forced to **bring**

177. **obey:** perhaps, order

178. **like:** likely

179. **commodity:** parcel of goods; **being taken up:** To "take up a commodity" was to obtain goods on credit and then sell them for cash. **bills:** (1) watchmen's weapons; (2) "bills of parcels" or itemized invoices

180. **in question:** in dispute; or, in a doubtful state

but the devil my master knew she was Margaret; 155
and partly by his oaths, which first possessed them,
partly by the dark night, which did deceive them,
but chiefly by my villainy, which did confirm any
slander that Don John had made, away went Claudio
enraged, swore he would meet her as he was 160
appointed next morning at the temple, and there,
before the whole congregation, shame her with
what he saw o'ernight and send her home again
without a husband.

FIRST WATCHMAN   We charge you in the Prince's name, 165
stand!

⌈SEACOAL⌉   Call up the right Master Constable. ⌈*Second
Watchman exits.*⌉ We have here recovered the most
dangerous piece of lechery that ever was known in
the commonwealth. 170

FIRST WATCHMAN   And one Deformed is one of them. I
know him; he wears a lock.

⌈*Enter Dogberry, Verges, and Second Watchman.*⌉

⌈DOGBERRY⌉   Masters, masters—

⌈FIRST⌉ WATCHMAN, ⌈*to Borachio*⌉   You'll be made bring
Deformed forth, I warrant you. 175

⌈DOGBERRY, *to Borachio and Conrade*⌉   Masters, never
speak, we charge you, let us obey you to go with us.

BORACHIO, ⌈*to Conrade*⌉   We are like to prove a goodly
commodity, being taken up of these men's bills.

CONRADE   A commodity in question, I warrant you.— 180
Come, we'll obey you.

They exit.

3.4 Early the next morning, Hero prepares for the wedding. Beatrice enters, suffering, she says, from a bad cold, but Hero and Margaret tease her about being in love with Benedick.

————————

2. **desire:** i.e., tell

5. **Well:** i.e., very **well**

6. **Troth:** i.e., faith, a mild oath; **rebato:** a tall, ornamental, stiff collar

8. **pray thee:** a phrase of apology

9. **'s:** i.e., it is

13. **tire:** attire, headdress; **within:** perhaps, in the next room

14. **hair:** i.e., hairpiece attached to the headdress; **a thought:** i.e., a bit

17. **that exceeds:** i.e., that's wonderful

18. **nightgown:** dressing gown

18–19. **in respect of:** i.e., compared to

19. **cloth o' gold:** fabric woven in part from **gold** thread; **cuts:** slashes in the outer fabric that show off the rich lining

19–20. **laced with silver:** i.e., trimmed **with silver** lace

20. **down sleeves:** tight-fitting long **sleeves; side sleeves:** long ornamental **sleeves** hanging from the shoulder

21. **underborne:** trimmed underneath; **tinsel:** rich fabric interwoven with silver or gold

22. **quaint:** elaborate, elegant

23. **on 't:** i.e., of it

25. **heavy:** sad, somber

30. **in a beggar:** i.e., even **in a beggar**

(continued)

⌜Scene 4⌝
Enter Hero, and Margaret, and Ursula.

HERO   Good Ursula, wake my cousin Beatrice and
desire her to rise.

URSULA   I will, lady.

HERO   And bid her come hither.

URSULA   Well.   ⌜*Ursula exits.*⌝   5

MARGARET   Troth, I think your other rebato were
better.

HERO   No, pray thee, good Meg, I'll wear this.

MARGARET   By my troth, 's not so good, and I warrant
your cousin will say so.   10

HERO   My cousin's a fool, and thou art another. I'll
wear none but this.

MARGARET   I like the new tire within excellently, if the
hair were a thought browner; and your gown's a
most rare fashion, i' faith. I saw the Duchess of   15
Milan's gown that they praise so.

HERO   O, that exceeds, they say.

MARGARET   By my troth, 's but a nightgown ⌜in⌝ respect
of yours—cloth o' gold, and cuts, and laced with
silver, set with pearls, down sleeves, side sleeves,   20
and skirts round underborne with a bluish tinsel.
But for a fine, quaint, graceful, and excellent fashion, yours is worth ten on 't.

HERO   God give me joy to wear it, for my heart is
exceeding heavy.   25

MARGARET   'Twill be heavier soon by the weight of a
man.

HERO   Fie upon thee! Art not ashamed?

MARGARET   Of what, lady? Of speaking honorably? Is
not marriage honorable in a beggar? Is not your   30
lord honorable without marriage? I think you
would have me say "Saving your reverence, a husband." An bad thinking do not wrest true speaking,

32. **Saving your reverence:** a request to be excused for using an indecent word

33. **An:** if; **do not wrest:** i.e., does not distort or twist the meaning of

36. **light:** licentious; or, frivolous

37. **heavy:** serious (with the obvious puns on both words); **else:** if it is otherwise

41. **in the sick tune:** i.e., as if you were **sick**

43. **Clap 's into:** i.e., let's **clap** (swing) **into; Light o' love:** the name of a popular song

44. **burden:** refrain; or bass accompaniment (The standard meaning of **burden** continues the puns on **light** and **heavy.**)

45. **light o' love with your heels:** a double accusation of wantonness (**light** meaning licentious and "light-heeled" meaning "unchaste")

47. **barns:** with a pun on "bairns" or children

48. **illegitimate:** inaccurate (with the obvious pun); **construction:** interpretation

48–49. **scorn that with my heels:** proverbial, meaning to reject something with contempt

52–53. **Heigh-ho . . . husband:** See note to 2.1.313.

54. **H:** The noun form of *ache* was pronounced like the letter *h*. The pun on *h* and *ache* was common.

55. **be . . . Turk:** have not renounced your old faith

55–56. **there's . . . star:** i.e., **there's** nothing one can trust (literally, one cannot use the North Star for navigation)

57. **trow:** i.e., I **trow,** I wonder

60. **they are:** i.e., they have

62. **I am stuffed:** i.e., my nose is **stuffed** up

(continued)

112

I'll offend nobody. Is there any harm in "the heavier
for a husband"? None, I think, an it be the right   35
husband and the right wife. Otherwise, 'tis light and
not heavy. Ask my lady Beatrice else. Here she
comes.

Enter Beatrice.

HERO   Good morrow, coz.

BEATRICE   Good morrow, sweet Hero.   40

HERO   Why, how now? Do you speak in the sick tune?

BEATRICE   I am out of all other tune, methinks.

MARGARET   Clap 's into "Light o' love." That goes
without a burden. Do you sing it, and I'll dance it.

BEATRICE   You light o' love with your heels! Then, if   45
your husband have stables enough, you'll see he
shall lack no barns.

MARGARET   O, illegitimate construction! I scorn that
with my heels.

BEATRICE   'Tis almost five o'clock, cousin. 'Tis time   50
you were ready. By my troth, I am exceeding ill.
Heigh-ho!

MARGARET   For a hawk, a horse, or a husband?

BEATRICE   For the letter that begins them all, *H*.

MARGARET   Well, an you be not turned Turk, there's no   55
more sailing by the star.

BEATRICE   What means the fool, trow?

MARGARET   Nothing, I; but God send everyone their
heart's desire.

HERO   These gloves the Count sent me, they are an   60
excellent perfume.

BEATRICE   I am stuffed, cousin. I cannot smell.

MARGARET   A maid, and stuffed! There's goodly catch-
ing of cold.

BEATRICE   O, God help me, God help me! How long   65
have you professed apprehension?

63. **stuffed:** perhaps, pregnant

66. **professed apprehension:** i.e., made wittiness your profession

67. **it:** i.e., **apprehension,** wit

68. **rarely:** excellently

71. **some of this:** i.e., **some**

71–72. **carduus benedictus:** i.e., the herb "blessed thistle," allegedly "a salve for every sore" (Lines 71–76 pun on **carduus**—which means "thistle" and which sounds like the Latin *cordis,* "of the heart"—and on **benedictus,** which means "holy" and contains Benedick's name.) See picture, below.

73. **qualm:** sudden illness

76. **moral:** hidden meaning

80. **list:** choose

84. **such another:** i.e., **another** who refused to love

86. **in despite of:** i.e., despite the opposition of

86–87. **eats . . . grudging:** perhaps, is content to be like other men

91. **false gallop:** literally, a canter (with a pun on **false** as "untrue, mistaken")

Blessed thistle *(Carduus benedictus).*
From John Gerard, *The herball . . .* (1597).

MARGARET   Ever since you left it. Doth not my wit
　become me rarely?
BEATRICE   It is not seen enough; you should wear it in
　your cap. By my troth, I am sick.   70
MARGARET   Get you some of this distilled *carduus bene-*
　dictus and lay it to your heart. It is the only thing for
　a qualm.
HERO   There thou prick'st her with a thistle.
BEATRICE   *Benedictus!* Why *benedictus?* You have some   75
　moral in this *benedictus?*
MARGARET   Moral? No, by my troth, I have no moral
　meaning; I meant plain holy thistle. You may think
　perchance that I think you are in love. Nay, by 'r
　Lady, I am not such a fool to think what I list, nor I   80
　list not to think what I can, nor indeed I cannot
　think, if I would think my heart out of thinking, that
　you are in love or that you will be in love or that you
　can be in love. Yet Benedick was such another, and
　now is he become a man. He swore he would never   85
　marry, and yet now, in despite of his heart, he eats
　his meat without grudging. And how you may be
　converted I know not, but methinks you look with
　your eyes as other women do.
BEATRICE   What pace is this that thy tongue keeps?   90
MARGARET   Not a false gallop.

　　　　　　　　　Enter Ursula.

URSULA   Madam, withdraw. The Prince, the Count,
　Signior Benedick, Don John, and all the gallants of
　the town are come to fetch you to church.
HERO   Help to dress me, good coz, good Meg, good   95
　Ursula.
　　　　　　　　　　　　　　⌐*They exit.*⌐

3.5 Dogberry and Verges try to tell Leonato about the arrest of Borachio and Conrade, but they are so unintelligible that Leonato impatiently dismisses them, telling them to examine the prisoners. He leaves for the wedding.

------

0 SD. **Headborough:** petty constable, with more limited authority than Dogberry's

2. **confidence:** a mistake for "conference, conversation"

3. **decerns:** a mistake for "concerns"; **nearly:** closely

9. **Goodman:** a term of address for a man below the rank of gentleman

10. **blunt:** a mistake for "sharp"

12. **honest . . . brows:** proverbial

15. **odorous:** Proverbial: **"Comparisons are** odious." **Palabras:** i.e., silence (The Spanish phrase *pocas palabras* means "few words.")

19. **the poor duke's officers:** a mistake for **"the duke's poor officers"**

20. **tedious as a king:** The following lines indicate that Dogberry thinks **tedious** means "rich."

21. **of:** i.e., on

23. **an 'twere:** if it were

24. **exclamation on:** probably a mistake for "acclamations of" ("To exclaim on" meant "to accuse loudly, to blame.")

28. **fain:** gladly

29. **tonight:** last night

(continued)

⌈Scene 5⌉

Enter Leonato, and ⌈*Dogberry,*⌉ *the Constable, and*
⌈*Verges,*⌉ *the Headborough.*

LEONATO   What would you with me, honest neighbor?

DOGBERRY   Marry, sir, I would have some confidence
with you that decerns you nearly.

LEONATO   Brief, I pray you, for you see it is a busy time
with me.   5

DOGBERRY   Marry, this it is, sir.

VERGES   Yes, in truth, it is, sir.

LEONATO   What is it, my good friends?

DOGBERRY   Goodman Verges, sir, speaks a little off the
matter. An old man, sir, and his wits are not so blunt   10
as, God help, I would desire they were, but, in faith,
honest as the skin between his brows.

VERGES   Yes, I thank God I am as honest as any man
living that is an old man and no honester than I.

DOGBERRY   Comparisons are odorous. *Palabras*, neigh-   15
bor Verges.

LEONATO   Neighbors, you are tedious.

DOGBERRY   It pleases your Worship to say so, but we
are the poor duke's officers. But truly, for mine
own part, if I were as tedious as a king, I could find   20
in my heart to bestow it all of your Worship.

LEONATO   All thy tediousness on me, ah?

DOGBERRY   Yea, an 'twere a thousand pound more
than 'tis, for I hear as good exclamation on your
Worship as of any man in the city, and though I be   25
but a poor man, I am glad to hear it.

VERGES   And so am I.

LEONATO   I would fain know what you have to say.

VERGES   Marry, sir, our watch tonight, excepting your
Worship's presence, ha' ta'en a couple of as arrant   30
knaves as any in Messina.

DOGBERRY   A good old man, sir. He will be talking. As

29–30. **excepting . . . presence:** Dogberry probably intends the complimentary phrase "respecting [showing respect to] **your presence.**" (His words mean, literally, "except for you, the men we have arrested are 'as arrant knaves as any in Messina.' ")

30. **ha' ta'en:** i.e., have taken, have arrested; **arrant:** unmitigated

33. **age:** The proverb actually states: **"When the ale is in, the wit is out."** (The rest of this speech is a collection of proverbs that are more accurately reproduced than this one.)

36. **ride of a horse:** i.e., **ride** on one **horse**

40. **he comes too short of you:** i.e., he can't measure up to you, or talk as much

41. **Gifts:** i.e., my virtues are **gifts**

44. **comprehended:** a mistake for "apprehended"; **aspicious:** a mistake for "suspicious"

50. **suffigance:** a mistake for "sufficient"

52. **stay:** i.e., wait

54. **wait upon:** attend

55–56. **Francis Seacoal:** This may be the Sexton who appears in 4.2. The watchman in 3.3 was named George Seacoal.

57. **examination:** a mistake for "examine"

59. **spare for no wit:** i.e., not hold back on wisdom

60. **noncome:** perhaps a confusion of *non plus* ("a state of perplexity") with *non compos mentis* ("not of sound mind")

61–62. **excommunication:** a mistake for "examination"

they say, "When the age is in, the wit is out." God
help us, it is a world to see!—Well said, i' faith,
neighbor Verges.—Well, God's a good man. An two   35
men ride of a horse, one must ride behind. An
honest soul, i' faith, sir, by my troth he is, as ever
broke bread, but God is to be worshiped, all men
are not alike, alas, good neighbor.

LEONATO Indeed, neighbor, he comes too short of you.   40

DOGBERRY Gifts that God gives.

LEONATO I must leave you.

DOGBERRY One word, sir. Our watch, sir, have indeed
comprehended two aspicious persons, and we
would have them this morning examined before   45
your Worship.

LEONATO Take their examination yourself and bring it
me. I am now in great haste, as it may appear unto
you.

DOGBERRY It shall be suffigance.   50

LEONATO Drink some wine ere you go. Fare you well.

⌈*Enter a Messenger.*⌉

MESSENGER My lord, they stay for you to give your
daughter to her husband.

LEONATO I'll wait upon them. I am ready.
                              He exits, ⌈with the Messenger.⌉

DOGBERRY Go, good partner, go, get you to Francis   55
Seacoal. Bid him bring his pen and inkhorn to the
jail. We are now to examination these men.

VERGES And we must do it wisely.

DOGBERRY We will spare for no wit, I warrant you.
Here's that shall drive some of them to a noncome.   60
Only get the learned writer to set down our excom-
munication and meet me at the jail.
                              ⌈*They exit.*⌉

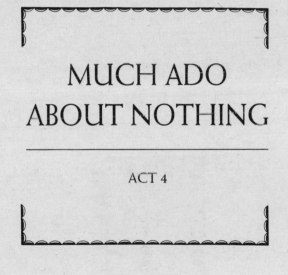

MUCH ADO
ABOUT NOTHING

ACT 4

4.1 At the wedding, Claudio publicly denounces Hero as a lewd woman. He is supported in his story by Don Pedro and Don John. Hero faints and her accusers depart. The Friar believes in her innocence and proposes that Leonato announce that she has died. This news, the Friar thinks, will make Claudio remember his love for her. After the others depart, Benedick and Beatrice admit they love each other, and Benedick reluctantly agrees to challenge Claudio to a duel.

---

12. **inward:** undisclosed
13. **charge:** command
21–22. **some . . . ha, he:** an echo of Lyly's Latin *Grammar,* where **interjections** are defined

A lute. (2.1.92, 3.61)
From Silvestro Pietrasanta,
Symbola heroica . . . (1682).

⌜ACT 4⌝

⌜Scene 1⌝
Enter Prince, ⌜John the⌝ Bastard, Leonato, Friar,
Claudio, Benedick, Hero, and Beatrice, ⌜with
Attendants.⌝

LEONATO   Come, Friar Francis, be brief, only to the
plain form of marriage, and you shall recount their
particular duties afterwards.

FRIAR, ⌜*to Claudio*⌝   You come hither, my lord, to marry
this lady?   5

CLAUDIO   No.

LEONATO   To be married to her.—Friar, you come to
marry her.

FRIAR   Lady, you come hither to be married to this
count?   10

HERO   I do.

FRIAR   If either of you know any inward impediment
why you should not be conjoined, I charge you on
your souls to utter it.

CLAUDIO   Know you any, Hero?   15

HERO   None, my lord.

FRIAR   Know you any, count?

LEONATO   I dare make his answer, none.

CLAUDIO   O, what men dare do! What men may do!
What men daily do, not knowing what they do!   20

BENEDICK   How now, interjections? Why, then, some
be of laughing, as ah, ha, he!

123

23. **Stand thee by:** i.e., stand aside; **Father:** i.e., Leonato

25. **maid:** virgin

28. **counterpoise:** counterbalance

30. **learn:** i.e., teach

33. **sign:** show or pretense

35. **authority:** power to inspire belief; **show:** outward appearance

36. **withal:** i.e., with

37. **modest evidence:** i.e., **evidence** of modesty

38. **witness:** i.e., act as a witness to

41. **luxurious:** lascivious, lecherous

45. **approvèd:** proved, convicted

46. **proof:** perhaps, experience; or, perhaps, trial or test of her

49. **known:** had sexual relations with

50. **embrace me as a husband:** Although the church forbade intercourse before the ritual celebration of marriage, custom allowed intercourse for formally betrothed couples.

Marriage ceremony.
From Richard Day, *A booke of christian prayers* . . . (1578).

CLAUDIO
  Stand thee by, friar.—Father, by your leave,
  Will you with free and unconstrainèd soul
  Give me this maid, your daughter?   25

LEONATO
  As freely, son, as God did give her me.

CLAUDIO
  And what have I to give you back whose worth
  May counterpoise this rich and precious gift?

PRINCE
  Nothing, unless you render her again.

CLAUDIO
  Sweet prince, you learn me noble thankfulness.—   30
  There, Leonato, take her back again.
  Give not this rotten orange to your friend.
  She's but the sign and semblance of her honor.
  Behold how like a maid she blushes here!
  O, what authority and show of truth   35
  Can cunning sin cover itself withal!
  Comes not that blood as modest evidence
  To witness simple virtue? Would you not swear,
  All you that see her, that she were a maid,
  By these exterior shows? But she is none.   40
  She knows the heat of a luxurious bed.
  Her blush is guiltiness, not modesty.

LEONATO
  What do you mean, my lord?

CLAUDIO   Not to be married,
  Not to knit my soul to an approvèd wanton.   45

LEONATO
  Dear my lord, if you in your own proof
  Have vanquished the resistance of her youth,
  And made defeat of her virginity—

CLAUDIO
  I know what you would say: if I have known her,
  You will say she did embrace me as a husband,   50

51. **forehand sin:** i.e., the sinfulness of the act committed in anticipation (of the marriage)

53. **too large:** improper, gross

55. **comely:** proper, decorous

57. **Out on thee:** i.e., curses on you; **seeming:** semblance, mere appearance

58. **Dian:** i.e., Diana, goddess of chastity and of the moon (here equated with the moon "in her [i.e., its] orb"); **orb:** sphere (In Ptolemaic astronomy, the moon, like the sun and the planets, moved around the earth in its own crystalline sphere.) See pictures below and on page xxxii.

59. **be blown:** i.e., has burst into flower

60. **blood:** sensual appetites

61. **Venus:** goddess of love, often depicted as promiscuous and highly sensual (See picture, page 172.)

63. **wide:** i.e., **wide** of the mark, wildly

68. **common stale:** lowest-class prostitute

72. **True:** an echo of Don John's word at line 70

77. **but move:** only pose

"Dian in her orb." (4.1.58)
From Vincenzo Cartari,
Le vere e noue imagini . . . (1615).

And so extenuate the forehand sin.
No, Leonato,
I never tempted her with word too large,
But, as a brother to his sister, showed
Bashful sincerity and comely love.   55

HERO
And seemed I ever otherwise to you?

CLAUDIO
Out on thee, seeming! I will write against it.
You seem to me as Dian in her orb,
As chaste as is the bud ere it be blown.
But you are more intemperate in your blood   60
Than Venus, or those pampered animals
That rage in savage sensuality.

HERO
Is my lord well that he doth speak so wide?

LEONATO
Sweet prince, why speak not you?

PRINCE   What should I   65
   speak?
I stand dishonored that have gone about
To link my dear friend to a common stale.

LEONATO
Are these things spoken, or do I but dream?

DON JOHN
Sir, they are spoken, and these things are true.   70

BENEDICK   This looks not like a nuptial.

HERO   True! O God!

CLAUDIO   Leonato, stand I here?
Is this the Prince? Is this the Prince's brother?
Is this face Hero's? Are our eyes our own?   75

LEONATO
All this is so, but what of this, my lord?

CLAUDIO
Let me but move one question to your daughter,

78. **kindly:** lawful

79. **in:** i.e., over

80. **charge thee:** order you to

81. **beset:** surrounded

82. **catechizing:** questioning

85. **just reproach:** justified blame

86. **Marry:** an oath "by the Virgin Mary"

87. **Hero itself can blot out Hero's virtue:** See longer note, page 203.

88. **yesternight:** last night

90. **maid:** maiden, virgin

92. **Why . . . maiden:** Since she does not answer his question by naming the man, she fails his test: "if you are a maid, answer. . . ."

94. **grievèd:** aggrieved; grief-stricken

97. **liberal:** plainspoken

104. **much misgovernment:** great immorality

And by that fatherly and kindly power
That you have in her, bid her answer truly.

LEONATO
I charge thee do so, as thou art my child.   80

HERO
O, God defend me, how am I beset!—
What kind of catechizing call you this?

CLAUDIO
To make you answer truly to your name.

HERO
Is it not Hero? Who can blot that name
With any just reproach?   85

CLAUDIO   Marry, that can Hero!
Hero itself can blot out Hero's virtue.
What man was he talked with you yesternight
Out at your window betwixt twelve and one?
Now, if you are a maid, answer to this.   90

HERO
I talked with no man at that hour, my lord.

PRINCE
Why, then, are you no maiden.—Leonato,
I am sorry you must hear. Upon mine honor,
Myself, my brother, and this grievèd count
Did see her, hear her, at that hour last night   95
Talk with a ruffian at her chamber window,
Who hath indeed, most like a liberal villain,
Confessed the vile encounters they have had
A thousand times in secret.

DON JOHN
Fie, fie, they are not to be named, my lord,   100
Not to be spoke of!
There is not chastity enough in language,
Without offense, to utter them.—Thus, pretty lady,
I am sorry for thy much misgovernment.

CLAUDIO
O Hero, what a Hero hadst thou been   105

106. **outward graces:** external beauties
107. **counsels:** secrets
108. **fair:** beautiful
110. **For:** i.e., because of
111. **conjecture:** suspicion
112. **thoughts of harm:** i.e., harmful **thoughts;** or, perhaps, **thoughts** about **harm**
113. **gracious:** attractive (to me)
115. **wherefore:** why
117. **spirits:** vital powers
122. **cover:** screen, concealment, cloak
130. **blood:** i.e., blushes

If half thy outward graces had been placed
About thy thoughts and counsels of thy heart!
But fare thee well, most foul, most fair. Farewell,
Thou pure impiety and impious purity.
For thee I'll lock up all the gates of love   110
And on my eyelids shall conjecture hang,
To turn all beauty into thoughts of harm,
And never shall it more be gracious.

LEONATO
Hath no man's dagger here a point for me?
                              ⌐*Hero falls.*⌐

BEATRICE
Why, how now, cousin, wherefore sink you down?   115
DON JOHN
Come, let us go. These things, come thus to light,
Smother her spirits up.
                    ⌐*Claudio, Prince, and Don John exit.*⌐
BENEDICK
How doth the lady?
BEATRICE   Dead, I think.—Help, uncle!—
Hero, why Hero! Uncle! Signior Benedick! Friar!   120
LEONATO
O Fate, take not away thy heavy hand!
Death is the fairest cover for her shame
That may be wished for.
BEATRICE   How now, cousin Hero?   ⌐*Hero stirs.*⌐
FRIAR, ⌐*to Hero*⌐   Have comfort, lady.   125
LEONATO, ⌐*to Hero*⌐
Dost thou look up?
FRIAR   Yea, wherefore should she not?
LEONATO
Wherefore? Why, doth not every earthly thing
Cry shame upon her? Could she here deny
The story that is printed in her blood?—
Do not live, Hero, do not ope thine eyes,   130
For, did I think thou wouldst not quickly die,

134. **on the rearward of reproaches:** i.e., after reproaching you; or, after this public scandal

135. **but one:** i.e., just one child

136. **Chid:** i.e., chided, found fault, uttered words of rebuke; **frame:** plan

137. **much:** i.e., many; **by:** i.e., in

140. **issue:** i.e., infant

141. **mired:** soiled

145. **proud on:** i.e., **proud of**

147. **Valuing of:** i.e., because I cared so much for

148. **that the:** i.e., so **that the**

150–51. **season give / To:** (1) preserve from decay (literally, embalm); (2) restore to soundness (literally, add flavor or relish to)

153. **wonder:** amazement

155. **is belied:** i.e., has been lied about

159. **that:** i.e., the charge against Hero

160. **before:** i.e., already

Vulcan. (1.1.181)
From Johann Basilius Herold,
Heydenweldt . . . [1554].

Thought I thy spirits were stronger than thy shames,
Myself would, on the rearward of reproaches,
Strike at thy life. Grieved I I had but one?   135
Chid I for that at frugal Nature's frame?
O, one too much by thee! Why had I one?
Why ever wast thou lovely in my eyes?
Why had I not with charitable hand
Took up a beggar's issue at my gates,   140
Who, smirchèd thus, and mired with infamy,
I might have said "No part of it is mine;
This shame derives itself from unknown loins"?
But mine, and mine I loved, and mine I praised,
And mine that I was proud on, mine so much   145
That I myself was to myself not mine,
Valuing of her—why she, O she, is fall'n
Into a pit of ink, that the wide sea
Hath drops too few to wash her clean again,
And salt too little which may season give   150
To her foul tainted flesh!
BENEDICK   Sir, sir, be patient.
For my part, I am so attired in wonder
I know not what to say.
BEATRICE
O, on my soul, my cousin is belied!   155
BENEDICK
Lady, were you her bedfellow last night?
BEATRICE
No, truly not, although until last night
I have this twelvemonth been her bedfellow.
LEONATO
Confirmed, confirmed! O, that is stronger made
Which was before barred up with ribs of iron!   160
Would the two princes lie and Claudio lie,
Who loved her so that, speaking of her foulness,
Washed it with tears? Hence from her. Let her die!
FRIAR   Hear me a little,

166. **given way ... fortune:** i.e., accepted **this course** of events

167. **noting of:** paying attention to; **marked:** noticed

168, 169. **blushing apparitions, shames:** The Friar describes Hero's alternately red and white face as if it were being visited by supernatural beings.

169. **start into:** i.e., appear suddenly in

172. **burn the errors:** an image in which the **errors** are heretics to be burned at the stake

174. **reading:** perhaps, **reading** of Hero's face

175. **experimental seal:** i.e., the **seal** of experience; **warrant:** guarantee (the truth of)

176. **tenor of my book:** i.e., what I find in my reading (The reference here is either to the books he has read or to Hero's face, which he reads as if it were a book.)

177. **reverence:** perhaps, age, position as a venerable person; **calling:** profession as priest; **divinity:** knowledge of theology

181. **grace:** goodness, virtue

188. **of:** i.e., about

189. **warrant:** sanction, allow

191. **Prove you:** i.e., if **you prove**

192. **unmeet:** unfitting, improper

193. **Maintained ... words:** i.e., talked

194. **Refuse:** reject, abandon

195. **misprision:** misunderstanding, error

196. **have the very bent of honor:** i.e., are totally disposed to be honorable

For I have only ⌜silent been⌝ so long,   165
And given way unto this course of fortune,
By noting of the lady. I have marked
A thousand blushing apparitions
To start into her face, a thousand innocent shames
In angel whiteness beat away those blushes,   170
And in her eye there hath appeared a fire
To burn the errors that these princes hold
Against her maiden truth. Call me a fool,
Trust not my reading nor my observations,
Which with experimental seal doth warrant   175
The tenor of my book; trust not my age,
My reverence, calling, nor divinity,
If this sweet lady lie not guiltless here
Under some biting error.
LEONATO   Friar, it cannot be.   180
Thou seest that all the grace that she hath left
Is that she will not add to her damnation
A sin of perjury. She not denies it.
Why seek'st thou then to cover with excuse
That which appears in proper nakedness?   185
FRIAR
Lady, what man is he you are accused of?
HERO
They know that do accuse me. I know none.
If I know more of any man alive
Than that which maiden modesty doth warrant,
Let all my sins lack mercy!—O my father,   190
Prove you that any man with me conversed
At hours unmeet, or that I yesternight
Maintained the change of words with any creature,
Refuse me, hate me, torture me to death!
FRIAR
There is some strange misprision in the princes.   195
BENEDICK
Two of them have the very bent of honor,

197. **wisdoms:** understanding, good judgment

198. **practice:** machination, plotting

199. **spirits:** vital powers; **frame of:** i.e., framing, contriving

200. **but:** merely

204. **invention:** inventiveness, ability to plot or scheme

205. **means:** (financial) resources

206. **reft:** i.e., bereft, deprived; **friends:** The term **friends** here includes kinsmen.

207. **they:** i.e., the princes; **kind:** manner

208. **policy:** cunning

210. **quit me of:** repay, settle the score with; **throughly:** i.e., thoroughly

215. **publish:** proclaim

216. **mourning ostentation:** display or show of **mourning**

217. **monument:** sepulcher, burial vault

220. **become of:** i.e., come from

221. **carried:** managed

223. **dream . . . on:** conceive . . . of, think . . . of

224. **on this travail:** i.e., from this effort (with a pun on **travail** as childbirth)

225. **maintained:** declared to be true

228. **Of:** i.e., by

229. **prize:** esteem, value; **the worth:** i.e., its true value

And if their wisdoms be misled in this,
The practice of it lives in John the Bastard,
Whose spirits toil in frame of villainies.

LEONATO
I know not. If they speak but truth of her,   200
These hands shall tear her. If they wrong her honor,
The proudest of them shall well hear of it.
Time hath not yet so dried this blood of mine,
Nor age so eat up my invention,
Nor fortune made such havoc of my means,   205
Nor my bad life reft me so much of friends,
But they shall find, awaked in such a kind,
Both strength of limb and policy of mind,
Ability in means and choice of friends,
To quit me of them throughly.   210

FRIAR   Pause awhile,
And let my counsel sway you in this case.
Your daughter here the princes left for dead.
Let her awhile be secretly kept in,
And publish it that she is dead indeed.   215
Maintain a mourning ostentation,
And on your family's old monument
Hang mournful epitaphs and do all rites
That appertain unto a burial.

LEONATO
What shall become of this? What will this do?   220

FRIAR
Marry, this well carried shall on her behalf
Change slander to remorse. That is some good.
But not for that dream I on this strange course,
But on this travail look for greater birth.
She, dying, as it must be so maintained,   225
Upon the instant that she was accused,
Shall be lamented, pitied, and excused
Of every hearer. For it so falls out
That what we have we prize not to the worth

231. **rack the value:** i.e., strain its worth to the limit

232. **possession:** i.e., possessing it

233. **fare:** happen

234. **upon:** i.e., when he spoke

236. **study of imagination:** imaginative reveries

237. **every . . . life:** i.e., all that gives **her life organ:** a means of action or operation

238. **habit:** clothing

240. **prospect:** range of vision

242. **interest in:** a claim upon, a share in; **liver:** the organ thought to be the seat of the passions

245. **doubt not but:** i.e., do **not doubt** that; **success:** i.e., that which follows

246. **event:** outcome

247. **lay . . . likelihood:** i.e., project as its probable outcome

248. **if all . . . false:** i.e., if we miss the mark in everything **but this** (i.e., the **supposition of the lady's death** [line 249])

250. **wonder of:** bewildered curiosity about

251. **it sort not:** i.e., **it** does **not** turn out

253. **reclusive:** cloistered

254. **injuries:** insults

256. **inwardness:** close friendship

261. **Being that:** i.e., since; **flow in:** perhaps, am flooded with, or am afloat in

263. **Presently:** at once

Whiles we enjoy it, but being lacked and lost,   230
Why then we rack the value, then we find
The virtue that possession would not show us
Whiles it was ours. So will it fare with Claudio.
When he shall hear she died upon his words,
Th' idea of her life shall sweetly creep   235
Into his study of imagination,
And every lovely organ of her life
Shall come appareled in more precious habit,
More moving, delicate, and full of life,
Into the eye and prospect of his soul,   240
Than when she lived indeed. Then shall he mourn,
If ever love had interest in his liver,
And wish he had not so accused her,
No, though he thought his accusation true.
Let this be so, and doubt not but success   245
Will fashion the event in better shape
Than I can lay it down in likelihood.
But if all aim but this be leveled false,
The supposition of the lady's death
Will quench the wonder of her infamy.   250
And if it sort not well, you may conceal her,
As best befits her wounded reputation,
In some reclusive and religious life,
Out of all eyes, tongues, minds, and injuries.

BENEDICK
Signior Leonato, let the Friar advise you.   255
And though you know my inwardness and love
Is very much unto the Prince and Claudio,
Yet, by mine honor, I will deal in this
As secretly and justly as your soul
Should with your body.   260
LEONATO   Being that I flow in grief,
The smallest twine may lead me.
FRIAR
'Tis well consented. Presently away,

264. **to strange sores:** i.e., to heal unusual wounds; **strangely:** in extraordinary ways

264–65. **they strain the cure:** i.e., people use extraordinary remedies

267. **prolonged:** postponed

272. **freely:** of my own accord

276. **right:** avenge

278. **even:** direct, straightforward

279. **May:** i.e., can

280. **office:** function, job

288. **By my sword:** a mild oath

289–93. **swear and eat it . . . devised to it:** The wordplay here is on the two phrases "to eat one's words" (i.e., to recant what one has said) and "to make someone eat one's sword" (i.e., to force someone to submit). **devised to it:** i.e., provided for it

294. **protest:** declare (as a formal affirmation or vow)

297. **stayed:** stopped; **in a happy hour:** at a fortunate moment

For to strange sores strangely they strain the
    cure.—   265
Come, lady, die to live. This wedding day
Perhaps is but prolonged. Have patience and
    endure.

            ⌜*All but Beatrice and Benedick*⌝ *exit.*

BENEDICK   Lady Beatrice, have you wept all this while?
BEATRICE   Yea, and I will weep a while longer.   270
BENEDICK   I will not desire that.
BEATRICE   You have no reason. I do it freely.
BENEDICK   Surely I do believe your fair cousin is
    wronged.
BEATRICE   Ah, how much might the man deserve of me   275
    that would right her!
BENEDICK   Is there any way to show such friendship?
BEATRICE   A very even way, but no such friend.
BENEDICK   May a man do it?
BEATRICE   It is a man's office, but not yours.   280
BENEDICK   I do love nothing in the world so well as
    you. Is not that strange?
BEATRICE   As strange as the thing I know not. It were as
    possible for me to say I loved nothing so well as you,
    but believe me not, and yet I lie not; I confess   285
    nothing, nor I deny nothing. I am sorry for my
    cousin.
BENEDICK   By my sword, Beatrice, thou lovest me!
BEATRICE   Do not swear and eat it.
BENEDICK   I will swear by it that you love me, and I will   290
    make him eat it that says I love not you.
BEATRICE   Will you not eat your word?
BENEDICK   With no sauce that can be devised to it, I
    protest I love thee.
BEATRICE   Why then, God forgive me.   295
BENEDICK   What offense, sweet Beatrice?
BEATRICE   You have stayed me in a happy hour. I was
    about to protest I loved you.

307. **I am gone . . . here:** i.e., I have left you even though you are detaining me

315. **approved:** proved to be; **height:** extreme

317–18. **bear her in hand:** i.e., deceive her, lead her on

319. **uncovered:** open, undisguised

323–24. **proper saying:** i.e., fine story (sarcastic)

327. **undone:** destroyed

329. **counties:** i.e., counts

330. **a goodly count:** a handsome count (with puns on **goodly** as "fine" and on **count** as "story" [i.e., account] and as "legal charge"); **Comfect:** comfit or confect, candy

331. **for his sake:** i.e., because of him

Adam and Eve. (5.1.191–92)
From Pedro Mexia, *The imperiall historie: or the liues of the emperours . . .* (1623).

BENEDICK   And do it with all thy heart.

BEATRICE   I love you with so much of my heart that   300
none is left to protest.

BENEDICK   Come, bid me do anything for thee.

BEATRICE   Kill Claudio.

BENEDICK   Ha! Not for the wide world.

BEATRICE   You kill me to deny it. Farewell.   305

⌜*She begins to exit.*⌝

BENEDICK   Tarry, sweet Beatrice.

BEATRICE   I am gone, though I am here. There is no
love in you. Nay, I pray you let me go.

BENEDICK   Beatrice—

BEATRICE   In faith, I will go.   310

BENEDICK   We'll be friends first.

BEATRICE   You dare easier be friends with me than
fight with mine enemy.

BENEDICK   Is Claudio thine enemy?

BEATRICE   Is he not approved in the height a villain   315
that hath slandered, scorned, dishonored my kins-
woman? O, that I were a man! What, bear her in
hand until they come to take hands, and then, with
public accusation, uncovered slander, unmitigated
rancor—O God, that I were a man! I would eat his   320
heart in the marketplace.

BENEDICK   Hear me, Beatrice—

BEATRICE   Talk with a man out at a window! A proper
saying.

BENEDICK   Nay, but Beatrice—   325

BEATRICE   Sweet Hero, she is wronged, she is slandered, she is undone.

BENEDICK   Beat—

BEATRICE   Princes and counties! Surely a princely testimony, a goodly count, Count Comfect, a sweet   330
gallant, surely! O, that I were a man for his sake! Or
that I had any friend would be a man for my sake!
But manhood is melted into curtsies, valor into

334. **compliment:** ceremonies of civility or courtesy

335. **trim ones:** i.e., fine, elegant talkers; **He:** i.e., any man; **now:** i.e., these days; **Hercules:** See note to 2.1.250.

336. **swears it:** i.e., **swears** that it's true

346. **engaged:** committed, pledged

346–47. **challenge him:** i.e., to a duel

348. **render me a dear account:** i.e., pay dearly

4.2 Dogberry ineptly questions Borachio and Conrade about the deception of Claudio and Don Pedro. The Sexton has Borachio and Conrade bound and orders them taken to Leonato.

———

0 SD. **gowns:** i.e., official black **gowns**

1. **dissembly:** a mistake for "assembly"

5. **exhibition:** perhaps a mistake for "commission"

Doublet. (2.3.18; 3.3.117)
From Robert Greene, *A quip for an vpstart courtier . . .* (1620).

compliment, and men are only turned into tongue,
and trim ones, too. He is now as valiant as Hercules   335
that only tells a lie and swears it. I cannot be a man
with wishing; therefore I will die a woman with
grieving.

BENEDICK   Tarry, good Beatrice. By this hand, I love
thee.   340

BEATRICE   Use it for my love some other way than
swearing by it.

BENEDICK   Think you in your soul the Count Claudio
hath wronged Hero?

BEATRICE   Yea, as sure as I have a thought or a soul.   345

BENEDICK   Enough, I am engaged. I will challenge
him. I will kiss your hand, and so I leave you. By
this hand, Claudio shall render me a dear account.
As you hear of me, so think of me. Go comfort your
cousin. I must say she is dead, and so farewell.   350
                                        ⌜*They exit.*⌝

                        ⌜Scene 2⌝
Enter the Constables ⌜*Dogberry and Verges,*⌝ *and the*
Town Clerk, ⌜*or Sexton,*⌝ *in gowns,* ⌜*with the Watch,*
                Conrade, and⌝ *Borachio.*

⌜DOGBERRY⌝   Is our whole dissembly appeared?

⌜VERGES⌝   O, a stool and a cushion for the Sexton.
                ⌜*A stool is brought in; the Sexton sits.*⌝

SEXTON   Which be the malefactors?

⌜DOGBERRY⌝   Marry, that am I, and my partner.

⌜VERGES⌝   Nay, that's certain, we have the exhibition to   5
examine.

SEXTON   But which are the offenders that are to be
examined? Let them come before Master Constable.

14. **sirrah:** a term of address to a male social inferior

21. **defend but:** forbid but that

24. **will go near to be:** i.e., **will** almost **be**

26. **none:** i.e., nothing of the kind

27. **witty:** clever

28. **go about with:** set to work upon

30. **false:** treacherous, deceitful

33. **both in a tale:** i.e., telling the same story

38. **eftest:** perhaps a mistake for "fastest" or "deftest"

44. **perjury:** a mistake for "treachery"

Hercules. (2.1.250)
From Vincenzo Cartari,
Le vere e noue imagini . . . (1615).

⌜DOGBERRY⌝ Yea, marry, let them come before me.   10
⌜*Conrade and Borachio are brought forward.*⌝
What is your name, friend?

BORACHIO Borachio.

⌜DOGBERRY⌝ Pray, write down "Borachio."—Yours,
sirrah?

CONRADE I am a gentleman, sir, and my name is   15
Conrade.

⌜DOGBERRY⌝ Write down "Master Gentleman Conrade."—Masters, do you serve God?

BORACHIO / CONRADE Yea, sir, we hope.

⌜DOGBERRY⌝ Write down that they hope they serve   20
God; and write God first, for God defend but God
should go before such villains!—Masters, it is
proved already that you are little better than false
knaves, and it will go near to be thought so shortly.
How answer you for yourselves?   25

CONRADE Marry, sir, we say we are none.

⌜DOGBERRY⌝ A marvelous witty fellow, I assure you,
but I will go about with him.—Come you hither,
sirrah, a word in your ear. Sir, I say to you it is
thought you are false knaves.   30

BORACHIO Sir, I say to you we are none.

⌜DOGBERRY⌝ Well, stand aside.—'Fore God, they are
both in a tale. Have you writ down that they are
none?

SEXTON Master constable, you go not the way to   35
examine. You must call forth the watch that are
their accusers.

⌜DOGBERRY⌝ Yea, marry, that's the eftest way. Let
the watch come forth. Masters, I charge you in the
Prince's name, accuse these men.   40

FIRST WATCHMAN This man said, sir, that Don John, the
Prince's brother, was a villain.

⌜DOGBERRY⌝ Write down Prince John a villain. Why,
this is flat perjury, to call a prince's brother villain!

52. **Flat burglary:** i.e., out-and-out treachery

56. **upon his words:** i.e., on the strength of Borachio's accusation

59. **redemption:** a mistake for "damnation"

65. **refused:** rejected

69. **opinioned:** a mistake for "pinioned" (i.e., bound by the arms)

71. **coxcomb:** i.e., fool (literally, the cap worn by a professional Fool) See picture, below.

72. **God's:** i.e., may God save

74. **naughty:** wicked

76. **suspect:** a mistake for "respect"; **place:** position

77. **years:** i.e., age

A Fool with his coxcomb. (4.2.71)
From Sebastian Brant, *Stultifera nauis* (1570).

BORACHIO Master constable—   45
⌜DOGBERRY⌝ Pray thee, fellow, peace. I do not like thy
    look, I promise thee.
SEXTON, ⌜to Watch⌝ What heard you him say else?
⌜SEACOAL⌝ Marry, that he had received a thousand
    ducats of Don John for accusing the Lady Hero   50
    wrongfully.
⌜DOGBERRY⌝ Flat burglary as ever was committed.
⌜VERGES⌝ Yea, by Mass, that it is.
SEXTON What else, fellow?
FIRST WATCHMAN And that Count Claudio did mean,   55
    upon his words, to disgrace Hero before the whole
    assembly, and not marry her.
⌜DOGBERRY, to Borachio⌝ O, villain! Thou wilt be con-
    demned into everlasting redemption for this!
SEXTON What else?   60
⌜SEACOAL⌝ This is all.
SEXTON And this is more, masters, than you can deny.
    Prince John is this morning secretly stolen away.
    Hero was in this manner accused, in this very
    manner refused, and upon the grief of this sudden- 65
    ly died.—Master constable, let these men be bound
    and brought to Leonato's. I will go before and show
    him their examination.   ⌜He exits.⌝
⌜DOGBERRY⌝ Come, let them be opinioned.
⌜VERGES⌝ Let them be in the hands—   70
⌜CONRADE⌝ Off, coxcomb!
⌜DOGBERRY⌝ God's my life, where's the Sexton? Let
    him write down the Prince's officer "coxcomb."
    Come, bind them.—Thou naughty varlet!
⌜CONRADE⌝ Away! You are an ass, you are an ass!   75
⌜DOGBERRY⌝ Dost thou not suspect my place? Dost
    thou not suspect my years? O, that he were here to
    write me down an ass! But masters, remember that
    I am an ass, though it be not written down, yet
    forget not that I am an ass.—No, thou villain, thou   80

81. **piety:** a mistake, perhaps for "impiety"

84. **pretty . . . flesh:** perhaps (unwittingly) obscene: in *Romeo and Juliet*, Sampson boasts, "Me they [i.e., maids] shall feel while I am able to stand, and . . . I am a pretty piece of flesh" (1.1.29–30).

85, 86. **go to:** an expression of dismissiveness

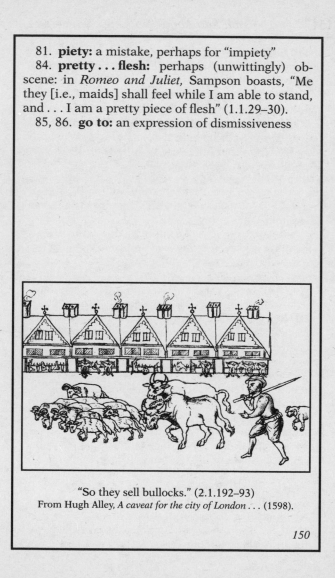

"So they sell bullocks." (2.1.192–93)
From Hugh Alley, *A caveat for the city of London . . .* (1598).

art full of piety, as shall be proved upon thee by
good witness. I am a wise fellow and, which is more,
an officer and, which is more, a householder and,
which is more, as pretty a piece of flesh as any is in
Messina, and one that knows the law, go to, and a   85
rich fellow enough, go to, and a fellow that hath had
losses, and one that hath two gowns and everything
handsome about him.—Bring him away.—O, that I
had been writ down an ass!

⌜*They*⌝ *exit.*

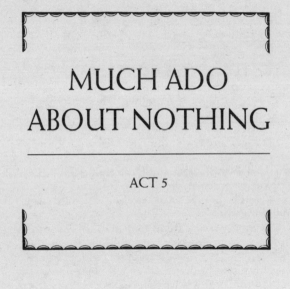

MUCH ADO
ABOUT NOTHING

ACT 5

5.1 Leonato and his brother tell Claudio and Don Pedro of Hero's death, and attempt to challenge them to a duel. Benedick succeeds in issuing his challenge to Claudio. Dogberry and the prisoners enter, and Claudio and Don Pedro learn about the trick that was played on them. They also learn that Don John has fled from Messina. Having been convinced of Hero's innocence, Claudio begs Leonato's forgiveness and is told that he must sing an epitaph at Hero's tomb that night. The next morning he is to marry Leonato's "niece."

———————

1 SP. **Leonato's brother:** See note to 1.2.0 SD.
2. **second:** reinforce, assist the effect of
8. **suit with:** correspond with, match
10. **of her:** i.e., in her
12. **Measure his woe:** i.e., let his grief equal
13. **answer . . . strain:** This is primarily a musical metaphor, where one **strain** or phrase of music answers another. One could paraphrase as "Let his woe match mine in detail or in intensity."
14. **such a grief for such:** i.e., **such a grief** matching **such** another grief
17. **wag:** depart; **hem:** i.e., "h'm" or "ahem" (the word used to represent the sound made when clearing the throat, when expressing doubt, or when coughing to attract attention before speaking)
19. **Patch . . . with proverbs:** mend . . . with proverbial sayings; **drunk:** i.e., stupefied, insensible
20. **With candle-wasters:** i.e., through (the words of) those who read and write late into the night
21. **of him:** i.e., from him

⌐ACT 5⌐

⌐Scene 1⌐
Enter Leonato and his brother.

LEONATO'S BROTHER
If you go on thus, you will kill yourself,
And 'tis not wisdom thus to second grief
Against yourself.

LEONATO   I pray thee, cease thy counsel,
Which falls into mine ears as profitless   5
As water in a sieve. Give not me counsel,
Nor let no comforter delight mine ear
But such a one whose wrongs do suit with mine.
Bring me a father that so loved his child,
Whose joy of her is overwhelmed like mine,   10
And bid him speak of patience.
Measure his woe the length and breadth of mine,
And let it answer every strain for strain,
As thus for thus, and such a grief for such,
In every lineament, branch, shape, and form.   15
If such a one will smile and stroke his beard,
⌐Bid⌐ sorrow wag, cry "hem" when he should
     groan,
Patch grief with proverbs, make misfortune drunk
With candle-wasters, bring him yet to me,   20
And I of him will gather patience.
But there is no such man. For, brother, men

155

25. **passion:** (1) strong emotion; (2) suffering; **which before:** i.e., who earlier

26. **preceptial med'cine:** i.e., medicinal precepts; **to rage:** i.e., to others' anguish or violent pain

28. **Charm:** subdue, control (as with a magic spell)

29. **office:** obligation (said sarcastically)

30. **wring:** twist in anguish, writhe

31. **virtue:** strength, power; **sufficiency:** ability, competency

32. **To be so moral:** i.e., to moralize in that manner

34. **than advertisement:** i.e., than (can be soothed by) instruction or precepts (pronounced **advèrtisement**)

35. **nothing:** not at all

39. **However:** i.e., however much; **writ . . . gods:** i.e., assumed in their writings the title **of gods** (in professing indifference to misfortune)

40. **a push at:** an attack on; **sufferance:** suffering

41. **bend not:** i.e., do not direct; **upon:** against

48. **e'en:** i.e., afternoon (literally, evening)

Can counsel and speak comfort to that grief
Which they themselves not feel, but tasting it,
Their counsel turns to passion, which before   25
Would give preceptial med'cine to rage,
Fetter strong madness in a silken thread,
Charm ache with air and agony with words.
No, no, 'tis all men's office to speak patience
To those that wring under the load of sorrow,   30
But no man's virtue nor sufficiency
To be so moral when he shall endure
The like himself. Therefore give me no counsel.
My griefs cry louder than advertisement.

LEONATO'S BROTHER
Therein do men from children nothing differ.   35

LEONATO
I pray thee, peace. I will be flesh and blood,
For there was never yet philosopher
That could endure the toothache patiently,
However they have writ the style of gods
And made a push at chance and sufferance.   40

LEONATO'S BROTHER
Yet bend not all the harm upon yourself.
Make those that do offend you suffer too.

LEONATO
There thou speak'st reason. Nay, I will do so.
My soul doth tell me Hero is belied,
And that shall Claudio know; so shall the Prince   45
And all of them that thus dishonor her.

Enter Prince and Claudio

LEONATO'S BROTHER
Here comes the Prince and Claudio hastily.

PRINCE
Good e'en, good e'en.

CLAUDIO   Good day to both of you.

54. **all is one:** i.e., it does not matter

56. **right:** avenge

57. **Some of us:** i.e., Claudio and Don Pedro; **lie low:** i.e., **lie** prostrate or dead

62. **beshrew:** a mild word for "curse"

63. **your age:** i.e., you as an old man

64. **my . . . sword:** perhaps, I had no plan to use my sword

65. **fleer:** jeer, mock

69. **to thy head:** i.e., to your face

71. **reverence:** state of being respected (because of age)

73. **trial of a man:** i.e., a **trial** by combat, a duel

79. **framed:** contrived

"Enfranchised with a clog." (1.3.31)
From Geoffrey Whitney, *A choice of emblemes* (1586).

LEONATO
  Hear you, my lords—   50
PRINCE   We have some haste,
    Leonato.
LEONATO
  Some haste, my lord! Well, fare you well, my lord.
  Are you so hasty now? Well, all is one.
PRINCE
  Nay, do not quarrel with us, good old man.   55
LEONATO'S BROTHER
  If he could right himself with quarreling,
  Some of us would lie low.
CLAUDIO   Who wrongs him?
LEONATO
  Marry, thou dost wrong me, thou dissembler, thou.
  Nay, never lay thy hand upon thy sword.   60
  I fear thee not.
CLAUDIO   Marry, beshrew my hand
  If it should give your age such cause of fear.
  In faith, my hand meant nothing to my sword.
LEONATO
  Tush, tush, man, never fleer and jest at me.   65
  I speak not like a dotard nor a fool,
  As under privilege of age to brag
  What I have done being young, or what would do
  Were I not old. Know, Claudio, to thy head,
  Thou hast so wronged mine innocent child and me   70
  That I am forced to lay my reverence by,
  And with gray hairs and bruise of many days
  Do challenge thee to trial of a man.
  I say thou hast belied mine innocent child.
  Thy slander hath gone through and through her   75
    heart,
  And she lies buried with her ancestors,
  O, in a tomb where never scandal slept,
  Save this of hers, framed by thy villainy.

85. **nice fence:** i.e., elegant fencing skills; **practice:** i.e., at swordplay

86. **lustihood:** vigor, robustness

88. **daff:** i.e., doff, discard

92. **Win me and wear me:** proverbial, meaning "defeat me and then boast"; **answer:** fight with

95. **foining fence:** thrusting swordplay (*To foin* is to pierce or thrust.)

102. **apes:** counterfeits; **jacks:** lowborn fellows

105. **scruple:** the twenty-fourth part of an ounce (a unit of apothecary weight)

106. **Scambling:** contentious; **outfacing:** i.e., brazen; **fashionmonging:** i.e., foppish

107. **cog:** cheat; or, flatter, wheedle; **flout:** jeer; **deprave:** vilify, disparage

108. **anticly:** i.e., grotesquely dressed; **show outward hideousness:** i.e., look terrifying

CLAUDIO
  My villainy? 80
LEONATO   Thine, Claudio, thine, I say.
PRINCE
  You say not right, old man.
LEONATO   My lord, my lord,
  I'll prove it on his body if he dare,
  Despite his nice fence and his active practice, 85
  His May of youth and bloom of lustihood.
CLAUDIO
  Away! I will not have to do with you.
LEONATO
  Canst thou so daff me? Thou hast killed my child.
  If thou kill'st me, boy, thou shalt kill a man.
LEONATO'S BROTHER
  He shall kill two of us, and men indeed, 90
  But that's no matter. Let him kill one first.
  Win me and wear me! Let him answer me.—
  Come, follow me, boy. Come, sir boy, come, follow
    me.
  Sir boy, I'll whip you from your foining fence, 95
  Nay, as I am a gentleman, I will.
LEONATO   Brother—
LEONATO'S BROTHER
  Content yourself. God knows I loved my niece,
  And she is dead, slandered to death by villains
  That dare as well answer a man indeed 100
  As I dare take a serpent by the tongue.—
  Boys, apes, braggarts, jacks, milksops!
LEONATO   Brother Anthony—
LEONATO'S BROTHER
  Hold you content. What, man! I know them, yea,
  And what they weigh, even to the utmost scruple— 105
  Scambling, outfacing, fashionmonging boys,
  That lie and cog and flout, deprave and slander,
  Go anticly and show outward hideousness,

110. **durst:** dared

114. **meddle:** concern yourself

115. **wake your patience:** perhaps, disturb your peace of mind any further

122. **some of us:** i.e., the two of you

128. **had like to have had:** i.e., nearly had

129. **with:** i.e., by

131. **doubt:** suspect

133. **false quarrel:** perhaps, a fight in which you are in the wrong

136. **high-proof:** i.e., impervious, impenetrable; **fain:** gladly

Map of the world with the Antipodes. (2.1.261)
From Macrobius, *In Somnium Scipionis . . .* (1492).

And speak off half a dozen dang'rous words
How they might hurt their enemies, if they durst, 110
And this is all.

LEONATO But brother Anthony—

LEONATO'S BROTHER Come, 'tis no matter.
Do not you meddle. Let me deal in this.

PRINCE
Gentlemen both, we will not wake your patience. 115
My heart is sorry for your daughter's death,
But, on my honor, she was charged with nothing
But what was true and very full of proof.

LEONATO My lord, my lord—

PRINCE I will not hear you. 120

LEONATO
No? Come, brother, away. I will be heard.

LEONATO'S BROTHER
And shall, or some of us will smart for it.
                         ⌈*Leonato and his brother*⌉ *exit.*

Enter Benedick.

PRINCE
See, see, here comes the man we went to seek.

CLAUDIO Now, signior, what news?

BENEDICK, ⌈*to Prince*⌉ Good day, my lord. 125

PRINCE Welcome, signior. You are almost come to
part almost a fray.

CLAUDIO We had ⌈like⌉ to have had our two noses
snapped off with two old men without teeth.

PRINCE Leonato and his brother. What think'st thou? 130
Had we fought, I doubt we should have been too
young for them.

BENEDICK In a false quarrel there is no true valor. I
came to seek you both.

CLAUDIO We have been up and down to seek thee, for 135
we are high-proof melancholy and would fain have
it beaten away. Wilt thou use thy wit?

141. **beside their wit:** i.e., out of their minds; **draw:** i.e., take out your wit (as you would **draw** your sword)

142. **draw . . . us:** Addressed to **minstrels,** this might mean "draw your instruments from their cases."

145. **What, courage, man:** The word **What** is used as an interjection introducing an exclamation.

146. **care killed a cat:** a common expression; **mettle:** spirit

148. **in the career:** at full speed (a term from tournaments, as are **charge** and **'cross**); **an:** if

149. **charge it:** i.e., use it as a weapon

150. **subject:** i.e., person to attack; or, perhaps, topic

151. **staff:** i.e., spear shaft (Using the continuing tournament metaphor, Claudio here says that Benedick's wit has failed him.)

152. **broke 'cross:** i.e., clumsily broken crosswise

153. **By this light:** a mild oath; **changes:** i.e., grows pale

155. **turn his girdle:** Proverbial: "If he be angry, let him **turn his girdle.**" The meaning of the proverb is not known.   **girdle:** a belt for carrying a light weapon or keys

159. **make it good:** i.e., enforce my accusation through combat; **how:** i.e., however

160. **Do me right:** i.e., give me satisfaction

161. **protest:** announce, proclaim

164. **meet you:** i.e., in a duel (Don Pedro's response suggests he hears this comment, along with the reference to **good cheer**—i.e., hospitable entertainment—and misinterprets it.)

167. **bid:** invited

(continued)
164

BENEDICK   It is in my scabbard. Shall I draw it?

PRINCE   Dost thou wear thy wit by thy side?

CLAUDIO   Never any did so, though very many have   140
    been beside their wit. I will bid thee draw, as we do
    the minstrels: draw to pleasure us.

PRINCE   As I am an honest man, he looks pale.—Art
    thou sick, or angry?

CLAUDIO, ⌈*to Benedick*⌉   What, courage, man! What   145
    though care killed a cat? Thou hast mettle enough
    in thee to kill care.

BENEDICK   Sir, I shall meet your wit in the career, an
    you charge it against me. I pray you, choose another
    subject.   150

CLAUDIO, ⌈*to Prince*⌉   Nay, then, give him another staff.
    This last was broke 'cross.

PRINCE   By this light, he changes more and more. I
    think he be angry indeed.

CLAUDIO   If he be, he knows how to turn his girdle.   155

BENEDICK   Shall I speak a word in your ear?

CLAUDIO   God bless me from a challenge!

BENEDICK, ⌈*aside to Claudio*⌉   You are a villain. I jest
    not. I will make it good how you dare, with what you
    dare, and when you dare. Do me right, or I will   160
    protest your cowardice. You have killed a sweet
    lady, and her death shall fall heavy on you. Let me
    hear from you.

CLAUDIO   Well, I will meet you, so I may have good
    cheer.   165

PRINCE   What, a feast, a feast?

CLAUDIO   I' faith, I thank him. He hath bid me to a
    calf's head and a capon, the which if I do not carve
    most curiously, say my knife's naught. Shall I not
    find a woodcock too?   170

BENEDICK   Sir, your wit ambles well; it goes easily.

PRINCE   I'll tell thee how Beatrice praised thy wit the
    other day. I said thou hadst a fine wit. "True," said

168, 170. **calf's head, capon, woodcock:** Each of these could be an item at a **feast** (dishes that Claudio is ready to **carve**), but each also has a symbolic, insulting meaning: **calf's head** and **woodcock** mean "simpleton"; **capon** (a castrated cock) means "eunuch." (See picture of **woodcock,** page 88.)

169. **curiously:** elaborately, exquisitely; **naught:** worthless

174. **fine:** excellent; extremely narrow

176. **Just:** exactly

178. **wise gentleman:** perhaps a sarcastic name for a fool

179. **tongues:** i.e., ability to speak many languages

181. **forswore:** repudiated, renounced

183. **transshape:** alter the shape of

185. **proper'st:** finest, handsomest

188. **an if:** i.e., **if**

191–92. **God saw him . . . in the garden:** In the book of Genesis, after Adam eats the fruit forbidden him in the Garden of Eden, he "and his wife hid themselves from the presence of the Lord God among the trees of the garden" (3.8). (See picture, page 142.)

193–96. **the savage bull's . . . married man:** a reference to 1.1.256–62

198. **gossip-like:** A **gossip** was a gossiping or tattling woman. **humor:** mood

199. **braggarts . . . blades:** a reference to the way **braggarts** damage their own weapons and then brag that they broke them in a fight

201. **courtesies:** kindnesses

205. **meet:** i.e., in a duel; **peace be with him:** a phrase used as a greeting or, as here, a farewell

she, "a fine little one." "No," said I, "a great wit."
"Right," says she, "a great gross one." "Nay," said I,   175
"a good wit." "Just," said she, "it hurts nobody."
"Nay," said I, "the gentleman is wise." "Certain,"
said she, "a wise gentleman." "Nay," said I, "he
hath the tongues." "That I believe," said she, "for he
swore a thing to me on Monday night which he   180
forswore on Tuesday morning; there's a double
tongue, there's two tongues." Thus did she an hour
together transshape thy particular virtues. Yet at
last she concluded with a sigh, thou wast the
proper'st man in Italy.   185

CLAUDIO   For the which she wept heartily and said she
cared not.

PRINCE   Yea, that she did. But yet for all that, an if she
did not hate him deadly, she would love him
dearly. The old man's daughter told us all.   190

CLAUDIO   All, all. And, moreover, God saw him when
he was hid in the garden.

PRINCE   But when shall we set the savage bull's horns
on the sensible Benedick's head?

CLAUDIO   Yea, and text underneath: "Here dwells Ben-   195
edick, the married man"?

BENEDICK   Fare you well, boy. You know my mind. I
will leave you now to your gossip-like humor. You
break jests as braggarts do their blades, which, God
be thanked, hurt not.—My lord, for your many   200
courtesies I thank you. I must discontinue your
company. Your brother the Bastard is fled from
Messina. You have among you killed a sweet and
innocent lady. For my Lord Lackbeard there, he and
I shall meet, and till then peace be with him.   205
⌜*Benedick exits.*⌝

PRINCE   He is in earnest.

CLAUDIO   In most profound earnest, and, I'll warrant
you, for the love of Beatrice.

211. **goes in:** i.e., walks around only in

212. **leaves off his wit:** i.e., forgets to wear his intelligence

213–14. **He is . . . man:** These lines have been variously (and unsatisfactorily) explained. **to an ape:** perhaps, in the eyes of the **ape;** or, in comparison to **an ape; doctor:** man of learning

215. **soft you:** wait a minute; **Pluck up:** i.e., pay attention

216. **sad:** serious

218. **she shall . . . balance:** The image is of Justice with **her balance** scales; since **reasons** was pronounced like *raisins*, there is a secondary image of a vendor weighing fruit to sell.

219. **an:** i.e., if; **once:** i.e., in a word

221. **bound:** in bonds, tied up

223. **Hearken after:** i.e., ask about

227. **slanders:** i.e., slanderers

228. **verified:** asserted

232. **committed:** i.e., being sent to prison

232–33. **lay to their charge:** i.e., charge them with

234. **division:** i.e., way of enumerating the parts

235. **meaning:** idea, topic; **suited:** perhaps, set out in a variety of ways

237–38. **bound to your answer:** i.e., tied up, compelled, and on your way to make your legal defense (a triple pun on **bound**)

238. **cunning:** clever

241. **Do you hear me:** i.e., listen to me

PRINCE   And hath challenged thee?

CLAUDIO   Most sincerely.   210

PRINCE   What a pretty thing man is when he goes in his
  doublet and hose and leaves off his wit!

CLAUDIO   He is then a giant to an ape; but then is an ape
  a doctor to such a man.

PRINCE   But soft you, let me be. Pluck up, my heart,   215
  and be sad. Did he not say my brother was fled?

*Enter Constables ⌜Dogberry and Verges, and the Watch,
      with⌝ Conrade and Borachio.*

⌜DOGBERRY⌝   Come you, sir. If justice cannot tame you,
  she shall ne'er weigh more reasons in her balance.
  Nay, an you be a cursing hypocrite once, you must
  be looked to.   220

PRINCE   How now, two of my brother's men bound?
  Borachio one!

CLAUDIO   Hearken after their offense, my lord.

PRINCE   Officers, what offense have these men done?

⌜DOGBERRY⌝   Marry, sir, they have committed false   225
  report; moreover, they have spoken untruths; sec-
  ondarily, they are slanders; sixth and lastly, they
  have belied a lady; thirdly, they have verified unjust
  things; and, to conclude, they are lying knaves.

PRINCE   First, I ask thee what they have done; thirdly, I   230
  ask thee what's their offense; sixth and lastly, why
  they are committed; and, to conclude, what you lay
  to their charge.

CLAUDIO   Rightly reasoned, and in his own division;
  and, by my troth, there's one meaning well suited.   235

PRINCE, ⌜to Borachio and Conrade⌝   Who have you of-
  fended, masters, that you are thus bound to your
  answer? This learned constable is too cunning to be
  understood. What's your offense?

BORACHIO   Sweet prince, let me go no farther to mine   240
  answer. Do you hear me, and let this count kill me.

246. **incensed:** incited

247. **orchard:** formal garden

250. **seal:** i.e., guarantee (the **record** of **my villainy**) to be true

252, 261. **upon:** i.e., because of

258–59. **the practice of it:** i.e., putting it in **practice**

260. **framed:** created, constructed

263. **semblance:** form, image

264. **plaintiffs:** a mistake for "defendants" or "prisoners"

265. **reformed:** a mistake for "informed"

Conjuring. (2.1.252–54)
From Christopher Marlowe, *The tragicall historie of . . .*
Doctor Faustus . . . (1631).

I have deceived even your very eyes. What your
wisdoms could not discover, these shallow fools
have brought to light, who in the night overheard
me confessing to this man how Don John your 245
brother incensed me to slander the Lady Hero, how
you were brought into the orchard and saw me
court Margaret in Hero's garments, how you dis-
graced her when you should marry her. My villainy
they have upon record, which I had rather seal with 250
my death than repeat over to my shame. The lady is
dead upon mine and my master's false accusation.
And, briefly, I desire nothing but the reward of a
villain.

PRINCE, ⌜*to Claudio*⌝
Runs not this speech like iron through your blood? 255

CLAUDIO
I have drunk poison whiles he uttered it.

PRINCE, ⌜*to Borachio*⌝
But did my brother set thee on to this?

BORACHIO   Yea, and paid me richly for the practice of
it.

PRINCE
He is composed and framed of treachery, 260
And fled he is upon this villainy.

CLAUDIO
Sweet Hero, now thy image doth appear
In the rare semblance that I loved it first.

⌜DOGBERRY⌝   Come, bring away the plaintiffs. By this
time our sexton hath reformed Signior Leonato of 265
the matter. And, masters, do not forget to specify,
when time and place shall serve, that I am an ass.

⌜VERGES⌝   Here, here comes Master Signior Leonato,
and the Sexton too.

Enter Leonato, his brother, and the Sexton.

277. **beliest:** tell lies about

282. **bravely:** (1) courageously; (2) splendidly

283. **pray:** i.e., beg

285. **Impose me to:** subject **me to,** make **me** undergo; **invention:** imagination

294. **Possess:** inform

296. **aught:** at all; **invention:** composing, devising (here, the writing of a poem or song)

297. **Hang her:** i.e., **hang** for **her**

Venus. (4.1.61)
From Vincenzo Cartari, *Le vere e noue imagini . . .* (1615).

LEONATO
Which is the villain? Let me see his eyes,   270
That, when I note another man like him,
I may avoid him. Which of these is he?
BORACHIO
If you would know your wronger, look on me.
LEONATO
Art thou the slave that with thy breath hast killed
Mine innocent child?   275
BORACHIO   Yea, even I alone.
LEONATO
No, not so, villain, thou beliest thyself.
Here stand a pair of honorable men—
A third is fled—that had a hand in it.—
I thank you, princes, for my daughter's death.   280
Record it with your high and worthy deeds.
'Twas bravely done, if you bethink you of it.
CLAUDIO
I know not how to pray your patience,
Yet I must speak. Choose your revenge yourself.
Impose me to what penance your invention   285
Can lay upon my sin. Yet sinned I not
But in mistaking.
PRINCE   By my soul, nor I,
And yet to satisfy this good old man
I would bend under any heavy weight   290
That he'll enjoin me to.
LEONATO
I cannot bid you bid my daughter live—
That were impossible—but, I pray you both,
Possess the people in Messina here
How innocent she died. And if your love   295
Can labor aught in sad invention,
Hang her an epitaph upon her tomb
And sing it to her bones. Sing it tonight.
Tomorrow morning come you to my house,

301. **yet:** nevertheless

304. **right:** fair treatment (with wordplay on rite of marriage)

311. **naughty:** wicked

313. **packed in:** i.e., an accomplice to

318. **by her:** i.e., of her

320. **under white and black:** i.e., written down; **plaintiff:** a mistake for "offender"

325–26. **the which he hath used:** i.e., a habit which he has practiced

326. **paid:** i.e., repaid

333. **God save the foundation:** i.e., **God** bless the founder (said at the doors of charitable religious houses)

"And sigh away Sundays." (1.1.197–98)
From *The whole psalmes in foure partes . . .* (1563).

And since you could not be my son-in-law,   300
Be yet my nephew. My brother hath a daughter,
Almost the copy of my child that's dead,
And she alone is heir to both of us.
Give her the right you should have giv'n her cousin,
And so dies my revenge.   305

CLAUDIO   O, noble sir!
Your overkindness doth wring tears from me.
I do embrace your offer and dispose
For henceforth of poor Claudio.

LEONATO
Tomorrow then I will expect your coming.   310
Tonight I take my leave. This naughty man
Shall face to face be brought to Margaret,
Who I believe was packed in all this wrong,
Hired to it by your brother.

BORACHIO   No, by my soul, she was not,   315
Nor knew not what she did when she spoke to me,
But always hath been just and virtuous
In anything that I do know by her.

⌐DOGBERRY, *to Leonato* ⌐   Moreover, sir, which indeed is
not under white and black, this plaintiff here, the   320
offender, did call me ass. I beseech you, let it be
remembered in his punishment. And also the watch
heard them talk of one Deformed. They say he
wears a key in his ear and a lock hanging by it and
borrows money in God's name, the which he hath   325
used so long and never paid that now men grow
hardhearted and will lend nothing for God's sake.
Pray you, examine him upon that point.

LEONATO   I thank thee for thy care and honest pains.

⌐DOGBERRY⌐   Your Worship speaks like a most thankful   330
and reverent youth, and I praise God for you.

LEONATO, ⌐*giving him money*⌐   There's for thy pains.

⌐DOGBERRY⌐   God save the foundation.

340. **give you leave:** a mistake for "ask your leave"

341. **prohibit:** a mistake for "permit" or "foster"

349. **lewd:** base, disreputable

5.2 Benedick tells Beatrice that he has challenged Claudio. They are summoned to Leonato's house with the news that Hero's innocence has been proved.

———

2. **to the speech of:** i.e., to speak with

7. **come over it:** Benedick plays with the fact that **style** sounds like "stile" (a set of steps built over a fence). **Come over it** can thus mean (1) write in a more elegant style; and (2) climb over the stile. **comely:** proper

9. **come over me:** i.e., make love to me

10. **keep below stairs:** remain in the servants' quarters (There seems to be an implied pun here on **mistress** (line 1) as "the lady of the house"—and therefore not **"below stairs"**—and as "a woman with a lover.")

LEONATO   Go, I discharge thee of thy prisoner, and I
    thank thee.   335
⌜DOGBERRY⌝   I leave an arrant knave with your Wor-
    ship, which I beseech your Worship to correct
    yourself, for the example of others. God keep your
    Worship! I wish your Worship well. God restore you
    to health. I humbly give you leave to depart, and if a   340
    merry meeting may be wished, God prohibit it.—
    Come, neighbor.   ⌜*Dogberry and Verges exit.*⌝

LEONATO
    Until tomorrow morning, lords, farewell.

LEONATO'S BROTHER
    Farewell, my lords. We look for you tomorrow.

PRINCE
    We will not fail.   345

CLAUDIO   Tonight I'll mourn with Hero.

LEONATO, ⌜*to Watch*⌝
    Bring you these fellows on.—We'll talk with
        Margaret,
    How her acquaintance grew with this lewd fellow.
                                                They exit.

                        ⌜Scene 2⌝
                Enter Benedick and Margaret.

BENEDICK   Pray thee, sweet Mistress Margaret, deserve
    well at my hands by helping me to the speech of
    Beatrice.

MARGARET   Will you then write me a sonnet in praise
    of my beauty?   5

BENEDICK   In so high a style, Margaret, that no man
    living shall come over it, for in most comely truth
    thou deservest it.

MARGARET   To have no man come over me? Why, shall I
    always keep below stairs?   10

16–17. I give thee the bucklers: i.e., **I give** up (in this wit combat) **bucklers:** small shields used in swordfighting (See picture, page 180.) The double entendre on **swords** and **bucklers** that begins in line 18 continues with **pikes, vice,** and **maids.**

21. pikes: spikes in the center of bucklers; **vice:** i.e., vise (a clamp used in carpentry or metalworking)

26–29. The god of love: This stanza is the beginning of a popular old song.

30. Leander: in Greek mythology, a famous lover who drowned swimming across the Hellespont to see his sweetheart (See picture, page 188, and longer note to 4.1.87, especially the final paragraph, page 204.)

31. Troilus: famed for his love for Cressida, whose uncle Pandarus made their affair possible

32. quondam: bygone, former; **carpetmongers:** i.e., pretend lovers (The word seems to have been constructed by analogy with "carpet knight," a man knighted not on the battlefield but at court, and thus a pretend warrior. The word means literally "sellers of carpets.")

33. even: smooth

37. an innocent: a childish, a silly

38. hard: (1) harsh, unpleasant sounding; (2) referring to the unpleasant idea of cuckoldry

40–41. under a rhyming planet: i.e., **under** the influence of **a planet** that bestows poetic gifts

41. festival: joyful, glad

BENEDICK   Thy wit is as quick as the greyhound's
    mouth; it catches.

MARGARET   And yours as blunt as the fencer's foils,
    which hit but hurt not.

BENEDICK   A most manly wit, Margaret; it will not hurt   15
    a woman. And so, I pray thee, call Beatrice. I give
    thee the bucklers.

MARGARET   Give us the swords; we have bucklers of our
    own.

BENEDICK   If you use them, Margaret, you must put in   20
    the pikes with a vice, and they are dangerous
    weapons for maids.

MARGARET   Well, I will call Beatrice to you, who I
    think hath legs.

BENEDICK   And therefore will come.   25

                              Margaret exits.

⌜*Sings*⌝   *The god of love*
              That sits above,
          And knows me, and knows me,
              How pitiful I deserve—

I mean in singing. But in loving, Leander the good   30
swimmer, Troilus the first employer of panders, and
a whole book full of these quondam carpetmongers, whose names yet run smoothly in the even
road of a blank verse, why, they were never so truly
turned over and over as my poor self in love. Marry,   35
I cannot show it in rhyme. I have tried. I can find out
no rhyme to "lady" but "baby"—an innocent
rhyme; for "scorn," "horn"—a hard rhyme; for
"school," "fool"—a babbling rhyme; very ominous
endings. No, I was not born under a rhyming   40
planet, nor I cannot woo in festival terms.

                    Enter Beatrice.

Sweet Beatrice, wouldst thou come when I called
thee?

47. **that I came:** i.e., what **I came** for

53. **noisome:** foul-smelling

55. **frighted:** i.e., frightened; **his:** i.e., its

58–59. **subscribe him:** write him down as

60. **parts:** attributes

63. **politic:** (1) judiciously governed; (2) cunning

65. **suffer:** (1) experience; (2) undergo the pains of

66. **epithet:** term, expression; **do suffer:** am subjected to

72. **wise:** clever (In Beatrice's response, **wise** has its usual meaning.)

73. **It appears not:** i.e., your wisdom does not reveal itself

76. **instance:** i.e., saying (literally, example or case)

77. **good neighbors:** Proverbial: "He has ill [i.e., bad] **neighbors** who is fain to praise himself."

78–79. **live no longer in monument:** i.e., be memorialized **no longer**

79. **bell:** i.e., church **bell** tolled for funerals

A buckler. (5.2.17)
From Louis de Gaya, *A treatise of the arms . . .* (1678).

BEATRICE   Yea, signior, and depart when you bid me.

BENEDICK   O, stay but till then!   45

BEATRICE   "Then" is spoken. Fare you well now. And
yet, ere I go, let me go with that I came, which is,
with knowing what hath passed between you and
Claudio.

BENEDICK   Only foul words, and thereupon I will kiss   50
thee.

BEATRICE   Foul words is but foul wind, and foul wind is
but foul breath, and foul breath is noisome. Therefore I will depart unkissed.

BENEDICK   Thou hast frighted the word out of his right   55
sense, so forcible is thy wit. But I must tell thee
plainly, Claudio undergoes my challenge, and either
I must shortly hear from him, or I will subscribe
him a coward. And I pray thee now tell me, for
which of my bad parts didst thou first fall in love   60
with me?

BEATRICE   For them all together, which maintained so
politic a state of evil that they will not admit any
good part to intermingle with them. But for which
of my good parts did you first suffer love for me?   65

BENEDICK   Suffer love! A good epithet. I do suffer love
indeed, for I love thee against my will.

BEATRICE   In spite of your heart, I think. Alas, poor
heart, if you spite it for my sake, I will spite it for
yours, for I will never love that which my friend   70
hates.

BENEDICK   Thou and I are too wise to woo peaceably.

BEATRICE   It appears not in this confession. There's not
one wise man among twenty that will praise himself.   75

BENEDICK   An old, an old instance, Beatrice, that lived
in the time of good neighbors. If a man do not erect
in this age his own tomb ere he dies, he shall live no
longer in monument than the bell rings and the
widow weeps.   80

82. **Question:** perhaps, a good question (and here is the answer); **clamor:** i.e., the tolling of the bell

83. **quarter:** i.e., **quarter** of an hour; **rheum:** i.e., weeping

84. **Don Worm, his conscience:** The traditional linking of pangs of **conscience** with a gnawing **worm** may derive from the biblical descriptions of the damned as those whose "worm shall not die, neither shall their fire be quenched" (Isaiah 66.24, echoed at Mark 9.44, 46, 48).

90. **ill:** badly

93. **mend:** get better

96. **old coil:** i.e., all kinds of turmoil

98. **abused:** deceived

99. **presently:** at once

101. **die:** (1) **die** for love; (2) experience sexual orgasm

5.3 Claudio appears at Leonato's family tomb, has a song sung for Hero, and hangs a scroll on the tomb.

———————

1. **monument of Leonato:** i.e., tomb of Leonato's family

BEATRICE   And how long is that, think you?

BENEDICK   Question: why, an hour in clamor and a
quarter in rheum. Therefore is it most expedient for
the wise, if Don Worm, his conscience, find no
impediment to the contrary, to be the trumpet of   85
his own virtues, as I am to myself. So much for
praising myself, who, I myself will bear witness, is
praiseworthy. And now tell me, how doth your
cousin?

BEATRICE   Very ill.   90

BENEDICK   And how do you?

BEATRICE   Very ill, too.

BENEDICK   Serve God, love me, and mend. There will I
leave you too, for here comes one in haste.

Enter Ursula.

URSULA   Madam, you must come to your uncle. Yon-   95
der's old coil at home. It is proved my Lady Hero
hath been falsely accused, the Prince and Claudio
mightily abused, and Don John is the author of all,
who is fled and gone. Will you come presently?
                              ⌜*Ursula exits.*⌝

BEATRICE   Will you go hear this news, signior?   100

BENEDICK   I will live in thy heart, die in thy lap, and be
buried in thy eyes—and, moreover, I will go with
thee to thy uncle's.
                              ⌜*They*⌝ *exit.*

⌜Scene 3⌝
Enter Claudio, Prince, and three or four ⌜*Lords*⌝ *with*
tapers, ⌜*and Musicians.*⌝

CLAUDIO   Is this the monument of Leonato?

⌜FIRST⌝ LORD   It is, my lord.

5. **guerdon:** recompense

12. **goddess of the night:** Diana, **goddess of the** moon and of chastity (hence the reference to Hero as Diana's **virgin knight**)

18. **Heavily:** sadly, mournfully

19. **yawn:** i.e., open

20. **Till death be utterèd:** The verb *to utter* could mean both "to express" and "to vanquish." This much-debated line might therefore mean "**till** Hero's **death be** fully expressed" or "until **death be** vanquished."

24. **morrow:** morning

25. **have preyed:** i.e., have finished their preying

26. **the wheels of Phoebus:** i.e., **the** chariot **of Phoebus,** god of the sun (See picture, below.)

29. **several:** separate

SOL

Phoebus in his chariot. (5.3.26)
From Hyginus, . . . *Fabularum liber* . . . (1549).

⌈CLAUDIO, *reading an*⌉ *Epitaph.*

>Done to death by slanderous tongues
>>Was the Hero that here lies.
>Death, in guerdon of her wrongs,   5
>>Gives her fame which never dies.
>So the life that died with shame
>Lives in death with glorious fame.
>>>>⌈*He hangs up the scroll.*⌉

Hang thou there upon the tomb,
Praising her when I am ⌈dumb.⌉   10
Now music, sound, and sing your solemn hymn.

Song

>Pardon, goddess of the night,
>Those that slew thy virgin knight,
>For the which with songs of woe,
>Round about her tomb they go,   15
>>Midnight, assist our moan.
>>Help us to sigh and groan
>>>Heavily, heavily.
>Graves, yawn and yield your dead,
>Till death be utterèd,   20
>>Heavily, heavily.

⌈CLAUDIO⌉
Now, unto thy bones, goodnight.
Yearly will I do this rite.

PRINCE
Good morrow, masters. Put your torches out.
The wolves have preyed, and look, the gentle day   25
Before the wheels of Phoebus, round about
Dapples the drowsy east with spots of gray.
Thanks to you all, and leave us. Fare you well.

CLAUDIO
Good morrow, masters. Each his several way.
⌈*Lords and Musicians exit.*⌉

30. **weeds:** clothing

32. **Hymen:** god of marriage (See picture, page 196.) **issue:** result; **speed 's:** i.e., **speed** us, favor us

5.4 Claudio and Don Pedro appear for the second wedding. The women enter masked. When Claudio takes the hand of Leonato's "niece," agreeing to marry her, she unmasks and he learns that she is Hero. Benedick and Beatrice agree to marry, but only out of pity for each other. Love poems each has written to the other are produced to prove that they do, in fact, love each other. Claudio is forgiven by all, and a double wedding is set to follow the closing dance.

———————

3. **Upon:** i.e., because of; **debated:** discussed

5. **against her will:** perhaps, unintentionally (The phrase more commonly means "unwillingly.")

6. **question:** investigation

7. **sorts:** turn out

8. **else:** otherwise; **by faith:** i.e., through my promise

9. **call . . . to a reckoning:** make . . . give an account of himself

14. **office:** part

PRINCE
Come, let us hence, and put on other weeds,   30
And then to Leonato's we will go.

CLAUDIO
And Hymen now with luckier issue speed 's,
Than this for whom we rendered up this woe.

They exit.

⌜Scene 4⌝

Enter Leonato, Benedick, ⌜Beatrice,⌝ Margaret, Ursula,
⌜Leonato's brother,⌝ Friar, Hero.

FRIAR
Did I not tell you she was innocent?

LEONATO
So are the Prince and Claudio, who accused her
Upon the error that you heard debated.
But Margaret was in some fault for this,
Although against her will, as it appears   5
In the true course of all the question.

LEONATO'S BROTHER
Well, I am glad that all things sorts so well.

BENEDICK
And so am I, being else by faith enforced
To call young Claudio to a reckoning for it.

LEONATO
Well, daughter, and you gentlewomen all,   10
Withdraw into a chamber by yourselves,
And when I send for you, come hither masked.
The Prince and Claudio promised by this hour
To visit me.—You know your office, brother.
You must be father to your brother's daughter,   15
And give her to young Claudio.   *The ladies exit.*

17. **confirmed countenance:** i.e., controlled facial expression

18. **pains:** i.e., help

20. **undo:** (1) unbind; (2) destroy

28. **for:** i.e., as **for; my will is:** i.e., **my** desire **is** that

37. **attend:** await, wait upon; **yet:** still

39. **hold:** i.e., not change; **Ethiope:** Ethiopian, or anyone with black skin (Dark hair and skin were not considered beautiful in Elizabethan England.)

Leander swimming the Hellespont. (5.2.30)
From Musaeus, [*Hero and Leander*] (1538).

LEONATO'S BROTHER
    Which I will do with confirmed countenance.
BENEDICK
    Friar, I must entreat your pains, I think.
FRIAR   To do what, signior?
BENEDICK
    To bind me, or undo me, one of them.—   20
    Signior Leonato, truth it is, good signior,
    Your niece regards me with an eye of favor.
LEONATO
    That eye my daughter lent her; 'tis most true.
BENEDICK
    And I do with an eye of love requite her.
LEONATO
    The sight whereof I think you had from me,   25
    From Claudio, and the Prince. But what's your will?
BENEDICK
    Your answer, sir, is enigmatical.
    But for my will, my will is your goodwill
    May stand with ours, this day to be conjoined
    In the state of honorable marriage—   30
    In which, good friar, I shall desire your help.
LEONATO
    My heart is with your liking.
FRIAR   And my help.
    Here comes the Prince and Claudio.

    Enter Prince, and Claudio, and two or three other.

PRINCE   Good morrow to this fair assembly.   35
LEONATO
    Good morrow, prince; good morrow, Claudio.
    We here attend you. Are you yet determined
    Today to marry with my brother's daughter?
CLAUDIO
    I'll hold my mind were she an Ethiope.

44. **savage bull:** a reference to 1.1.256
45. **horns:** (1) of the bull; (2) of the cuckold
46. **Europa:** Europe
47–48. **Europa . . . love:** Jove, king of the Roman gods, fell in love with a girl named Europa, transformed himself into a bull, and, when she climbed on his back, carried her off to Crete. (See picture, page 192.)
50. **leapt:** mounted, mated with
51. **got:** begot
53. **I owe you:** i.e., I'll pay you back; **reck'nings:** i.e., matters to be dealt with

55 SP. **Leonato:** Most editions change this speech prefix, since Leonato's brother had agreed to act as the "niece's" father. However, since the "niece" is really Hero, one can argue that Leonato changes his mind, or that he forgets himself and resumes his fatherly role.
60. **like of:** i.e., **like**

LEONATO
  Call her forth, brother. Here's the Friar ready. 40
                ⌜*Leonato's brother exits.*⌝

PRINCE
  Good morrow, Benedick. Why, what's the matter
  That you have such a February face,
  So full of frost, of storm, and cloudiness?

CLAUDIO
  I think he thinks upon the savage bull.
  Tush, fear not, man. We'll tip thy horns with gold, 45
  And all Europa shall rejoice at thee,
  As once Europa did at lusty Jove
  When he would play the noble beast in love.

BENEDICK
  Bull Jove, sir, had an amiable low,
  And some such strange bull leapt your father's cow 50
  And got a calf in that same noble feat
  Much like to you, for you have just his bleat.

CLAUDIO
  For this I owe you. Here comes other reck'nings.

  Enter ⌜*Leonato's*⌝ *brother, Hero, Beatrice, Margaret,*
      Ursula, ⌜*the ladies masked.*⌝

  Which is the lady I must seize upon?

LEONATO
  This same is she, and I do give you her. 55

CLAUDIO
  Why, then, she's mine.—Sweet, let me see your face.

LEONATO
  No, that you shall not till you take her hand
  Before this friar and swear to marry her.

CLAUDIO, ⌜*to Hero*⌝
  Give me your hand before this holy friar.
                  ⌜*They take hands.*⌝
  I am your husband, if you like of me. 60

68. **but whiles:** only as long as

69. **amazement:** a strong word, meaning "bewilderment," "complete confusion" (as if lost in a maze); **qualify:** mitigate, calm, pacify

70. **after that:** i.e., **after**

71. **largely:** fully, at length

72. **let wonder seem familiar:** i.e., treat these miraculous events as if they were everyday happenings

73. **let us presently:** i.e., **let us** go at once

74. **Soft and fair:** i.e., wait a moment

Europa and "Bull Jove." (5.4.46–49)
From Gabriele Simeoni, *La vita . . . d'Ouidio* (1559).

HERO
  And when I lived, I was your other wife,
  And when you loved, you were my other husband.
                     ⌜*She unmasks.*⌝

CLAUDIO
  Another Hero!
HERO   Nothing certainer.
  One Hero died defiled, but I do live, 65
  And surely as I live, I am a maid.
PRINCE
  The former Hero! Hero that is dead!
LEONATO
  She died, my lord, but whiles her slander lived.
FRIAR
  All this amazement can I qualify,
  When after that the holy rites are ended, 70
  I'll tell you largely of fair Hero's death.
  Meantime let wonder seem familiar,
  And to the chapel let us presently.
BENEDICK
  Soft and fair, friar.—Which is Beatrice?
BEATRICE, ⌜*unmasking*⌝
  I answer to that name. What is your will? 75
BENEDICK
  Do not you love me?
BEATRICE   Why no, no more than reason.
BENEDICK
  Why then, your uncle and the Prince and Claudio
  Have been deceived. They swore you did.
BEATRICE
  Do not you love me? 80
BENEDICK   Troth, no, no more than reason.
BEATRICE
  Why then, my cousin, Margaret, and Ursula
  Are much deceived, for they did swear you did.

86. **'Tis no such matter:** i.e., it isn't true

88. **cousin:** i.e., niece

91. **halting:** lame, limping; **of ... brain:** i.e., purely or entirely from **his own brain**

96. **hands:** i.e., handwriting

96–97. **against our hearts:** i.e., as evidence to prove **our hearts** guilty (of love)

97, 99. **by this light, by this good day:** mild oaths

101. **consumption:** wasting disease (i.e., love-sickness)

102. **stop your mouth:** i.e., compel you to be silent (literally, with a gag or muzzle; here, with a kiss)

104. **a college:** i.e., an (entire) company

105. **wit-crackers:** i.e., those who make sarcastic remarks; **flout:** mock, jeer; **humor:** inclination, state of mind

106. **care for:** i.e., **care** about, am bothered by

107. **brains:** i.e., witticisms

109. **do purpose:** intend

109–10. **to any purpose:** i.e., of any use

BENEDICK
　They swore that you were almost sick for me.
BEATRICE
　They swore that you were well-nigh dead for me.   85
BENEDICK
　'Tis no such matter. Then you do not love me?
BEATRICE
　No, truly, but in friendly recompense.
LEONATO
　Come, cousin, I am sure you love the gentleman.
CLAUDIO
　And I'll be sworn upon 't that he loves her,
　For here's a paper written in his hand,   90
　A halting sonnet of his own pure brain,
　Fashioned to Beatrice.　　　⌐*He shows a paper.*⌐
HERO　　　　　　　　　　And here's another,
　Writ in my cousin's hand, stol'n from her pocket,
　Containing her affection unto Benedick.   95
　　　　　　　　　　　⌐*She shows a paper.*⌐
BENEDICK　A miracle! Here's our own hands against
　our hearts. Come, I will have thee, but by this light
　I take thee for pity.
BEATRICE　I would not deny you, but by this good day, I
　yield upon great persuasion, and partly to save your   100
　life, for I was told you were in a consumption.
⌐BENEDICK⌐　Peace! I will stop your mouth.
　　　　　　　　　　　　⌐*They kiss.*⌐
PRINCE
　How dost thou, Benedick, the married man?
BENEDICK　I'll tell thee what, prince. a college of
　wit-crackers cannot flout me out of my humor.   105
　Dost thou think I care for a satire or an epigram?
　No. If a man will be beaten with brains, he shall
　wear nothing handsome about him. In brief, since I
　do purpose to marry, I will think nothing to any
　purpose that the world can say against it, and   110

114. **like:** likely

116. **denied:** i.e., refused to marry

118. **single:** (1) individual; (2) unmarried; (3) weak, feeble; **double-dealer:** (1) someone no longer single, but part of a couple; (2) one who acts duplicitously

118–19. **out of question:** i.e., without any doubt

119–20. **look exceeding narrowly to thee:** i.e., watch you extremely closely

125. **of my word:** i.e., on **my word**

127. **staff:** (1) i.e., wood or ivory rod carried as a symbol of a position's authority (hence, here, a high-ranking man, like Don Pedro); **reverend:** worthy of veneration

127–28. **tipped with horn:** (1) with a tip of ivory or other animal horn; (2) wearing the cuckold's horns (See longer note to 1.1.194–95, page 199.)

132. **brave:** splendid

Hymen, god of marriage. (5.3.32)
From Vincenzo Cartari, *Imagines deorum . . .* (1581).

therefore never flout at me for what I have said
against it. For man is a giddy thing, and this is my
conclusion.—For thy part, Claudio, I did think to
have beaten thee, but in that thou art like to be my
kinsman, live unbruised, and love my cousin.   115

CLAUDIO   I had well hoped thou wouldst have denied
Beatrice, that I might have cudgeled thee out of thy
single life, to make thee a double-dealer, which out
of question thou wilt be, if my cousin do not look
exceeding narrowly to thee.   120

BENEDICK   Come, come, we are friends. Let's have a
dance ere we are married, that we may lighten our
own hearts and our wives' heels.

LEONATO   We'll have dancing afterward.

BENEDICK   First, of my word! Therefore play, music.—   125
Prince, thou art sad. Get thee a wife, get thee a wife.
There is no staff more reverend than one tipped
with horn.

Enter Messenger.

MESSENGER, ⌈*to Prince*⌉
My lord, your brother John is ta'en in flight,
And brought with armed men back to Messina.   130

BENEDICK, ⌈*to Prince*⌉   Think not on him till tomorrow.
I'll devise thee brave punishments for him.—Strike
up, pipers!   ⌈*Music plays. They*⌉ *dance.*
                                        ⌈*They exit.*⌉

Longer Notes

1.1.0 SD. Enter Leonato: In the early printed texts of the play, Leonato's wife, Innogen, is listed here and in the opening entrance for Act 2, among the characters entering. She is given no speeches, is never spoken to, and is not listed in later scenes—for example, at Hero's wedding. It is assumed by editors that Shakespeare decided not to develop this character, though some recent scholars have argued that she should be a silent presence in the play. Her presence in this opening scene when Benedick jokes about her possible adultery, and her silence in the wedding scene as Hero is being attacked, would certainly alter the tone of the play.

1.1.194–95. but he will wear his cap with suspicion: Fears about husbands being betrayed by their wives and thereby turning into cuckolds are expressed throughout this play, as Gail Kern Paster points out in her "Modern Perspective." The word *cuckold* comes from the name of the cuckoo, a bird which does not build a nest but instead leaves its eggs for other birds to hatch and feed. The association of cuckolds with horns growing from the forehead goes back to ancient times and may originate with the early and prevalent practice of "grafting the spurs of a castrated cock on the root of the excised comb, where they grew and became horns, sometimes of several inches long" (*OED*, "horn" 7a).

1.2.0 SD. brother to Leonato: In the early printed versions of *Much Ado* there is a character, "an old man, brother to Leonato," who is identified in stage directions and speech prefixes throughout the play as "old" or "brother"; in one scene of the play (2.1) there is also

199

a masked character addressed as "Signior Antonio" and identified in speech prefixes as "Antho." Because Leonato calls his brother "Anthony" in 5.1 and because the masked Signior Antonio who dances with Ursula in 2.1 is spoken of by Ursula as if he, like Leonato's brother, were an "old man," with his head "waggling" and his hand "dry," Nicholas Rowe (in 1709) and all editors since have identified Leonato's brother with the Signior Antonio of 2.1 and have thus called the brother "Antonio" in all speech prefixes and stage directions. Unfortunately, this conflation of the brother with Signior Antonio creates a problem in 2.1, where Leonato and his brother (who enters with Leonato at the beginning of the scene) are the hosts of the supper to which Don Pedro and his company are invited. For Leonato's brother to join with the maskers (as "Signior Antonio") and dance with Ursula, either he has to be sent offstage (with, "Brother, give good room") and for some unexplained reason put on a mask and reenter with the masked guests, or (as some current editors would have it) both Leonato and the brother must mask as the masked guests enter. To have Leonato's brother (and Leonato) mask is to break with the convention of masking in other plays of the period—for example, in *Romeo and Juliet* and *Henry VIII*—where the outside revelers come in masked and the unmasked hosts greet them. We do not find the reasons for conflating the brother and "Signior Antonio" persuasive enough to outweigh the awkwardness that occurs when they are conflated; we therefore keep separate the masked Signior Antonio of 2.1 and Leonato's unmasked brother, whom we designate "Leonato's brother" throughout the play.

2.1.83 SD–152 SD. **Drum . . . Dance:** The dialogue that appears in lines 84–149 can be imagined as spoken as the couples move forward and aside in an opening stately processional dance, or pavan; such a dance would be accompanied by the tabor and probably one or two other instruments. The **Music for the dance** called for in the Folio (in our text at line 148 SD) and the **Dance** called for in the quarto (in our text at line 152 SD) would likely call for a larger number of musicians as the couples join in a galliard or some other dance appropriate for masked "reveling." It is quite possible, however, that the dialogue in lines 84–149 precedes any dancing, and simply reflects the conversation of the couples as they begin to pair off for the dance that begins at line 152.

2.1.98 SP. **Benedick:** The early printed texts give this speech and the two following to Benedick and the remaining two to Balthasar. Most editors assume that the speech prefixes are in error and either give all of the speeches to Balthasar or, because of what happens later in the play, give all of them to Borachio. Given the play's emphasis on Benedick as a womanizer, and given his flirtation with Margaret in 5.1, we have decided to follow the early printed texts in the speech assignments.

2.1.196–98. **now . . . post:** Editors find parallels with a story in *Lazarillo de Tormes* about a boy and his blind master. In this mid-sixteenth-century picaresque novel, the boy steals the blind man's meat and tricks the blind man into knocking himself unconscious on a stone pillar, at one point called a "post." Although there are a few points of similarity, the Lazarillo story does not in any way illustrate the moral of Benedick's statement.

2.1.250. **Hercules:** Hercules was briefly the slave of the queen of Lydia, Omphale, and on surviving Greek vases is pictured as spinning wool for her. Turning the roasting spit would be a more demeaning occupation.

2.2.44. Claudio: Those who substitute "Borachio" for "Claudio" in this speech argue that the plot that Borachio is setting up would require Margaret, in her role as Hero, to call Borachio by his own name; to call him "Claudio," they argue, would suggest to onlookers that she was being deceived by an impostor rather than being unfaithful. Those who follow the early printed text and retain "Claudio" argue that Margaret may be led to think that she and Borachio are pretending to be Hero and Claudio. Since we never learn how Borachio persuades Margaret to take part in the deception, we have no way of knowing if she calls him "Claudio" as part of the game they are playing or whether the text is in error here.

3.3.117–18. the fashion . . . is nothing to a man: Editors have suggested that Borachio here begins leading up to a major point—either that Claudio, in turning against Hero, has been more inconstant than the fickleness of the fashions, or that Hero's clothing has led Claudio to mistake Margaret for Hero. In either case, Borachio's "fashion is nothing to a man"—which might mean "the style of his clothes does not matter to a man" or "clothes do not make the man"—is understood by Conrade to mean "*clothes* are nothing to a man," a statement he rejects by saying that "clothes are apparel."

3.3.172 SD. Enter Dogberry: We agree with J. C. Meagher (*Shakespeare Quarterly,* 1972) and F. H. Mares (The New Cambridge Shakespeare *Much Ado*) that Dogberry should reenter at this point. Dogberry, at line 84, ordered the Watch to summon him if anything important happened, and Seacoal tells a fellow watchman to "Call up the right Master Constable" at line 167. The speeches and speech headings for lines 173–77 are so garbled in the early printed text that editorial intervention is almost mandatory. Our solution to the textual problems here is to have Dogberry reenter and to assign lines 173 and 176–77 to him. In the quarto, the speech headings for these lines read *Conr;* Mares suggests that *Con.*, for "Constable," could have been intended. (*Con* is, in fact, what is printed in the quarto in its earlier [its so-called uncorrected] state.) Despite his own persuasive argument, Mares does not have Dogberry reenter.

4.1.87. Hero itself can blot out Hero's virtue: The dialogue in lines 82–87—

HERO
    What kind of catechizing call you this?
CLAUDIO
    To make you answer truly to your name.
HERO
    Is it not Hero? Who can blot that name
    With any just reproach?
CLAUDIO   Marry, that can Hero!
    Hero itself can blot out Hero's virtue—

has suggested to many editors connections with the Anglican catechism and with the legends about the lovers named Hero and Leander, made popular through Christopher Marlowe's poem named for the lovers.

The "Catechism for Children" included in the section on "Confirmation" in the Anglican Book of Common Prayer (1559) opens with the question "What is your name?" (Other Anglican catechisms—such as King Edward's Catechism of 1553 and *A Briefe and necessary Catechism or Instruction* of 1575—begin with quite different questions.) Even though other catechisms did not ask the child its name, and even though "catechizing" could simply mean "questioning," it is quite possible that the combination of Hero's question about "catechizing" and Claudio's response about her answering to her name might have echoed, for Shakespeare's original audiences, the opening of the Book of Common Prayer catechism and its emphasis on the connection between naming, baptism, and a Christian life.

The relationship between Hero's name and that of the heroine of Marlowe's *Hero and Leander* is much more problematic. It has been argued that the legendary Hero had come to be seen as an example of female constancy, since she killed herself when her lover, Leander, drowned while swimming the Hellespont to visit her. It is equally likely that the legendary Hero (who was a nun—although, in Marlowe, a nun of Venus) was seen as an example of the way a good Renaissance woman should not behave, since she broke her vows by admitting Leander into her bed. How a Renaissance audience would have responded to the legendary Hero's name would give two possible, opposite readings of line 87. The line could mean: "You, as a wanton woman, put a blot on the virtues of the name of the legendary Hero," or "The very name of the unchaste legendary Hero puts a blot on any virtues you might have."

Textual Notes

The reading of the present text appears to the left of the square bracket. Unless otherwise noted, the reading to the left of the bracket is from **Q**, the First Quarto text (upon which this edition is based). The earliest sources of readings not in Q are indicated as follows: **F** is the First Folio of 1623; **F2** is the Second Folio of 1632; **F3** is the Third Folio of 1663–64; **F4** is the Fourth Folio of 1685; **Ed.** is an earlier editor of Shakespeare, beginning with Rowe in 1709. No sources are given for emendations of punctuation or for corrections of obvious typographical errors, like turned letters that produce no known word. **SD** means stage direction; **SP** means speech prefix; **uncorr.** means the first or uncorrected state of the First Quarto; **corr.** means the second or corrected state of the First Quarto; ~ stands in place of a word already quoted before the square bracket; ʌ indicates the omission of a punctuation mark.

1.1
    0. SD *Messina*] Ed.; *Messina, Innogen his wife* Q

  2, 10. Pedro] Q (Peter)

    15. lion.] ~, Q

    41. bird-bolt] Q (Burbolt)

    58. stuffing—well] ~ ʌ ~ Q

    63. that.] ~, Q

    87. Claudio] ~, Q

    87. Benedick] Q (Benedict)

    90. Do,] ~ ʌ Q

    94 *and hereafter to 2.1.314.* SP PRINCE] This ed.; *Pedro* Q

   111. SP BENEDICK] Q (*Be.*)

 114–15. talking, . . . Benedick,] Q

141. i'] Q (a)
144. all, Leonato.—] ~: ~, Q
152–53. lord, ... brother,] ~, ... ~: Q
154. *and hereafter to 2.2.55.* SP DON JOHN]
        Ed.; *Iohn* Q
199. SD *Pedro*] Ed.; *Pedro, Iohn the bastard* Q
259. vilely] Q (vildly)
261. hire"] ~: Q
268. hours.] ~, Q
274. you—] ~. Q
276. it—] ~. Q
280. sometimes] Q (sometime)
281. neither.] ~, Q
302. words.] ~, Q

1.2   0. SD *meeting*] Ed.; *and* Q
     3. *and hereafter in this scene.* SP LEONATO'S
        BROTHER] this ed.; *Old* Q
    27. skill] F; shill Q

1.3 22–23. root∧ ... yourself.] ~, ... ~, Q
    38. SD *1 line later in* Q
    47. brother's] F; bothers Q
    52. on] Q (one)
    67. me?] ~. Q
    70. o'] Q (a)

2.1   0. SD *brother, Hero ... niece, with ...*
        Margaret] Ed.; *brother, his wife, Hero*
        ... neece, and a kinsman. Q
     2. *and hereafter in this scene.* SP LEONATO'S
        BROTHER] This ed.; *brother* Q
    40. bearherd] Q (Berrord)
    42. SP LEONATO] Lenoato Q
    66. you.] ~, Q
    72, 74. jig] ijgge Q
    83. SD *with a Drum ... all in masks*] F
        (*Maskers with a drum*); not in Q
    83. SD *Prince∧ Pedro ... and Don John*]
        Ed.; *prince, Pedro ... or dumb Iohn* Q

	84.	a bout] about Q
	86.	So∧] ~, Q
	148.	SD F, *4 lines later; not in* Q
	192.	drover] Q (Drouier)
	207.	SD *Leonato*] This ed.; *Leonato, Iohn and Borachio, and Conrade.* Q
	293–94.	father∧ . . . obtained.] ~, . . . ~, Q
	299.	cue] Q (Qu)
	307.	it, . . . fool,] ~, . . . ~∧ Q
	325.	o'] Q (a)
	340.	SP PRINCE] This ed.; *Pedro* Q
	365.	too,] ~∧ Q
2.2	43.	Margaret term] Q (Marg terme)
2.3	7.	SD *1 line earlier in* Q
	25.	an] Q (and)
	36.	SD *Claudio . . . music*] Ed.; *Claudio, Musicke* Q; "Enter Balthaser with musicke" *6 lines later in* Q
	64.	SP BALTHASAR *sings*] Ed.; *The Song* Q *corr.;* *The Son*ʒ Q *uncorr.*
	76–79.	so, . . . nonny] so, &c. Q
	87.	lief] Q (liue)
	94.	SD *1 line earlier in* Q
	108–9.	it, . . . affection,] Q
	143.	us of] F; of vs Q
	159.	sometimes] Q (sometime)
	184–85.	well. . . . love,] ~, . . . ~, Q
	249.	Against] Aganst Q
3.1	0.	SD and 4 *Ursula*] Q (Ursley)
	9.	enter,] ~: Q
	63.	featured,] ~. Q
	67.	antic] Q (antique)
	69.	vilely] Q (vildly)
	101.	bearing,] ~∧ Q
	117.	on; . . . will] on . . . will Q *corr.;* one . . . wil Q *uncorr.*
3.2	19–20.	love. . . . sad,] ~, . . . ~, Q

27. can] Ed.; cannot Q
39. o'] Q (a)
51. SP PRINCE] F; *Bene.* Q
65. toothache.—] ~, Q
73 *and hereafter to 4.1.70.* SP DON JOHN]
    Ed.; *Bastard* Q
74. e'en] Q (den)
79. of∧] Q *uncorr.;* ~, Q *corr.*
90. manifest.] ~, Q
90–91. brother, I . . . heart∧] Ed.; ~, ~ . . . ~,
    Q *uncorr.;* ~ (~ . . . ~) Q *corr.*
91. holp] Q *corr.* (holpe); hope Q *uncorr.*
96–97. shortened, for . . . of,] ~ (~ . . . talking of)
    Q *corr.;* ~∧ ~ . . . talking, Q *uncorr.*
105. me∧] Q *corr.;* ~, Q *uncorr.*
107. her∧ then,] ~, ~∧ Q
117. her,] ~∧ Q
117. congregation,] Q *corr.;* ~∧ Q *uncorr.*

3.3
15. name.] ~, Q *uncorr.;* ~: Q *corr.*
17, 27. SP SEACOAL] Ed.; *Watch 2* Q
17. constable—] ~. Q
24. lantern] Q (lanthorne)
37, 66. SP SECOND WATCHMAN] This ed.; *Watch* Q
44, 48, 53. SP SEACOAL] This ed.; *Watch* Q
87, 95, 105. SP SEACOAL] Ed.; *Watch* Q
107. Don] F; Dun Q
123. deformed] Q *corr.;* defermed Q *uncorr.*
125. SP FIRST WATCHMAN] This ed.; *Watch* Q
126–27. year. He . . . down] yeere, a . . . downe
    Q *corr.;* yeere∧ a . . . down Q *uncorr.*
127. I] Q *corr.;* omit Q *uncorr.*
134. reechy] Q (rechie)
134, 135. sometimes] Q (sometime)
148. vilely] Q (vildly)
149–50. Prince, . . . planted∧] ~∧ . . . ~. Q

153. SP CONRADE] *Conr.* Q *corr.; Con.* Q *uncorr.*
154. SP BORACHIO] *Bar.* Q
156. oaths,] ~. Q
167. SP SEACOAL] This ed.; *Watch 2* Q
173, 176. SP DOGBERRY] This ed. (*after J. C. Meagher, "Conrade Conned: or, the career of Hugh Oatcake," Shakespeare Quarterly 24 (1972): 90–92; Conr* Q *corr.; Con. or Con* Q *uncorr.*
173. masters—] ~. Q
174. SP FIRST WATCHMAN] Ed.; *Watch 2* Q
177. speak, . . . you,] Q
180. SP CONRADE] *Conr.* Q *corr.; Con.* Q *uncorr.*

3.4   1. Good] Q *corr.;* God Q *uncorr.*
18. in] F; it Q
19, 43, 45. o'] Q (a)

3.5   0. SD *Leonato, and*] Q *uncorr.; Leonati, and* Q *corr.*
2, 6, 9, 15, 18, 23, 32, 41, 43. SP DOGBERRY] Ed.; *Const. Dog.* Q
7, 13, 27, 29. SP VERGES] Ed.; *Headb.* or *Head.* Q
9. off] Q (of)
23. an] and't Q
32. talking.] ~ˇ Q
34. see!—] ~, Q *uncorr.;* ~: Q *corr.*
37. troth he is, as] Q *corr.;* ~, ~ ~ˇ ~ Q *uncorr.*
50. SP DOGBERRY] Ed.; *Constable* Q
54. SD *4 lines earlier in* Q

4.1   4. SP FRIAR] *Fran.* Q
26. SP LEONATO] *Leonata* Q
29. SP PRINCE] *Princn* Q
48. virginity—] ~. Q
57. thee,] ~ˇ Q

91. SP HERO] Q *corr.* (*Hero*); *Bero* Q *uncorr.*
100. SP DON JOHN] Ed.; *Iohn* Q
116. SP DON JOHN] Ed.; *Bastard* Q
120. Benedick!] ~, Q *corr.;* ~∧ Q *uncorr.*
126. up?] Q *corr.* (vp?); ~. Q *uncorr.*
128. Why,] ~∧ Q
131. eyes,] Q *uncorr.* (eies,); ~: Q *corr.*
145. on,] ~∧ Q
146–47. mine, . . . her—] ~: . . . ~, Q
156. Lady,] Q *corr.;* ~∧ Q *uncorr.*
165. silent been] Ed.; bin silent Q
166–67. fortune, . . . lady.] ~, . . . ~, Q
176. tenor] Q (tenure)
200–201. not. . . . her,] ~, . . . ~, Q
213. princes . . . dead.] Q *as* "princesse (left for dead,)"
228. out∧] ~. Q
239. moving,] ~∧ Q
307. here.] ~, Q
309, 322, 325. Beatrice—] ~. Q
318. hand∧] ~. Q
328. Beat—] ~? Q
4.2   0. SD *Enter . . . Borachio.*] Ed.; *Enter the Constables, Borachio, and the Towne clearke in gownes.* Q
1. SP DOGBERRY] Ed.; *Keeper* Q
2, 5, 70. SP VERGES] Ed.; *Cowley* Q
4. SP DOGBERRY] Ed.; *Andrew* Q
7. offenders∧] ~? Q
10,13, 17, 20, 27, 32, 38, 43, 46, 52, 58, 72,
76. SP DOGBERRY] Ed.; *Kemp* or *Ke.* or *Kem.* Q
19. SP BORACHIO/CONRADE] Q (*Both*)
45. constable—] ~. Q
49. SP SEACOAL] This ed.; *Watch 2* Q
53. SP VERGES] *Const.* Q

61. SP SEACOAL] This ed.; *Watch* Q
69. SP DOGBERRY] *Constable* Q
70–71. hands— | CONRADE Off, coxcomb!] Ed.;
      hands of Coxcombe. Q
74. them.—] ~, Q
75. SP CONRADE] Ed.; *Couley* Q

5.1   1 *and hereafter throughout this scene.* SP
      LEONATO'S BROTHER] This ed.; *Brother*
      Q
17. Bid] Ed.; And Q
48. e'en . . . e'en] Q (den . . . den)
50. lords—] ~? Q
97. Brother—] ~. Q
103, 112. Anthony—] ~. Q
108. anticly] Q (antiquely)
109. off] Q (of)
119. lord—] ~. Q
121. No?] ~∧ Q
122. SD *Leonato . . . exit.*] This ed.; *Exeunt*
      amb. Q, *1 line earlier*
128. likc] F2; likt Q
130. brother.] ~∧ Q
141. wit.] ~, Q
149. me.] ~, Q
161. sweet] sweeete Q
167. him.] ~∧ Q
169. naught.] ~, Q
194. on] Q (one)
204. Lackbeard∧ there,] ~, ~∧ Q
215. up.] ~∧ Q
216. SD *4 lines earlier in* Q
217,225, 264, 319, 330, 333, 336. SP DOGBERRY] Ed.;
      Const. Q
268. SP VERGES] Ed.; *Con. 2* Q
278–79. men— . . . fled—] ~, . . . ~∧ Q

5.2   9. me? Why,] ~, ~∧ Q

25. SD *1 line earlier in* Q
29. *deserve*—] ~. Q
41. SD *2 lines later in* Q
68. think.] ~, Q
86. myself.] ~∧ Q

5.3 3. *slanderous*] slauderous Q
10. dumb] F (dombe); dead Q
11. Now] Ed.; *Claudio* Now Q
17. *groan*∧] ~. Q
22. SP CLAUDIO] Ed.; *Lo.* Q
32. speed 's] Q (speeds)

5.4 0. SD *Leonato's brother*] This ed.; *old man* Q
5. will, . . . appears∧] ~∧ . . . ~, Q
7 *and hereafter.* SP LEONATO'S BROTHER] This ed.; *Old* Q
41. Benedick] Q (Bened.)
53. SD *1 line earlier in* Q
69–70. qualify, . . . ended,] Q
82. cousin,] ~∧ Q
102. SP BENEDICK] Ed.; *Leon.* Q
102. Peace!] ~∧ Q
125. play,] ~∧ Q

Much Ado About Nothing:
A Modern Perspective

Gail Kern Paster

Cuckoldry jokes are in the air in Messina. Its governor, Leonato, snatches one out of it when he jokes feebly about having to ask his wife repeatedly for reassurance as to his daughter's legitimacy:

PRINCE I think this is your daughter.
LEONATO Her mother hath *many times* told me so.[1]
(1.1.102–3)

Benedick draws our attention to this trace of an old suspicion: "Were you in doubt, sir, that you asked her?" (1.1.104). But Benedick, we soon learn, is also suspicious of women as the agents of men's humiliation and defeat. He expresses an almost pathological fear of betrayal in marriage: to be married is to wear the conventional horns of a cuckold, to have one's own military bugle snatched away, to have it sounded in one's own face:

> That a woman conceived me, I thank her; that she brought me up, I likewise give her most humble thanks. But that I will have a recheat winded [i.e., a bugle-call blown] in my forehead or hang my bugle in an invisible baldrick, all women shall pardon me. Because I will not do them the wrong to mistrust any, I will do myself the right to trust none.
> (1.1.234–40)

213

Benedick's extraordinary self-portrait of his relations with women yields readily to a psychoanalytic
reading. Moving without pause from his conception
to his upbringing to his cuckolding, he conflates his
relations to mother and to wife, collapses past and
future, memories and fears.[2] What seems to unify all
these stages of a man's life, for Benedick, is humiliating dependence on women, beginning with the infant's
dependence on maternal women for life and nurture.
But that early dependence, instead of being outgrown,
is seen here as forerunner to the later sexual humilia-
tions of the adult male. Furthermore, Benedick's dis-
missive mention of his mother as the "woman [who]
conceived me" betrays her real importance to the structure of repressed memory. In psychoanalytic narratives
of male repression, the mother's lack of the phallus is
a disturbing image for the child—an image of his own
fear of castration and of his overmastering by another
male. But for Benedick, the returning soldier, this fear
of women seems less generic than personal: the cuckold's horns that he envisions as his own future headdress are specifically those of a defeated soldier who
has lost his bugle to another soldier. It is not surprising, then, that Benedick's anticipation of a farewell
to arms here parallels Othello's lament for the loss of
heroic identity through an imagined sexual betrayal by
Desdemona:

> Farewell the tranquil mind! Farewell content!
> Farewell the plumèd troops and the big wars
> That makes ambition virtue! O, farewell!
> Farewell the neighing steed and the shrill trump,
> The spirit-stirring drum, th' ear-piercing fife,
> The royal banner, and all quality,
> Pride, pomp, and circumstance of glorious war!
>   (*Othello* 3.3.400–406)

Musicians with drums and fife. (2.3.14)
From Thomas Lant, *Sequitur celebritas & pompa funeris* . . . (1587).

For soldiers like Benedick and Othello, marriage threatens loss of a valued form of masculine singleness, a loss of control.

More interesting, perhaps, in a comic action like *Much Ado*'s which is organized around the imagining of sexual betrayal, is that the fear of being associated with the cuckold's horns is not peculiar to men nor is resistance to marriage a symptom of only masculine identity. Though her uncles worry that Beatrice's sharp tongue makes her "too curst" (2.1.20) to get a husband, she jokes that she will thereby avoid making her husband wear horns: "I shall lessen God's sending that way, for it is said 'God sends a curst cow short horns,' but to a cow too curst, he sends none" (2.1.21–24). Even the devil, no mere mortal, wears the signs of betrayal; Beatrice imagines having him meet her looking "like an old cuckold with horns on his head" (2.1.44–45). The horn motif continues to sound in the play even after it ostensibly has been silenced by the exposure of Don John's sexual slander against Hero. Thus Benedick, though converted to love in the person of Beatrice, nonetheless misogynistically urges the play's remaining eligible bachelor, Don Pedro, to join in the march to the altar in the spirit of accepting a universal, age-old humiliation: "Get thee a wife, get thee a wife. There is no staff more reverend than one tipped with horn" (5.4.126–28). If betrayal is the universal fate of the married, it is no wonder that Beatrice regards marriage as a form of repentance:

> wooing, wedding, and repenting is as a Scotch jig, a measure, and a cinquepace. The first suit is hot and hasty like a Scotch jig, and full as fantastical; the wedding, mannerly modest as a measure, full of state and ancientry; and then comes repentance, and

with his bad legs falls into the cinquepace faster and
faster till he sink into his grave.

$$(2.1.72–78)^3$$

As all these quotations suggest, anxiety about sexual
betrayal in marriage seems endemic in Messina, spar-
ing neither the old nor the young, neither male nor
female. What is clear in the men's cuckoldry jokes is
their willful silence, for the sake of male friendship and
preservation of the status quo, about the male betrayer
and a contrasting emphasis on his female partner. It
is not the desires of other men that Benedick mis-
trusts but those of womenkind. It is only when they are
among themselves that the Men's Club of Messina—to
borrow Harry Berger's wonderful appellation—allows
Balthasar's song to register an alternative truth: "Sigh
no more, ladies, sigh no more, / Men were deceivers
ever, / One foot in sea and one on shore, / To one thing
constant never" (2.3.64–67).[4]

Much Ado is not unusual in its reiterated wordplay
on horns, since jokes about the wearing of cuckolds'
horns are commonplace throughout the literature of
this period. But, in the drama of the period, there is a
marked disparity between the frequency of the jokes
and the infrequency of wifely infidelity. Many more
wives are falsely accused than are, in fact, guilty. This
discrepancy between fears of betrayal and actual guilt
suggests that we should focus less on the infidelity
itself than on the real source of patriarchal anxiety,
which was patriarchy's inevitable dependence on (and
inability to verify) the chastity of wives and mothers.
For only such chastity secured a social structure based
on legitimate inheritance of lands, wealth, property,
rank, and name.

In *Much Ado*, I want to suggest, this patriarchal anxiety gives cuckoldry jokes a particular, local function. They work to resolve a social contradiction in Elizabethan society, a moment of double bind in the cultural history of marriage in which an authoritarian official tradition collided with an emergent ideal. Sixteenth-century English society had not yet dispensed with forms of overt, virulent misogyny inherited from medieval Catholicism which made marriage, especially for men, a less perfect way of life than celibacy. But it could not readily accommodate these inherited forms of misogyny to a post-Reformation celebration of marriage, particularly in its modern form of companionate, consensual unions in which the emotional satisfaction of both partners assumes new importance. Elizabethan society could not dispense with misogyny because the most general, even ancient function of antifeminist discourse is to justify patriarchy's unequal distribution of power and property, its subordination of women. But virulent suspicion of wifely chastity—the kind of suspicion that destroys lives and marriages in *Othello* and *The Winter's Tale*, for example—must have seemed incompatible with an emergent theory of marriage focused upon the initial consent of both partners and upon their long-term fulfillment of a set of mutual obligations which were in part material, in part emotional.[5] Even Don Pedro, in seeking to promote the marriage of Hero and Claudio, assumes that winning the consent of Hero comes before anything else: "I will break *with her* and with her father" (1.1.304), while Beatrice slyly urges her cousin not to say "Father, as it please you" but rather "Father, as it please me" (2.1.53, 55–56). If women's feelings matter, then so, it would seem, do feelings about women: medieval misogyny and post-Reformation marriage theory could not comfortably coexist. From the tension between them, the double plots of Shakespeare's comedy come into being.

Perhaps such a reading of *Much Ado* seems obvious. Any reader of the play can see how much of its action is devoted to overcoming, through Don Pedro's theatrical manipulations, the resistance to love expressed by both Beatrice and Benedick. But to follow this reading to its logical conclusion will require the replacement of a character-based interpretation of the play with one which dissolves boundaries between the text as an autonomous work of art and the culture in which it is produced. Such a reading will attend to the widely dispersed misogyny in Elizabethan culture which speaks in and through Benedick, and to the effects of that misogyny as they register in Beatrice's resistance. Thus, where I depart from traditional critics is in refusing to accept Beatrice and Benedick's resistance to marriage as finally psychological in significance, even if it is expressed in psychological form in their language and behavior. I do not wish to explain resistance to marriage as idiosyncratic aspects of the personalities of Beatrice and Benedick, even though such resistance is what most sets them apart from their friends and kinfolk. Nor do I wish to interpret their eventual declarations of mutual affection as the manifestation of a hidden attraction that was there all along. I take their love as the creation of Don Pedro, who would "fain have it a match," he says, to enliven the time between Claudio's betrothal and nuptials by accomplishing a difficult thing. And presumably he also wishes to make sure that no person in his lordly jurisdiction escapes from the paradoxical cultural requirement to pair off *freely*.

But the uncomfortable truth is that in a misogynistic culture, resistance to marriage is rational, not idiosyncratic, because misogyny—defined as the systematic denigration of women—gives men and women well-founded reasons to suspect one another. Beatrice and Benedick are given the function in this play of wittily enacting for our benefit the conventional postures of mutual antagonism so that their eventual union will seem both to ratify the irrational force of desire (no matter how it is brought into being) and to dissolve the larger social tensions exemplified by their mutual mistrust. Because, even though marriage might appear incompatible with individual peace of mind, it remains the basic form of social organization, the central distribution point in Elizabethan society for the social and sexual goods of adult maturity. This paradox about marriage may serve to explain why Don Pedro, rather than take a laissez-faire position with regard to the wooing and resistance to wooing in his midst, intervenes personally as head of the social order in the double matchmakings of Hero to Claudio, Beatrice to Benedick. Indeed, he has a notable, almost quantifying pragmatism with regard to affection, assuaging Claudio's fear that his "liking might too sudden seem" with a breezy "What need the bridge much broader than the flood? / The fairest grant is the necessity. / Look what will serve is fit" (1.1.309, 311–13).

It is important for my argument to emphasize that the history of misogyny is also the history of romantic love, that cultivation of antifeminist feeling has, since the early twelfth century in Europe, coexisted with, indeed depended upon, a counterbalancing idealization of woman. As Howard Bloch has argued, "Misogyny and courtly love are coconspiring abstractions of the feminine whose function was from the start, and continues to be, the diversion of women from history by the annihilation of the identity of individual women . . . and thus the transformation of woman into an ideal."[6]

The marriage yoke. (1.1.197)
From Henry Peacham, *Minerua Britanna* . . . (1612).

That is to say, the idealism of romantic love and the denigration of antifeminist rhetoric are alike in functioning to erase differences between women in order to make women anonymous and invisible to historical action. Such an erasure of differences in women is precisely what occurs in Benedick's lines quoted above, where the distinct roles of mother and wife are subsumed into the one undifferentiated category, Woman. In the logic of misogyny, if one woman is treacherous, all women are condemned: "Because I will not do them the wrong to mistrust any, I will do myself the right to trust none." The point is not only, as Harry Berger has argued, that "the difference between men and women in this respect . . . is that women are responsible for their sins but men are not."[7] Even more crucial is to recognize the instability between a misogyny which posits all Women-as-the-Same and an idealization which posits Women-as-Different.[8] In the conversations between Claudio and Benedick—as in the similar conversations between Romeo and Mercutio—this instability in the categorization of women is easy to detect: "Can the world buy such a jewel" as Hero, idealist Claudio asks rhetorically. "Yea," comes the misogynist's bawdy reply, "and a case [vagina] to put it into" (1.1.177–78).

Indeed, this instability in the way women are categorized would seem to motivate the different rhetorics by which Benedick and Beatrice are each persuaded to love. While Benedick must be led to believe in Beatrice as Different from all other women, Beatrice must be brought to accept herself as just the Same. Hence Benedick is made to overhear a conversation among the men which describes Beatrice as a compendium of virtues—"an excellent sweet lady," "out of all suspicion . . . virtuous," "exceeding wise" (2.3.166–68)—except for her dotage on Benedick. Beatrice,

Maye

Now pleasaunt may spreds forth swete smelling flowers
Fresh sprouting buds green fieldes & springing trees
And all delights enfort by Aprill showers
She forceth ther with to glade man as he sees

Gemini

A pleached bower. (1.2.9–10; 3.1.7–9)
From T[homas] F[ella],
A book of diverse devices . . . (1585–1622).

by contrast, learns from Hero and Ursula less about Benedick's virtues than about her own faults, the chief of which is the nonconformity of resistance: "to be so odd and from all fashions / As Beatrice is cannot be commendable" (3.1.76–77). Both resisters are asked to understand the other's alleged passion as unwilled and uncontrollable—the real thing, in other words. Beatrice and Benedick experience their separate reactions to this surprising news as free and fortuitous. Benedick, on cue, vows to "be horribly in love with her" (2.3.237). Beatrice, stung by what she has overheard, thereupon commits herself to a course of action she names self-taming, "taming my wild heart to thy loving hand" (3.1.118). But we have heard Don Pedro gloat, "The sport will be when they hold one an opinion of another's dotage, and no such matter" (2.3.218–20), and we thus have reason to think otherwise about the relative freedom of their actions. We witness the conspirators glorying in the emotional transformations which, in the guise of "love gods" (2.1.377), they claim to have achieved; and we note in their language a deterministic vocabulary of contagion and entrapment. Claudio whispers to the Prince that Benedick has "ta'en th' infection" (2.3.129); Hero and Ursula congratulate themselves on having "limed," or trapped, Beatrice (3.1.109). Thus in the contrast between Beatrice and Benedick's subjective experience of free choice in love and the undeniable presence of social manipulation in bringing them to imagine that freedom, we can recognize the powerful, because invisible, workings of ideological conditioning to make people act, so they think, naturally: "The world," as Benedick grandiosely declares, "must be peopled" (2.3.244–45).

But since early modern English patriarchy required both marriage and misogyny, the social inscription that works so hard to create romantic love works equally hard to destabilize it. Thematic links between the two institutions of marriage and misogyny are emphasized because, in the double plot of *Much Ado About Nothing*, the actions to make and to break nuptials employ the same kinds of theatrical means. Shakespeare assigns the function of destroyer with evident symmetry to Don Pedro's brother, Don John the Bastard, whose sense of self-expression in trying to abort the nuptials of Claudio and Hero matches Don Pedro's in bringing them about. If the moral differences between the two brothers seem too insistently coded, that may be—as Jean Howard has argued—because the play is ambivalent about the social and moral function of theatrical practice.[9] By making the Iago-like Don John a bastard who is so determined to avenge his defeat at the hands of Claudio that he does not scruple to scapegoat Hero in the process, Shakespeare defines one kind of theatrical manipulation as evil, that is, as motivated by the urge to destroy. But is the moral character of Don Pedro's delight in theatrical practices thereby enhanced? The answer to that question cannot be unproblematical, given that Don Pedro's surrogate wooing of Hero leads to a series of early misapprehensions—that the Prince woos for himself; that Hero or her father might have preferred to accept the Prince's suit; that love of women breeds mistrust between male friends because, as Claudio says, "beauty is a witch / Against whose charms faith melteth into blood [i.e. sensual appetite]" (2.1.177–78). Nor does Don Pedro's devotion to theatrical practice give him any advantage in seeing through his brother's deception: when the Prince and Claudio witness the scene at Hero's chamber window in which Margaret allows herself to be courted as Hero in Hero's clothes, they see and hear only what Don John has prepared them to: "Go but with me tonight, you shall see her chamber window entered, even the night before her wedding day" (3.2.105–7). The potential moral hollowness and material harm of theatrical practices are later emblematized, in this play, when Claudio stands before what we know to be an empty tomb to read an epitaph for Hero.

The play takes pains to construct Claudio as inexperienced and to emphasize the superficiality of a love which arises, he says, at a moment of postcombat mental vacancy:

> . . . now I am returned and that war thoughts
> Have left their places vacant, in their rooms
> Come thronging soft and delicate desires,
> All prompting me how fair young Hero is,
> Saying I liked her ere I went to wars.
>   (1.1.296–300)

The prolongation of courtship—which seems the goal of Shakespeare's other conventional lovers such as Orlando in *As You Like It*, or even Romeo—holds no attraction for the two-dimensional Claudio, nor does Hero use the courtship period as Rosalind does in *As You Like It* to investigate the quality of her lover's desire and imagination. The too-compliant Hero accepts the marriage proposal of a man in a mask and then learns to transfer her consent from the wearer of that mask, Don Pedro, to his young favorite. Claudio does not even plan to spend much time getting acquainted with Hero after their marriage and has to be told that his astonishing plan to accompany Don Pedro home to Aragon would be a great "soil in the new gloss of your marriage" (3.2.5–6). (Indeed, the lovers' activity of courtship as mutual interrogation is taken over in this play by Beatrice and Benedick. Even though this delight in mutual interrogation is one reason why we are conditioned to expect their eventual union, it is also the case that Beatrice and Benedick use the resulting information to bolster resistance to marriage and to improve their jests at each other's expense.) Shakespeare uses Claudio's passivity and inexperience as a wooer to rationalize the young count's readiness to believe Don John's slander of Hero and to prepare us eventually to forgive the misogynistic brutality with which he shames her before the assembled wedding guests:

> O, what authority and show of truth
> Can cunning sin cover itself withal!
> Comes not that blood as modest evidence
> To witness simple virtue? Would you not swear,
> All you that see her, that she were a maid,
> By these exterior shows? But she is none.
>
> (4.1.35–40)

Claudio's willed commitment to reading Hero's blush as "guiltiness, not modesty" (42) suggests that the real problem linking the two plots of the play is the collapse of the tension between women-as-different and women-as-the-same into one incoherent category of woman-as-different-from-herself. The audience then and the audience now are in a position to understand that widespread cultural suspicion of women, surrogate wooing, and Don John's theatrical illusionism have combined to interrupt the wedding of Hero and Claudio. The audience is also in a position to appreciate the irony of Benedick and Beatrice relinquishing their resistance to marriage and exchanging protestations of love at the very moment when the grounds for mutual suspicion between the sexes seem to have widened. A subtler irony may reside in the complexities of Benedick's situation as the lapsed misogynist learns of one danger in love he had not foreseen, one other rational reason to remain resistant. That is, even as he gives up misogyny and trusts Beatrice's word for Hero's innocence, he finds a new way in which love may be hazardous to one's health: when he rashly asks Beatrice to "bid me do anything for thee," she promptly replies, "Kill Claudio" (4.1.302–3). "Ha! Not for the wide world," comes his automatic reply (304).

The recuperative necessities of comic closure that will not allow Hero to die or remain dishonored by an unforgiven Claudio also prevent Benedick from having to follow up on the challenge he flings at Claudio and Don Pedro, from having to act irrevocably upon his decision to sacrifice old loyalties to male companions to new loyalties to his future companion in marriage. But the final entrance of the bridal party, with not just the reborn Hero but all the women wearing masks, suggests that the old cultural categories that produce suspicion and slander remain largely untouched by the theatrical manipulations of the Friar and the rapprochement of Beatrice and Benedick. Even the words of Claudio's question, "Which is the lady I *must seize* upon?" (5.4.54), in their traditional suggestions of coercion and violence suggest the social manipulations that are required to separate men and women from the companionship of their own sex and precipitate them into the terrifying private world of heterosexual union for life. Perhaps this is why Benedick insists on ending the play not with a wedding but with the stately, regulated movements of a communal dance in which the couples move not singly, but together, and no man is yet wearing horns.

---

1. My emphasis. Note here that the original stage directions include the entrance of Leonato's wife, Innogen, but that editors in this text like others omit

her on the plausible ground that she has no words at all, appearing in the text no place but here and in the entrance direction for 2.1. This essay is much indebted to the essays by Carol Cook and Jean E. Howard, which are cited in full in the suggestions for further reading.

2. See Carol Cook, " 'The Sign and Semblance of Her Honor': Reading Gender Difference in *Much Ado About Nothing*," *PMLA* 101 (1986): 187.

3. For a brilliant application of this speech, see Harry Berger, Jr., "Against the Sink-a-Pace: Sexual and Family Politics in *Much Ado About Nothing*," *Shakespeare Quarterly* 33 (1982): 302 3.

4. Ibid., p. 308.

5. See Ralph A. Houlbrooke, *English Family Life, 1576–1716* (Oxford: Basil Blackwell, 1988), pp. 15–17. For an extended discussion of seventeenth-century discussions of marriage conduct books, see Mary Beth Rose, *The Expense of Spirit: Love and Sexuality in English Renaissance Drama* (Ithaca: Cornell University Press, 1988), pp. 116–31.

6. Howard Bloch, *Medieval Misogyny and the Invention of Western Romantic Love* (Chicago: University of Chicago Press, 1991), pp. 196–97.

7. Berger, "Against the Sink-a-Pace," p. 307.

8. On this categorical instability, see Peter Stallybrass, "Patriarchal Territories: The Body Enclosed," in *Rewriting the Renaissance: The Discourses of Sexual Difference in Early Modern Europe*, ed. Margaret W. Ferguson, Maureen Quilligan, and Nancy Vickers (Chicago: University of Chicago Press, 1986), p. 133.

9. Jean E. Howard, "Renaissance Antitheatricality and the Politics of Gender and Rank in *Much Ado About Nothing*," in *Shakespeare Reproduced*, ed. Jean E. Howard and Marion F. O'Connor (London: Methuen, 1987), pp. 172–73.

Further Reading

In addition to the following books and articles, see www.folger.edu/shakespeare and www.folger.edu/online-resources.

Much Ado About Nothing

Abbreviations: *Ado* – *Much Ado About Nothing; Ant.* = *Antony and Cleopatra;* AWW = *All's Well That Ends Well;* AYLI = *As You Like It; Cym.* = *Cymbeline;* F = First Folio (1623); LLL = *Love's Labor's Lost, MM* – *Measure for Measure;* MND = *A Midsummer Night's Dream;* MV = *The Merchant of Venice; Oth.* = *Othello;* Q = Quarto (1600); RSC = Royal Shakespeare Company; *Shr.* = *The Taming of the Shrew;* TGV = *The Two Gentlemen of Verona; Tro.* = *Troilus and Cressida;* Wives = *The Merry Wives of Windsor;* WT = *The Winter's Tale*

Alfar, Cristina León. " 'Manhood is melted into curtsies': Shifting masculine honor in *Much Ado About Nothing.*" Chapter 3 in *Women and Shakespeare's Cuckoldry Plays: Shifting Narratives of Marital Betrayal*, pp. 103–34. New York: Routledge, 2017.

Alfar's book investigates female characters' responses to accusations of cuckoldry in *Tro., Wives, Ado, Oth., WT,* and *Cym.* She contends that "the dramatic and rhetorical disruption the women enact . . . uncovers the power of female bonds and works both to critique and to reject men's anxieties about female sexual betrayal." The chapter on *Ado*, a play "more interested in male faithlessness than female faithlessness," begins with an exploration of masculine honor and its codes as a way to foreground Beatrice's inter-

vention on behalf of Hero and her critique of marriage
that accompanies it. "Because the play simultaneously
reinscribes and rejects the inequities between men
and women in marriage, as encapsulated by the Hero/
Claudio union, Beatrice's distrust of marriage can be
traced to women's subjection to 'a piece of valiant dust'
[2.1.61]." Having laid "the groundwork for understanding the men's vexed relations with one another" in the
early scenes, the play goes on to reveal "the contradiction that lies at the heart of male bonds, which are
the opposing, but also corresponding, competitions
between men for preferment and power." These same
competitions animate the men's anxieties about cuckoldry, underscored in the figure of Don John, whose
bastardy "works to expose the double bind of male
bonds and [rivalries] as dependent on and enabled by
the chaste female body." In Alfar's reading, the broken
nuptial scene (4.1) pivots the play from a relentless
privileging and foregrounding of a masculinist perspective to a female counternarrative of masculine betrayal:
"[T]he accusation against Hero of whoredom and Beatrice's defense of her cousin tip the discursive formation into an alternate territory, both reiterating and
shifting the standards, merits, definitions, and goals
of masculine honor." Beatrice proposes a new ideal of
manhood as 4.1 concludes, and Benedick performs it
(4.1.269–350). Through their union, "honor shifts so
that it defines itself not on narratives about the female
body but on trust over suspicion and constancy over
slander." Alfar's commentary on the cuckoldry joking
that returns at 5.4.44–52 and on Hero's declaration of
innocence (5.4.61–66) counters critical assessments of
the ending as a reaffirmation of an "aristocratic, masculinist moral order," complete with its fear of "law-
less female sexuality": the exchange between Claudio
and Benedick is less "light banter" than a "rebuke" to

the Count. Moreover, Hero's words, moving from past to present tense, "impl[y] that she has undergone an ontological shift" marking the birth of "a new woman." Alfar concludes that the women's "defenses against accusations of [infidelity] are more than reifications of virtue"; they are, in the words of Judith Butler, "labor[s] of self-definition" (*Excitable Speech: A Politics of the Performative* [1997], 163), "insurrectionary acts of resistance that must change how we think not only about the cuckoldry plays but also about female agency and feminist criticism itself."

Berger, Harry, Jr. "Against the Sink-a-Pace: Sexual and Family Politics in *Much Ado About Nothing.*" *Shakespeare Quarterly* 33 (1982): 302–13.

In this frequently cited essay, Berger writes of *Ado*'s Hero, its men, and male solidarity. He uses Beatrice's "little lecture" to Hero on "wooing, wedding, and repenting . . . as a Scotch jig, a measure, and a cinquepace" (2.1.71–78) to focus his discussion of "the premises of power, cost-avoidance, and fear of love and women" in what he calls "the Men's Club of Messina." Central to Berger's reading is Hero's virtual silence in the play's first two acts ("the correlative of Beatrice's witty noise"). If Hero "notes what we note, she hears enough to make her feel that her fate in life is to be her father's passport to self-perpetuation, a commodity in the alliance market." But even this "most male-dominated of heroines," Berger argues, is more interesting than is generally thought by critics. Singling out 2.1.86–93 and several passages in 3.1 (see especially lines 7–11, 53–58, and 76–81), he makes a case for a Hero who "both accepts and resents her fate as commodity," one who seems "both to admire and . . . to disapprove of [Beatrice]," one who, in short, "betrays [from time to time a 'dim awareness'] of her complicity in the sexual politics of Messina." In 3.1, "by putting down Beatrice and helping her to a husband, Hero will either eliminate the shadow cast over her own self-effacing commitment, or else she will triumph over Beatrice by reducing her to her own level," thereby "condemning her into everlasting redemption." Hero's words at 5.4.61–62 declare that Claudio's " 'love' is no more real than her 'death.' " Not Claudio's "another Hero" (63) but, as Don Pedro astutely notes, "The former Hero! Hero that is dead!" (67), this " 'new Hero' is simply the old with a vengeance," a Hero more certain than ever of her triumphant virtue (64–66). Unlike critics who emphasize a happy ending marked by a new Messina, Berger claims that nothing has changed in the cultural community of Messina's men's club, where the male bonds that opened the play—fashioned by "apprehensive reliance on power . . . secret worship of self-gratification, and . . . excessive attachment to *machismo*"—close it.

Cartmell, Deborah and Peter J. Smith, eds. *Much Ado About Nothing: A Critical Reader.* Arden Early Modern Drama Guides. London: Bloomsbury Arden Shakespeare, 2018.

Besides examining key themes and the evolution of critical preoccupations, this guide to the play provides a detailed and up-to-date history of *Ado*'s stage and screen afterlife: contemporary productions receiving close attention include Josie Rourke's 2011 Globe revival in London starring David Tennant and Catherine Tate, Vanessa Redgrave's Beatrice and James Earl Jones's Benedick in a 2013 staging directed by Mark Rylance at the Old Vic, and the RSC's 2016 pairing of *LLL* and *Ado* (the former serving as prologue to the latter, designated in the director's note as the lost *Love's Labours Won*). Four new critical essays address

(1) contemporary directors' deployment of older actors within the lead roles, (2) the play's relationship to *LLL*, (3) its presence on YouTube, and (4) the ways in which tales and ruses in the play belong to a wider concern with varieties of crime. Rounding out the volume is a guide to critical, Web-based and production-related resources and an annotated bibliography. The table of contents reads as follows: Introduction (Deborah Cartmell and Peter J. Smith), "The Critical Backstory" (Alison Findlay), "Performance History" (Kathryn Prince), "The State of the Art" (Elinor Parsons), "New Directions: Vile Tales in *Ado*" (Duncan Salkeld), "New Directions: Much Ado About Aging" (Liz Schafer), "New Directions: *Much Ado* or *Love's Labour's Won*? Does it matter which?" (Lois Potter), "New Directions: YouTube *Much Ado*" (Christy Desmet), and " 'How apt it is to learn': Resources for Staging, Studying and Teaching [*Ado*]" (Brett Hirsch and Sarah Neville).

Cook, Carol. " 'The Sign and Semblance of Her Honor': Reading Gender Difference in *Much Ado About Nothing*." *PMLA* 101 (1986): 186–202.

Unlike critics who claim that *Ado* "privileges the feminine and provides moral closure," Cook argues that while the play's sexual conflict illuminates "the question of gender differences and what is at stake in them," it "cannot resolve its contradictions from within its own structures of meaning": gender differences as presented point to "a masculine prerogative in language, which the play itself sustains," the final scene reiterating what has been problematic throughout— namely, the status of women "as ciphers until named by men." (See the entry of all four women in 5.4 masked, only two of whom speak and only when called to do so by their betrothed husbands.) Cook begins by focusing on the play's cuckoldry jokes as a signal of profound anxiety in both the male characters and in Beatrice, all of whom she reads as desiring phallic power. For all her feisty assertions of independence, Beatrice "tacitly accepts her culture's devaluation of 'feminine' characteristics of weakness, dependence, vulnerability." She therefore poses no threat to the patriarchal ideology informing the social order of Messina. For her part, the usually silent Hero has an identity written and rewritten in the male interest. She is first a Diana figure, then a Venus figure, and, in the final scene when she is "resurrected," again a Diana figure. As to whether Claudio changes enough to merit his ultimate good fortune, the mourning ritual in 5.3, which "reassert[s] . . . Messina's old order in new terms," makes the question not only "impossible" to answer but also "irrelevant." *Ado*'s ritual mode of comic closure "masks, as well as exposes, the mechanisms of masculine power," leading Cook to call the ending "something of an artful dodge": "Hero remains dead in her resurrection, as she is reappropriated to the mode of perception that killed her"; the men return to their verbal aggression and cuckoldry joking (5.4.44–52, 127–28); and Don John, expediently cast in the role of scapegoat, "deflect[s] attention from the unresolved anxieties about language and gender that led up to the catastrophe of Act 4."

Crunelle-Vanrigh, Anny. "Much Ado about Dancing." *Studies in English Literature* 57 (2017): 276–301.

Revisiting "the discourse of courtly dancing" in *Ado* in the light of Thoinot Arbeau's *Orchesography* (1589) and Sir John Davies's *Orchestra or A Poeme of Dauncing* (1596), the author explores "the extent to which dance imposes its own idiom in the play's negotiations with marriage and patriarchy." She argues that the kinetic system of dance "imparts to *Ado* a choreographic rather than a strictly dramatic format," the

details of which can be found in *Orchesography*: "Dancing informs the space of the play and the movement
of bodies across that space, turning the stage into a
dancing floor, words into steps, action into choreography, and [*Ado*] into a dance suite of which the masked
ball in Act 2 is the paradigm." The conventional image
set forth in the dance manuals of the time—i.e., that
dance figured social and marital concord, the "dancing prince emblematizing the promise of a well-gov-
erned society"—informs the play, with Don Pedro in
the sociopolitical role of patriarchal matchmaker.
Crunelle-Vanrigh, however, contends that the conventional meaning is subverted at times, most notably in
the "suite" of four dancing couples (?.1.85–152). If Don
Pedro and Hero begin the sequence with the stately
and "heavily ritualized" movements of the pavan and
Benedick and Beatrice end it with the fiery spirit of the
egalitarian canary or jig ("danced at rather than with
the partner"), the courtly suite may be seen as introducing an "undertow of subversiveness" that questions
"the gender structures deployed in courtly dancing":
"The performance of patriarchy sinks apace while the
carnival mood of topsy-turvydom takes over." Crunelle-
Vanrigh suggests the *branle*, with its sideways steps
and swaying movements, as an appropriate dance to
end the play at 5.4.133. Homophonous with brawl
(the "ordinary relational mode" of Benedick and Beatrice), the *branle* does not hold a "cosmic promise of
concord but the pragmatic commitment to contain discord." About two years after the publication of Davies's
Orchestra, which "rehearsed the motif of cosmic order
as a dance," *Ado* appears as " 'a play of dauncing,' in
which, unlike Davies, Shakespeare exposes the limits of prevailing discourses of dancing." The article
includes illustrations depicting the various movements
and tabulations associated with the dances discussed.

Evans, Bertrand. *"Much Ado About Nothing."* In *Shakespeare's Comedies*, pp. 68–87. Oxford: Clarendon Press, 1960.

Evans examines the comedies through the dramaturgical lens of "awareness and control." Noting how writers may opt to keep the reader/spectator less aware than the participants in the action, equally aware, or more aware, he observes that Shakespeare consistently chooses the third way, thereby "open[ing] exploitable gaps [of awareness] both between audience and participants and between participant and participant." In his study of "discrepant awareness"—i.e., differing levels of "who knows what" at any given moment in a play—Evans establishes that the viewer of *Ado* holds an advantage over at least some of the participants during fourteen of the play's seventeen scenes. He organizes the chapter around the eight "practices" that impel the action: Don Pedro's "gratuitous offer" to woo Hero for Claudio, Don John's perversion of that well-intentioned strategy, the gulling of Benedick followed by that of Beatrice, Don John's malicious trick to slander Hero, Claudio's cruel humiliation of Hero at the altar, the Friar's scheme to feign and "publish" Hero's "death," and the orchestration of the "resurrected" Hero in the final scene. Evans focuses at length on Don John's first "practice" on Claudio, which, while averted, illustrates in microcosm a world in which later misunderstandings are possible, Messina being inhabited by characters with a predilection for alternating the roles of deceiver and deceived. Subsequent misunderstanding casts an especially harsh light upon Claudio, whose callousness throws into relief the "humane and noble sympathy" of Beatrice and Benedick's love. In Evans's estimation, "no comedy of Shakespeare's is more aptly named than [*Ado*], all the ado of which, from our vantage-point, is indeed about nothing." And no other play "demonstrate[s] more conclusively the dramatist's devotion to situations characterized by exploitable differences in awareness."

Findlay, Alison. "Surface Tensions: Ceremony and Shame in *Much Ado About Nothing*." *Shakespeare Survey* 63 (2010): 282–90.

Findlay's focus is the "ceremonial idiom central to the social politics" of *Ado*, an idiom "brilliantly captur[ed]" in Beatrice and Benedick's first onstage "skirmish of wit" (1.1.112–19; see also 60–61). Their simultaneous combination of overplayed "deferential formality" and insults that "flout . . . the [ceremonial] code of politeness . . . immediately establishes Messina as a high-risk environment for face-to-face interactions." Drawing on studies of semiotics, particularly as they relate to ceremony and the concept of shame, Findlay reads *Ado* as a play that "explores how engaging in social discourse is an expression of, or investment of, interest that always involves deep risk to the self: the shame of that interest not being reciprocated." Messina's "network of ceremonies is designed to mitigate the risks to identity in everyday encounters and life-changing rites of passage," but in the "brittle" social fabric of *Ado* ceremony often fails to protect the fragile self, and shame is the result. Findlay develops her argument through an analysis of the stiff and awkward first betrothal of Claudio and Hero (2.1.283–310) and three subsequent scenes in which "ceremonial surfaces are subject to intolerable tensions": the broken nuptial (4.1), the superficial mourning ritual (5.3), and the second betrothal of Claudio and Hero (5.4). These three episodes are "failures in terms of being disrupted or somehow lacking in authenticity," each illustrative of a pattern in which "ceremonial practice is desecrated." Findlay pays special attention to Hero's "blush" (4.1.34–42), arguing that her "shame" is rooted in the "ceremonia[l] constructing and packaging" of her as a bride to accommodate early modern masculine anxieties about sexuality. The final celebratory scene may promise renewal, but here, as elsewhere in *Ado*, ceremony "offers no guarantee that Hero, or any other woman, will not be misread in the future." Shame for Hero is not "a transient experience. . . . Instead it is a life sentence to play the part of 'another Hero,' another male construction of female identity on the s(h)ame model: 'the former Hero, Hero that is dead!' "

Friedman, Michael D. " 'Get thee a wife, get thee a wife!': *Much Ado About Nothing.*" Chapter 3 in *The World Must Be Peopled: Shakespeare's Comedies of Forgiveness*, pp. 76–111. London: Associated University Presses; Madison, N.J.: Fairleigh Dickinson University Press, 2002.

Friedman considers *Ado* (along with *TGV, AWW,* and *MM*) under the generic heading "comedies of forgiveness." The chapter on *Ado* centers on the "problem of Claudio," a comic hero in the vein of Proteus (*TGV*), Bertram (*AWW*), and Angelo (*MM*): all four reveal a "glaring discrepancy between what they seem to deserve for their offenses against women and the punishment they actually receive." The first part of the chapter reviews the critical commentary on the Count. For his supporters, Claudio is "a congenial romantic lead," whose youth and inexperience make him an easy victim of Don John's malicious practicing, but who is ultimately "redeemed" and thus made worthy of a "happily ever after" future with Hero. For his detractors, Claudio is a "hateful young cub," "a worm," a "miserable specimen of humanity" (just a few of the terms used to describe him in the scholarship). His repudiation of Hero is "too callous," his subsequent apology and mourning "less than convincing," and his eagerness to "seize . . . [a]nother Hero" (5.4.54–63) "too expedient" to merit audience sympathy. The second half of the chapter examines select passages and scenes (among them 2.2.40–49; 3.3.144–52; 4.1.114 SD; 5.3; and 5.4) to show how editors and directors—through interpolation, emendation, and treatment of stage business and speech prefixes—have handled the Claudio problem. (Kenneth Branagh's 1993 film receives more than passing mention.) As Friedman reads *Ado*, textual evidence roots Claudio's forgiveness and the nuptial joy at the end of 5.4 in early modern social and patriarchal conventions—i.e., in male bonding and the marrying off of a daughter in a profitable exchange. A close reading of the Q and F texts allows for a conventional lover, neither perfect nor monstrous, in a play performed so that the "forces that orchestrate" matches between innocent young women and unworthy men are "revealed and questioned." Such a performance choice results in "the pleasures of a multifaceted response to the play's Forgiven Comic Hero."

Gottlieb, Derek. "*Much Ado About Nothing*." Chapter 3 in *Skepticism and Belonging in Shakespeare's Comedy*, pp. 53–86. New York: Routledge, 2016.

Gottlieb extends Stanley Cavell's influential study of the intersection of Shakespearean tragedy and epistemology (*Disowning Knowledge in Six Plays of Shakespeare* [1987]) to Shakespeare's comedies, specifically *Ado*, *MND*, and *AYLI*. Like the tragedies, Shakespeare's comedies demonstrate that "exposure or vulnerability to others is the source of both human happiness and human misery." But unlike the tragic plays, which (as Cavell argues) are "drama[s] of skepticism," Shakespeare's comic worlds are "drama[s] of acknowledgment." Gottlieb organizes his chapter on *Ado* under two subheadings: "Disquietudes and Problems" and "A Miracle" (a "resurrection" for one plot, and a pair of sonnets for the other). Two different types of disquietude afflict the play's two couples. In the case of Claudio and Hero, he (like Othello) "struggles with the urge to transform his love for Hero, originally experienced as something that happens to or . . . befalls him, into something like an object that he possesses . . . and can have stolen from him"; the case of Beatrice and Benedick is different in that both characters "grapple with a view of loving as dependent upon verifiable facts; that is, as following from or requiring the truth of another's love as a first condition." As Benedick's query "Do not you love me?" and Beatrice's response "Why no, no more than reason" (5.4.76–77) indicate, something—reason, truth, fact—keeps them from formally and publicly acknowledging feelings that they have already admitted to themselves (2.3, 3.1) and to each other in private (4.1.281–301). What is needed to break the impasse is a miracle, conveniently supplied in the form of self-penned verses (5.4.89–96), whose testamentary power forces Benedick and Beatrice to stop "disowning knowledge" and return to what has been in front of them the whole time. Similarly, Claudio returns, by way of the "resurrection," to the original character of his love for Hero, when the circumstances of his return from the wars—and not Hero's beauty or virtue—led him to see her in a new light that disposed him to desire her (1.1.291–300). "Conceiving of Claudio in terms of a return enables the *forgetting* (as opposed to forgiving) necessary to the play's happy conclusion": Claudio's error must be "undone just as his original experience of love must be *re*-done." In both plots, "the movements from engagement in the world to skeptical withdrawal and back again to engagement trace a pattern of learning [not as the discovery of new facts but] as the recovery or acknowledgment of that which one cannot fail to know."

Gueron, Claire. "Rumour and Second-Hand Knowledge in *Much Ado About Nothing*." In *The Circulation of Knowledge in Early Modern English Literature*, edited by Sophie Chiari, pp. 93–103. Burlington, Vt.: Ashgate, 2015.

The essays gathered in this volume investigate the multiple ways that ideas circulated in Shakespeare's time through the cultural processes of initiation, transmission, and transgression. In her essay, Gueron draws on critical and theoretical concerns about transmission and initiation in reading *Ado*, the only play in the Shakespeare canon to begin and end with a messenger's report. The roundabout trajectory of the false rumor about Don Pedro being in love with Hero in the early scenes illustrates how "information follows tortuous routes" in a Messina that "teems" with messengers, teachers, storytellers, gossips, and various forms of textual authority. While some critics view the play as "a pessimistic depiction of epistemological failure and a skeptical illustration of the limits of human understanding," Gueron argues that it "is less an affirmation of a power-based epistemology than an exploration of the complex entanglement of knowledge transmission and social [as well as gender] identity." As evidence of this entanglement, she cites Leonato's refusal to interrogate Don John's accomplices himself, a dereliction of duty that arises from the social conventions informing Messina's hierarchical orthodoxy: he does not wish to associate with social inferiors, the marginalized Dogberry and associates, let alone think that he can learn from them. To further illustrate the nexus of "epistemological, moral and social forces at work in society," Gueron singles out the line "my daughter says so"

(2.3.157). On one level, the line functions solely as an epistemological guarantee that the report Benedick overhears is authentic, but for the Hero–Claudio plot, it assumes moral and social significance that carries implications for the events in Acts 3 and 4. Presenting Hero as "violating decorum," the line places her in the position of "one who [improperly] reveals the secrets of the maidenly bedchamber to the male ear"; like the biblical Eve, she becomes "the victim of a male discourse [casting] her as the transmitter of forbidden knowledge." Gueron contrasts the "obsessive" emphasis on Hero as the conduit of credible information in 2.3 (see lines 118–19, 141, 142–43, 157, 179, and 208–9) with the single reference to reliance on the authority of the male voice in the following scene when Beatrice is eavesdropping (3.1.40). In *Ado*, Shakespeare "depicts a world in which the access to the truth is complicated by decorum as much as it is by the world's opacity and the deceptiveness of signs and where every act of information-sharing involves both the foregrounding and the possible undermining of class and gender barriers." Poised on the threshold of the scientific revolution, the play "reflects contemporary concerns about transmission while pondering the possibility of achieving a type of knowledge dissociated from moral and social considerations."

Howard, Jean. E. "Renaissance Antitheatricality and the Politics of Gender and Rank in *Much Ado About Nothing.*" In *Shakespeare Reproduced: The Text in History and Ideology*, edited by Jean E. Howard and Marion F. O'Connor, pp. 163–87, esp. 172–83. London: Methuen, 1987. [Chapter 3 of Howard's *The Stage and Social Struggle in Early Modern England* (New York: Routledge, 1994) incorporates a revised version of the 1987 essay: see "Antitheatricality Staged: The Workings of Ideology in Dekker's *The Whore of Babylon* and Shakespeare's *Much Ado About Nothing*," pp. 47–72, esp. 57–72.]

Howard examines *Ado* against a body of antitheatrical Elizabethan texts concerned with the "nature, control, and 'morality' of theatrical power." While one might expect *Ado*—filled with "playlets, staged shows, actors, and interior dramatists"—to be unequivocally positive in regard to theatricality, the play disciplines those who illegitimately aspire to control such power and ultimately returns control to the "better sort." Howard pursues the ideological implications of a text that both limits theatricality and—in its material production—gives it unrammeled expression. Arguing that issues of patriarchal and hierarchical social order are at the heart of the play's theatrical practices, Howard finds male assumptions about women responsible for the success of Don John's trick in slandering Hero; she also attributes the success of the lower-class Dogberry and Verges in solving "society's problems without ever threatening its central values or power relations" to their outsider status, a marginality underscored by "a gift of intuition . . . bought at the price of speech and rationality." The most graphic representation of the "role of theatrical functions as instruments of power and as a means of compelling belief in a particular view of truth," however, is found in Don Pedro's sociopolitical manipulation of Benedick and Beatrice. Whereas most critics view these characters as denying a mutual attraction present from the beginning of the play, Howard contends that Don Pedro's pageants "produc[e] their love," his goal being the "reproduc[tion of] existing social relations (both gender and class relations) and [the] control [of] threats to the social order." By investing his "established authority" in matters of courtship, the Prince furthers early modern motives—

political, economic, and social—governing upper-class marriages. In Howard's reading, the final scene "legitimates male, aristocratic theatricality." Contrary to being "above ideology," *Ado*, as both "text *and* stage play," emerges as a "site of ideological and political contestation . . . within the Elizabethan . . . social formation."

Johnson, Laurie, John Sutton, and Evelyn Tribble, eds. *Embodied Cognition and Shakespeare's Theatre: The Early Modern Body-Mind.* New York: Routledge, 2014.

Building on the scholarship of the past two decades on understandings of mind and body in Shakespeare's world, the essays in this collection reject a simple binary of the material (body) and the psychological (mind) in favor of the notion of an early modern "body-mind." The goal of the editors is to show how the concept of "embodied cognition" can "reinvigorate our understanding of the social and extended nature of cognition" in the early modern period. Two chapters deal with *Ado*: Ros King's "Plays, Playing, and Make-Believe: Thinking and Feeling in Shakespearean Drama" (pp. 27–45, esp. 38–42) and James A. Knapp's "Mental Bodies in *Much Ado About Nothing*" (pp. 86–103).

King uses *Ado* as a test case to explore Shakespeare's use of the concept of play—i.e., everything beyond the basics of life, "everything that involves reflection, creativity, choice, skill"—and "the extent to which mindfulness and the expression of feeling among performers and audience can be tested in the dynamic play of the playhouse." References to playing and acting abound in Shakespeare's works, but *Ado*, "as signaled by its title's claim to insignificance," captures the concept of play more fully than most. The language in the opening dialogue on the wars from which Don Pedro and his followers will be returning (1.1.5–9) is "nothing if not a game." The "gaming aspect" continues immediately in the exchange between the courtly messenger's extravagant account of Claudio's feats and Beatrice's very different assessment of martial exploits (12–17, 30–31, 38–44), setting the stage for the "gaming" that will follow in subsequent scenes (notably 2.1, 2.3, and 3.1). For all this sense of play and game, however, a "withdrawal from play" (personified throughout in the silent and "actively antisocial" Don John) becomes more pronounced in the slandered bride sequence of 4.1; even the final marriage trick "problematize[s the] supposedly happy ending . . . [by] rais[ing] more questions than it answers." A sense of play, however, returns with the comic "miracle" of the suddenly produced love sonnets and the final dance. Moreover, as Benedick's refusal (5.4.104–13) to be "flout[ed]" out of his humor attests, "man is always and inevitably a playful, 'giddy thing.'" Experiencing *Ado* in performance reveals the complex relationships set up between stage and auditorium, between word and gesture, and between mind and body.

Designating the two themes of *Ado* as recognition and misrecognition, Knapp organizes his essay around Claudio's rejection of Hero in 4.1 and the epistemological problem it raises (a recurrent one in Shakespeare): namely, "the gap between perception and knowledge, particularly the knowledge of another person," tied to the relationship between outward appearance and immaterial character. Focusing specifically on Hero's blush (4.1.34) and its different significations as interpreted by Claudio (35–42) and the Friar (167–73), he argues that Shakespeare "exploited contradictions in contemporary accounts of immateriality to open up theatrical possibilities in a play aptly titled *Much Ado About Nothing*." (The pun of the play's title—nothing

as "noting"—"points to the mental activity of pro-
cessing the input of the senses through cognition at
the same time that it references the immateriality of
the thoughts produced by such activity.") As early as the
exchange between Claudio and Benedick at 1.1.158–99,
Shakespeare invites his audience to contemplate the
difference between perception and cognition, "between
apprehension and comprehension—between Hero's
body provided by the senses and her body as seen
through the lens of cognitive judgment." Knapp views
Benedick's misrecognition of Beatrice's demeanor at
the end of 2.3 as a preview of Claudio's later misrecognition of Hero. In both cases, misrecognition occurs
because of the confusion that arises "when the characters are invited to compare [the perceptual bodies
in front of them with the] mental bodies derived from
the imagination's ability to create false images in the
mind without any immediate external stimulus." For
Benedick, the false image is that of a Beatrice madly in
love with him planted in his mind earlier in the scene;
for Claudio, the one planted by Don John at 3.2.105–7.
Closely "noting" Hero's appearance and drawing on his
extensive training in the comparison of perceptual and
mental bodies (4.1.165–79), the Friar outlines a plan
(213–19, 221–33) to "reconstruct Hero's mental body
in Claudio's brain" (233–41), on the assumption that
"the innocence that Hero's material body is unable
to confirm, her [reconstructed] mental body will."
Throughout *Ado* Shakespeare explores the "mysterious
interplay between the material body, corporeal spirit
(thought), and immaterial soul." The various examples
of recognition and misrecognition in the play "reveal
both the fallibility of the senses and the fallibility of
reason," thus underscoring the need to "think . . . with
the embodied mind."

Kreps, Barbara. "Two-Sided Legal Narratives: Slander, Evidence, Proof, and Turnarounds in *Much Ado About Nothing*." In *Taking Exception to the Law: Materializing Injustice in Early Modern English*, edited by Donald Beecher, pp. 162–78. Toronto: University of Toronto Press, 2015.

Kreps's essay appears in a collection that uses a range of early modern writings to engage with how legal questions were discussed in the period. Focusing on *Ado*, with its "two competing narratives: truth and false or erroneous witness," Kreps observes that the "apparently pointless plan" involving Don Pedro's proxy wooing of Hero for Claudio (1.1.315–23) "set[s] the stage for the display of contrasting attitudes towards the issues, fundamental to the play, of reliable evidence and what constitutes proof," and also "helps to distinguish appropriate and inappropriate reactions to hearsay evidence," especially "hearsay at several removes" (1.2.9–16, 21–24; 1.3.56–63). Noting the play's preoccupation with language games, Kreps discusses the ability to argue different sides of a question that was the cornerstone of early modern legal training at the Inns of Court, specifically in the moot court exercises that required young lawyers to interpret the same evidence and testimony in their arguments for the plaintiff one day and for the defense the next. Such mental facility, for both good and ill, is apparent in the linguistic and narrative skills of *Ado*'s characters in both plots: see the effective staging of evidence by the friends of Beatrice and Benedick in the gulling episodes of 2.3 and 3.1 "sandwiched between" the development of Don John's defamation plot against Hero in 2.2 and 3.2. While Dogberry's inversion of the correct legal order— suspicions leading to proof—provokes laughter in 3.3 and 3.5, the same "materializing of injustice" occurs in

4.1 but to a different end: staging a "trial" after he has already determined the outcome, Claudio "compresses arraignment and conviction into a brusque parody of the (civil) law's inquisitorial trial formulae, with the relevant linguistic paraphernalia of 'evidence,' 'witness,' 'guiltiness,' and 'proof.'" Drawing on archival records relating to early modern defamation cases, Kreps notes that the Friar never mentions the legal avenue open to Hero of seeking redress in an ecclesiastical court; instead, opting for a strategy that "will quench the wonder of her infamy" (4.1.250), he proposes the false report of Hero's death. Kreps concludes that the legal apparatus operating in *Ado* is generally ineffective and impedes rather than leads to the discovery of the truth. It is the "great judicial irony" of the play that the inept constables, Messina's official representatives of the law, stumble by accident on the evidence that vindicates Hero. Legal competence in Messina ultimately comes in the person of one whose role as church caretaker did not require legal knowledge, the Sexton (4.2.35–37, 48, 54, 60, 62–68). "If one does not look too deeply and accepts as felicitous the solution that unites Hero to the undeserving Claudio, a happy ending of sorts ostensibly gets patched together. But the legal process that leads to it is far from reassuring."

Leggatt, Alexander. *"Much Ado About Nothing."* In *Shakespeare's Comedy of Love*, pp. 151–83. London: Methuen, 1974.

Leggatt considers *Ado* an experimental attempt at retaining the range and fluidity of *MV* while producing the "harmony of disparate elements" that distinguishes *MND*. Forgoing thematic analysis for a more directly theatrical approach, he discovers a complex interplay of formality and naturalism that complicates placing the pure convention of the Claudio and Hero plot against the casual naturalism of the Benedick and Beatrice subplot. Among the passages and scenes he examines are the two gulling episodes (2.3 and 3.1), wherein the tentative prose of Benedick's soliloquy (2.3.223–46) contrasts with the formal verse of Beatrice's (3.1.113–22); both idioms, however, are equally revealing, as we hear Benedick's "anxious rationalizations" and Beatrice's simple and direct surrender to the power of love. In the "big theatrical scene" of the broken nuptial (4.1), Claudio's formal tirade sharply contrasts with Beatrice's "spontaneous, explosive, and unpredictable" demand that Benedick "Kill Claudio" (4.1.303). Just as the formal mating of Claudio and Hero provokes "the more psychologically determined mating" of Benedick and Beatrice in the gulling episodes, so in the first wedding scene, "the formalized suffering of the one love affair provokes psychological complications in the other. Beneath their differences, the two stories can be seen as moving in fundamentally the same way: love must pass through an ordeal. But the way the ordeal is dramatized is radically different." Throughout *Ado*, Shakespeare uses conventional devices (the eavesdropping trick, the mock death, the challenge issued to the lover to prove his love for the beloved, the unmasking of the bride, and customary wedding rituals) to reveal "the tensions and uncertainties of the characters' minds," thereby asserting the "human reality at the heart of convention." In its interplay of the naturalistic and the formal, *Ado* exemplifies the variety of Shakespeare's dynamic comic art, ever changing and self-questioning.

Neely, Carol Thomas. "Broken Nuptials in Shakespeare's Comedies: *Much Ado About Nothing*." In *Broken Nuptials in Shakespeare's Plays*, pp. 24–57. New Haven: Yale University Press, 1985.

With their emphasis on power in courtship, Neely's feminist reinterpretations of *Ado, AWW, Othello, Ant.,* and *WT* demonstrate how all five plays "embody the conflicts attendant on marriage by the incorporation of broken nuptials," which the author defines as "anything that disrupts the process of wooing, betrothal, wedding, and marriage." The broken nuptials that are Neely's focus "express the anxieties, desires, and conflicts of the couples who enter into marital unions as well as the external pressures placed on these unions by parents, rulers, the community." Whether achieved or broken, marriage "influences the themes and structure of the plays and serves as the focus for the social and emotional relation of the sexes." In a reading that underscores the parallels and differences between the Claudio–Hero and Benedick–Beatrice plots, both of which play out against a backdrop of patriarchal authority, Neely contends that the comedy's "tensions and its poise are achieved by the interaction" of the two couples in 4.1: there the interrupted wedding "provides the impetus" for Benedick and Beatrice, who have already acknowledged their love to themselves (see the gulling scenes in 2.3 and 3.1, respectively), now to reveal it to each other. Beatrice's and Benedick's "merry wars" are thus "transformed by the broken nuptials into romantic attachment, and Hero's mock death [brought on by that interrupted ceremony] and the revelation of her innocence transform Claudio's degradation of her into a ritualistic penance." Throughout the comedies, broken nuptials "give women the power to resist, control, or alter the movement of courtship. But with the celebration of completed nuptials at the end of the [plays], male control is reestablished, and women take their subordinate places in the dance." The kiss shared by Benedick and Beatrice in 5.4 illustrates this development. On the one hand, it suggests mutuality;

on the other, it silences Beatrice for the remainder of the play, thus heralding "the beginning of the inequality that [she] feared in marriage," an inequality also implicit in Benedick's control of the wedding festivities framed by male jokes about cuckoldry. Neely locates *Ado* at the "center of [Shakespeare's] comedies": the play looks backward to the so-called festive plays like *MND* and forward to the complex ethical issues of the so-called problem comedies like *MM*.

Osborne, Laurie. "Dramatic Play in *Much Ado About Nothing*: Wedding the Italian Novella and English Comedy." *Philological Quarterly* 69 (1990): 167–88.

Osborne pursues Shakespeare's treatment of the primary source behind *Ado*—the slandered maiden tale found in the Italian novellas by Ariosto and Bandello—to suggest that the playwright's principal interest lies in the "dangerous powers of dramatic play—staging scenes, acting roles, and creating spectacle." What she finds most striking in Shakespeare's use of these novella tales "is his fascination with figures who manipulate their worlds by dramatic means" and who "draw together the discourses of different genres" (which, in *Ado*, are melodrama and comedy). She calls these figures "player-dramatists" and analyzes the passing of power from Don Pedro and Don John to characters such as the Friar and Leonato. In choosing to add a comic subplot—the courtship of Beatrice and Benedick—Shakespeare adjusts the main novella plot of the slandered maiden to include comic principles. But the linkage of the two principal schemers—Don Pedro and Don John—reveals the difficulties of absorbing the noncomic, nondramatic materials of the source material into comic conventions. For Osborne, the process of creating comedy from noncomic sources requires the manufacture of disasters and oppositions, a process that reveals contradictions at the heart of comedy itself and that, in the case of *Ado*, called for the playwright's "ongoing reworking" of his source materials. Among the changes singled out by Osborne are the omission of the window scene; the "disturbing silence" of Margaret, whose "prototype" in Ariosto's tale is the one who reveals the trick of the bedroom scene; and the disappearance of Don John after the broken nuptial. Throughout the essay, Osborne's focus is on "comedy as a genre in process rather than a conventional dramatic form determined by its end."

Pellegrini, Ann. "Closing Ranks, Keeping Company: Marriage Plots and the Will to Be Single in *Much Ado about Nothing*." In *Shakesqueer: A Queer Companion to the Complete Works of Shakespeare*, edited by Madhavi Menon, pp. 245–53. Durham: Duke University Press, 2011.

This collection of essays attempts to integrate Shakespeare and queer theory, not to "provide 'queer readings' " of Shakespeare texts but to bring the non-normative stance of queerness into varied engagements with "the odd, eccentric, and unexpected" in the canonical Shakespeare. For Pellegrini, *Ado* is "one of Shakespeare's great plays on the power of theatricality to convert nothing into something." She begins her essay with a discussion of the 1970 musical *Company* (music and lyrics by Stephen Sondheim; book by George Furth). In contrast to musicals that have strong books (i.e., plots), *Company* struck many reviewers as a musical about nothing: a series of vignettes about a single man named Bobby, who keeps "evad[ing] . . . marriage as destination," and whose only friends are five married couples, ambivalent about his single status—on the one hand, wanting him to get married and be like them; on the other, preferring that he remain unattached and stay in their company as an ever-present "go to" friend. In part 2 of the essay ("Interlude: As If"), Pellegrini introduces Eve Kosofsky Sedgwick's formation of the nonce category "periperformative" to denote a class of negative performatives—disavowal, demurral, renunciation, deprecation, and repudiation (see "Around the Performative," in *Touching Feeling: Affect, Pedagogy, Performativity* [2003], pp. 67–92). Such speech acts are a way of "falling out with conventional and conventionalized performatives" on the order of "I do" and "I now pronounce you man and wife." Turning specifically to *Ado* in the final section of the essay, Pellegrini argues that the scowling Don John "emerges as something of a queer anti-hero." While ultimately "fail[ing] to derail the 'happy' ending" for Hero and Claudio, Don John's periperformative in setting up Claudio's "performative un-performance of the wedding vow" does "temporarily stun the marital plot, starkly illuminating—in or as a kind of freeze frame— not just marriage as theater, but marriage as a closing of ranks." Writing that theatricality is both an obstacle to and instrument of *Ado*'s linked marriage plots, Pellegrini observes that much of the play's wit stems from watching the "sworn marriage resisters," Beatrice and Benedict, propelled by gossip, acknowledge their desire to marry. Gossip—bad in the case of the Claudio–Hero plot; good in the Beatrice–Benedick plot—"insinuates itself into social relations as a kind of theatre," mobilizing and feeding off "profoundly gendered concerns" over how one is perceived by others. *Ado* is the only play in the Shakespeare canon to end with a call for a dance involving the entire company. The audience has enjoyed the witty tirades of Benedick and Beatrice, but "in the end the will to be single cannot hold against . . . [society's binary] call to be married or be no one at all." The concluding harmony figured in the "social choreography of marriage" comes at a cost, however, for not all are included. Offstage, Don John awaits his punishment. Returning to *Company*, Pellegrini detects a fleeting "space of possibility" in the final image of Bobby, all alone on stage, blowing out his candles. "Reach[ing] toward other ways of being in and desiring company," the theatrical moment contrasts with the social world dramatized in both the musical and *Ado*, a world that forces—or, at least, vigorously urges—people into married life, shutting off all possibility for "alternative social horizons."

Prouty, Charles Tyler. *The Sources of "Much Ado About Nothing": A Critical Study.* New Haven: Yale University Press, 1950.
    Prouty explores the "sea change which took place in Shakespeare's mind" in light of the "intertextual totality" of the eighteen versions of the Claudio–Hero story available in the sixteenth century prior to *Ado*. The book consists of four chapters and an extensive appendix (pp. 65–142) that reprints the only extant copy of Peter Beverley's *Ariodanto and Ieneura*, the first English appearance of the Claudio–Hero story (c. 1566). Chapter 1 outlines the major problems that need to be addressed in dealing with *Ado*'s sources: (1) Why did Shakespeare feel the need to introduce a second plot and what is the connection between the two plots? and (2) How should we view the nature of the main plot—as a courtship story leading to a marriage of convenience or to one based on romantic attachment; and by extension, how are we to respond to the character of Claudio? Chapter 2 briefly surveys the scholarship on the then-known sources of *Ado* for plot lines, characters, scenes, incidents, and passages. Chapter 3, titled "The Significance of the Sources," explores the "ideological provenance" of the main story as found in the

primary nondramatic sources: Ludovico Ariosto's tale in Canto V of his *Orlando Furioso* (1516; available to Shakespeare in Sir John Harington's 1591 translation); Matteo Bandello's twenty-second *Novella* (1554) and its French translation by François de Belleforest in *Histoires Tragiques* (1574); and the works of "sequent adaptors," namely, Beverley and George Whetstone (*The Rock of Regard* [1576]). The heart of the book is chapter 4 ("The Play"), wherein Prouty's emphasis is "upon the structure, characters, and thematic unity of [*Ado*] rather than the background." Thus he records and interprets Shakespeare's alterations to the Hero-Claudio plot as received from the sources. Prouty then shows how Shakespeare, having reduced the role of Hero and having recast Claudio, required a comic counterpart—the story of Beatrice and Benedick, apparently Shakespeare's invention. Prouty argues that Benedick and Beatrice are an integral part of the play and are not solely introduced for comic relief: the joining of the two plots, one borrowed and one original, was purposeful, not capricious. Finally, Prouty urges an understanding of the main plot and the figure of Claudio in Elizabethan terms.

Rossiter, A. P. *"Much Ado About Nothing."* In *Angels with Horns*, pp. 67–81. London: Longmans, Green, 1961. Reprinted in *Shakespeare, The Comedies: A Collection of Critical Essays*, edited by Kenneth Muir, pp. 47–57. Englewood Cliffs, N.J.: Prentice-Hall, 1965.

Describing *Ado* as a text filled with "Messinans [who] have dancing minds, and [who] make words dance or caper to their unpremeditated tunes," Rossiter examines the play's different types of humor, ranging from the verbal to the situational: quibbles, malapropisms, repartee, and "hyperbolic comic inventiveness" in which "exuberance . . . leaps beyond expectation in 'improving the occasion.' " Some of the wittiest passages, he argues, are found in the interrelations of the three plots—the Claudio-Hero, the Benedick-Beatrice, and the Dogberry and associates—all of which turn on "misapprehensions, misprisions, misunderstandings, misinterpretations and misapplications." The potentially disastrous element of the play that resides in the church scene (4.1) is "balanced neatly on a tonal frontier: not between comedy and tragedy, but between comedy and tragi-comedy" (in which "seeming and being . . . have a quite different seriousness"). In *Ado*'s "glittering world of amiable fools of all sorts," equivocations are restricted to appearance and do not extend into ambivalence toward things themselves (love, for example). This quality leads Rossiter to place *Ado* within Shakespeare's canon "just at the point" before the equilibrium between jest and fortune ("where fortune favors the laughers") turns to cynicism.

Ryan, Kiernan. "Strange Misprision: *Much Ado About Nothing.*" Chapter 8 in *Shakespeare's Comedies*, pp. 164–97. New York: Palgrave Macmillan, 2009.

Ryan focuses on the playwright's ten farcical and festive Elizabethan comedies as the first phase of "a kind of comedy which Shakespeare quite consciously brought to an end with *Twelfth Night* and to which he never returned." (He assigns the problem plays and romances to subsequent phases of Shakespearean comedy.) In the chapter on *Ado*, Ryan claims that the repeated use of the word "strange" (beginning as early as 1.2.4–5) provides "the best clue" both to the play's distinctive mood and to the "spectral quality" of its characters. The latter feature first emerges in the "textual ghosts" of Leonato's wife Innogen and "a kinsman," characters announced in initial stage directions of the early printed texts (at 1.1.0 and 2.1.0) but who neither speak nor act and are never mentioned again.

(On Innogen, see the longer note to 1.1.0 in the present edition [p. 199].) Their "spectral presence" on the margins of *Ado* is "peculiarly apt in a play that advertises its preoccupation with insubstantiality in its title." Further swelling "the ranks of the incorporeal are ... figurative or virtual dramatis personae," the most conspicuous of which is the resurrected Hero of 5.4, whose own words (line 61) and those of Don Pedro (line 67) "intimate that Claudio will be marrying a dead woman, . . . a shadow of her former self." A different but "equally uncanny, disembodied" figure is the thief called "Deformed" (3.3.122–27; 5.1.322–27). As the personification of fashion, "Deformed" controls the world of Messina. Ryan reads the Watchman's aside (3.3.125–27) as "an encrypted understanding" of the "capacity of clothes [only one aspect of fashion] to conceal [and distort] character," thereby underscoring "the vulnerability of perception and judgement." The iterated "strange," building on the "connotations it has accrued over the previous three acts[,] . . . comes into its own" in Act 4, its "full resonance" achieved in Beatrice and Benedict's "confessional *tête-à-tête* [4.1.269–350]." Held in thrall by the conventions of "Deformed Fashion," the characters inhabiting Shakespeare's Messina appear as strangers, the forces fashioning their identities and destinies "neither natural nor necessary but artificial and arbitrary." Reality for such characters, Ryan concludes, "appears . . . [as] a mirage created by misconceptions"—a world that "persistently deceives" its inhabitants, one "to which they can never fully belong. . . . And that's why the title of this comedy ultimately means just what it says."

Wynne-Davies, Marion, ed. *"Much Ado About Nothing" and "The Taming of the Shrew."* New Casebooks. New York: Palgrave, 2001.

Wynne-Davies presents a broad range of critical

essays exemplifying different approaches—feminist, historicist, deconstructionist, psychoanalytic, and performative—to *Ado* and *Shr.*, explaining in her introduction the development of the critical pieces included. The first half of this collection of critical essays is devoted to *Ado*. The items reprinted or excerpted are Harry Berger, Jr., "Against the Sink-a-Pace: Sexual and Family Politics in *Much Ado About Nothing*" (1982; see Berger above); S. P. Cerasano, "Half a Dozen Dangerous Words" (1992); Barbara Everett, "*Much Ado About Nothing*: The Unsociable Comedy" (1994); Penny Gay, "*Much Ado About Nothing*: A Kind of Merry War" (from Gay's 1994 book *As She Likes It: Shakespeare's Unruly Women*); and Jean E. Howard, "Antitheatricality Staged: The Workings of Ideology in Dekker's *The Whore of Babylon* and Shakespeare's *Much Ado About Nothing*" (from Howard's 1994 book *The Stage and Social Struggle in Early Modern England*; see Howard item above). Cerasano's essay examines Hero's "honest slander" and Claudio's rejection of her (4.1) in the context of early modern law and patriarchal orthodoxy. Everett's essay focuses on the psychological complexity behind comic conventions to argue that *Ado* "is serious in its concerns while always wearing the air of being entertainingly 'About Nothing'"; she calls *Ado* Shakespeare's "most psychologically interesting romantic comedy." The excerpted chapter from Gay's book on gender and performance considers how depictions of Beatrice in post–World War II British productions depend on the "perceived relation between women and the patriarchy at the moment of the play's embodiment."

Films

Branagh, Kenneth, director. *Much Ado About Nothing*. Samuel Goldwyn Co., 1993. 111 min.

Branagh's popular film features the director as Benedick with Emma Thompson opposite him as Beatrice. Denzel Washington's Don Pedro, Keanu Reeves's Don John, and Michael Keaton's Dogberry support the principals in this lavish treatment, set in a sun-drenched Italian villa.

Wheedon, Josh, director. *Much Ado About Nothing*. Bellweather Pictures, 2012. 109 min.

In contrast to Kenneth Branagh, whose popular 1993 film was lavishly set with period costumes, Wheedon directed and shot this critically acclaimed black-and-white, modern-dress, minimalist treatment in twelve days at his home in Santa Monica, California. Supporting the principals—Amy Acker as Beatrice and Alexis Denisof as Benedick—are Reed Diamond (Don Pedro), Clark Gregg (Leonato), Fran Kranz (Claudio), Jillian Morgese (Hero), Sean Maher (Don John), and Nathan Fillion (Dogberry).

Shakespeare's Language

Abbott, E. A. *A Shakespearian Grammar*. New York: Haskell House, 1972.

This compact reference book, first published in 1870, helps with many difficulties in Shakespeare's language, especially with respect to syntax, grammar, and prosody. Abbott systematically accounts for a host of differences between Shakespeare's usage and sentence structure and our own. As he observes, Shakespearean English "presents the English language in a transitional . . . condition, rejecting and inventing much that the verdict of posterity has retained and discarded. It was an age of experiments, and the experiments were not always successful." For more than a century, Abbott's book was the chief resource for questions of grammar; see Jonathan Hope (below) for a twenty-first-century approach to the subject.

Adamson, Sylvia, Lynette Hunter, Lynne Magnusson, Ann Thompson, and Katie Wales, eds. *Reading Shakespeare's Dramatic Language: A Guide.* London: Arden Shakespeare, 2001.

This interdisciplinary collection draws on literary criticism, performance, and the history of language to explore both the similarities and differences between "the writing and language use" of Shakespeare's time and our own. The first part of the book, "The Language of Shakespeare's Plays," consists of twelve essays that bring together "an understanding of Renaissance rhetoric and modern conversation theory, with some issues of reading, writing, and staging": Ann Thompson, "Heightened Language"; Lynne Magnusson, "Style, Rhetoric and Decorum"; Sylvia Adamson, "The Grand Style"; George T. Wright, "Shakespeare's Metre Scanned"; Walter Nash, "Puns and Parody"; William C. Carroll, "Description"; David Scott Kastan, "Narrative"; Lynette Hunter, "Persuasion"; Lynne Magnusson, "Dialogue"; Pamela Mason, "Characters in Order of Appearance"; Peter Lichtenfels, "Shakespeare's Language in the Theatre"; and Keir Elam, "Language and the Body." The second part, "Reading Shakespeare's English," contains four essays that examine Shakespeare's sounds, grammar, and word-making strategies, in addition to his "rich repertoire of regional and social varieties": Katie Wales, "Varieties and Variation"; Sylvia Adamson, "Understanding Shakespeare's Grammar: Studies in Small Words"; Terttu Nevalainen,

"Shakespeare's New Words"; and Roger Lass, "Shakespeare's Sounds." The volume also includes a list of rhetorical terms and an annotated bibliography.

Crystal, David. *"Think on my words": Exploring Shakespeare's Language*. Cambridge: Cambridge University Press, 2008.

Crystal's introduction to the linguistic nuts and bolts of Shakespeare's language is governed by the principle that "one should never examine a linguistic nut or bolt without asking 'what does it do?' And 'what does it do?' means two things: how does it help us understand the meaning of what is said (a semantic explanation), and how does it help us appreciate the dramatic or poetic effect of what is said (a pragmatic explanation)?" The book's chapters cover Shakespearean graphology, punctuation, phonology, pronunciation, grammar, vocabulary, and conversational style. The epilogue, " 'Your daring tongue,' " locates the hallmark of Shakespearean linguistic creativity not in the words and expressions that Shakespeare coined but in an "economy of expression" that trades on the "relationship between lexicon and grammar" in "service of the poetic imagination." The appendix, "An A-to-Z of Shakespeare's False Friends," considers words that seem familiar but are not because their meanings have changed since Shakespeare's time (examples include "awful," "belch," "dainty," "ecstasy," "fancy," "honest," and "jog"). Two tables deal, respectively, with (1) shared lines in relation to the number of verse lines in the plays, and (2) the proportions of verse and prose in the plays. Notes, references, and suggested further reading conclude the study.

Crystal, David, and Ben Crystal. *Shakespeare's Words: A Glossary and Language Companion*. London: Penguin, 2002.

In this comprehensive compilation of Early Modern English vocabulary found in Shakespeare, the authors provide definitions of nearly 14,000 words along with treatments of selected language topics (e.g., frequently encountered words, archaisms, greetings, currency terms, and swearwords). To be included in the glossary, a word must "present . . . the reader with a difficulty arising out of the differences between Elizabethan and Modern English." Following the glossary is a series of "Shakespearean Circles" for each play, diagramming the family, social, and occupational relationships entered into by the characters; lines of connection between circles "identify important points of contact between different groups." Several appendices "collate . . . the way characters are named, the names of the people and places they talk about, and the foreign languages that some of them use." The editors also provide information on figures of classical mythology and nonclassical legend, religious beings and personalities, historical personages, and contemporary figures (factual and fictitious). The glossary is one part of the Crystals' larger digital project bringing computer-based Shakespeare resources into the Internet age. See their *Shakespeare's Words*, http://www.shakespeareswords .com/, which provides a list of all the definitions associated with a word. When one clicks on a particular definition, the user is directed to other instances in the canon where the same meaning applies. A concordance accompanies the *Shakespeare's Words* website.

Hope, Jonathan. *Shakespeare's Grammar*. London: Arden Shakespeare, 2003.

Commissioned as a replacement for E. A. Abbott's *Shakespearian Grammar* (see above), Hope's book is organized in terms of the two basic parts of speech, the noun and the verb. After extensive analysis of the noun phrase and the verb phrase come briefer discussions of subjects and agents, objects, complements, and adverbials. The book targets three different audiences: Shakespeare specialists who will utilize it as a reference grammar, general readers/beginners who will benefit from the descriptive grammar provided, and literary critics who potentially will put the volume's stylistic overviews to good use in their analysis, explication, and interpretation of Shakespeare's plays and poems. Hope aims "to present Shakespeare's idiolect (that is, his particular version of Early Modern English) within a coherent linguistic structure" that will enable readers "to get a sense of the interrelatedness of many of the features of Early Modern English."

Houston, John. *Shakespearean Sentences: A Study in Style and Syntax.* Baton Rouge: Louisiana State University Press, 1988.

Houston studies Shakespeare's stylistic choices, considering matters such as sentence length, treatment of subordinate clauses, and the relative positions of subject, verb, and direct object. Examining plays throughout the canon in roughly chronological, developmental order, he analyzes how sentence structure is used in setting tone, in characterization, and for other dramatic purposes. Houston pays extensive attention to the effects of certain rhetorical devices—e.g., asyndeton, syndeton, polysyndeton, parataxis, and hypotaxis—on sentence construction.

Johnson, Keith. *Shakespeare's English: A Practical Linguistic Guide.* Harlow: Pearson, 2013.

With chapters on phonetics, grammar, vocabulary, word usage, pragmatics, rhetoric, the printed word, and prosody, this guide examines Shakespeare's early modern English within the history of the English language as a whole. In addition to discussing rhyme, meter, and pronunciation, Johnson specifically explores declensions, pronouns, compounds, speech acts (such as curses, insults, and commands), archaic word choices and forms, word clusters, word order, wordplay, spelling, punctuation, and Shakespeare's use of Anglo-Saxon, French, and Latinate vocabulary. Along with the pervasive influence of Cicero's *De inventione* and the pseudo-Ciceronian *Ad Herennium* on the writing practices of Shakespeare and his contemporaries, Johnson considers the importance of such humanist works as Thomas Wilson's *The Arte of Rhetorique* (1553) and George Puttenham's *The Arte of English Poesie* (1589). Although criticism is not the author's purpose, he does on occasion offer readings to illustrate how Shakespeare's linguistic and rhetorical choices chart changes in a character's trajectory. Throughout the book Johnson reminds the reader of shifts in lexical meaning over the centuries.

Robinson, Randal. *Unlocking Shakespeare's Language: Help for the Teacher and Student.* Urbana, Ill.: National Council of Teachers of English and the ERIC Clearinghouse on Reading and Communication Skills, 1989.

Specifically designed for the high school and undergraduate college teacher and student, Robinson's book addresses the problems that most often hinder present-day readers of Shakespeare. Through work with his own students, Robinson found that many readers today are particularly puzzled by such stylistic characteristics as subject-verb inversion, interrupted structures, and compression. He shows how our own colloquial language contains comparable structures, and thus helps students recognize such structures when they find them in Shakespeare's plays. This book supplies worksheets—with examples from major plays—to illuminate and remedy such problems as unusual sequences of words and the separation of related parts of sentences.

Williams, Gordon. *A Dictionary of Sexual Language and Imagery in Shakespearean and Stuart Literature.* 3 vols. London: Athlone Press, 1994.

Drawing on theatrical works, broadside ballads, newsbooks, jestbooks, and pamphlets, Williams provides a comprehensive list of words and expressions to which Shakespeare, his contemporaries, and later Stuart writers gave sexual meanings. He supports his identification of these meanings by extensive quotations, which, taken together, reveal how the language and imagery of sexuality reflect both linguistic development and sociocultural change across the early modern period.

Wright, George T. *Shakespeare's Metrical Art.* Berkeley: University of California Press, 1988. (Reissued as a paperback in 1991.)

Wright examines "the basic forms of Shakespeare's iambic pentameter line, its relation to other patterns (such as short lines, long lines, and prose), its changes over his career, and, most of all, the expressive gestures and powers this system provides for Shakespeare and his dramatis personae." To better understand Shakespeare's achievement (the primary focus of chapters 5 to 16), the author historicizes it in the "context of the decasyllabic line [Shakespeare] inherited and strongly influenced." For Wright, Shakespeare's metrical art is the culmination of a metrical chain that "runs back to Chaucer," through the verse of Thomas Wyatt, George Gascoigne, Henry Howard (Earl of Surrey), Philip Sidney, Edmund Spenser, and Christopher Marlowe. Chapter 17 considers the "extravagant turns" the pentameter line would take in John Donne and John Milton. Chapter 14, "The Play of Phrase and Line," explores the "creative equilibrium" Shakespeare maintains between "the continually recurring metrical pattern and the rhythmic phrase," a balance he achieves by varying the placement of the line break from the traditional fourth syllable slot of earlier poets to any position in the line, thereby yielding "phrases of three, five, or seven syllables as readily as phrases of four or six." The result of such freedom, especially in Shakespeare's later plays, is a more flexible and "sinuous" iambic pentameter line. For Wright, "the drama of Shakespeare is played out not only through a dialogue of characters but also through a dialogue of differently formed and framed verse lines, which speak to each other and to us of the variety, grace, and plenitude of human speech and trouble." Three appendices conclude the volume: (1) "Percentage Distribution of Prose in Shakespeare's Plays," (2) "Main Types of Deviant Lines in Shakespeare's Plays," and (3) "Short and Shared Lines." (Chapter 14 first appeared in *Shakespeare Quarterly* 34 [1983]: 147–58.)

Shakespeare's Life

Baldwin, T. W. *William Shakspere's Petty School.* Urbana: University of Illinois Press, 1943.

Baldwin here investigates the theory and practice of the petty school, the first level of education in Elizabethan England, where boys from the ages of four or five until the age of seven would learn the rudiments of reading and writing, with the aid of a hornbook (a leaf of paper framed in wood and covered with a thin layer of translucent horn) that contained the letters of the alphabet (preceded by a cross), combinations of vowels, and the Lord's Prayer. Students also mastered ABC books (introductory books to a subject, usually in question and answer form), the Catechism from the Book of Common Prayer, and the Primer (a fuller version of the catechism with additional prayers and psalms). As Baldwin states, the goal of the petty school was "to teach to read and write always, and to cast accounts [numbers] frequently," but, more importantly, the "predominantly religious" curriculum aimed at providing children with the fundamentals (in both theory and practice) of their orthodox Protestant religion. Baldwin focuses on the petty school educational system primarily as it is reflected in Shakespeare's art; see, for example, references to the life of a typical schoolboy in *As You Like It* (2.7.152–54), to the hornbook in *Love's Labors Lost* (5.1.46–49) and *Richard III* (1.1.58–63), and to the ABC book in *King John* (1.1.202).

Baldwin, T. W. *William Shakspere's Small Latine and Lesse Greeke*. 2 vols. Urbana: University of Illinois Press, 1944.

Baldwin refutes the view that Shakespeare was an uneducated genius—a view that had been dominant among Shakespeareans since the eighteenth century. Instead, Baldwin shows, the educational system of Shakespeare's time would have given the playwright a strong background in the classics, and there is much in the plays that shows how Shakespeare benefited from such an education. Volume 1 deals with the evolution of the grammar school curriculum in the sixteenth century from 1509 to 1600; Baldwin devotes chapters to the work of Erasmus; the education of royalty; specific models such as the Winchester, Eton, Westminster, and Paul's systems under Queen Elizabeth; the King's Free Grammar School at Stratford; and the Latin curriculum of the lower grammar school. Turning in volume 2 to the curriculum of the upper school (primarily Latin and, to a lesser degree, Greek), Baldwin considers the emphasis on rhetorical training (by way of the key texts of Cicero, Erasmus, Susenbrotus, and Quintilian), prose and verse composition, Latin poets (namely, Ovid, Virgil, Horace, Juvenal, Catullus, and Seneca), moral history, and moral philosophy. As Baldwin concludes, "If William Shakspere had the grammar school training of his day—or its equivalent—he had as good a formal literary training as had any of his contemporaries. At least, no miracles are required to account for such knowledge and techniques from the classics as he exhibits. Stratford grammar school will furnish all that is required. The miracle lies elsewhere; it is the world-old miracle of genius."

Beier, A. L., and Roger Finlay, eds. *London 1500–1700: The Making of the Metropolis.* New York: Longman, 1986.

Focusing on the economic and social history of early modern London, the nine essays in this collection probe aspects of metropolitan life under the headings "Population and Disease," "Commerce and Manufacture," and "Society and Change." The essays are as follows: Roger Finlay and Beatrice Shearer, "Population Growth and Suburban Expansion"; Paul Slack, "Metropolitan Government in Crisis: The Response to Plague"; Margaret Pelling, "Appearance and Reality: Barber-Surgeons, the Body and Disease"; A. L. Beier, "Engines of Manufacture: The Trades of London"; John Chartres, "Food Consumption and International Trade"; Brian Dietz, "Overseas Trade and Metropolitan Growth"; M. J. Kitch, "Capital and Kingdom: Migration to Later Stuart London"; M. J. Power, "The Social Topography of Restoration London"; and Stephen MacFarlane, "Social Policy and the Poor in the Later Seventeenth Century." The collection reveals a London caught up in the redistribution of socioeconomic and political power, the result of developments in capitalism and changes in class structure.

Callaghan, Dympna. *Who Was William Shakespeare? An Introduction to the Life and Works*. Oxford: Wiley-Blackwell, 2013.

Callaghan devotes the first part of her study to an examination of Shakespeare's life in the context of the social, cultural (particularly theatrical), political, intellectual, and religious climate of early modern England. She carries this focus on period and context into the second half of the volume in short essays on twenty-four plays, grouped under the following headings: "Comedies: Shakespeare's Social Life," "English and Roman Histories: Shakespeare's Politics," "Tragedies: Shakespeare in Love and Loss," and "Romances: Shakespeare and Theatrical Magic." The strictly biographical portion of the book considers "three of the most significant issues that shaped Shakespeare's identity": education (chapter 2), religion (chapter 3), and social status (chapter 4). Callaghan contends that Shakespeare's grammar school education was "the most important factor in allowing him as a gifted individual to become a writer." Religion furnished more than the backdrop for Shakespeare's canon, forming instead "the crucible in which his secular drama was generated." Callaghan is not concerned with Shakespeare's religious affiliation ("staunch Protestant, devout crypto-Catholic, furtive nonbeliever, or the holder of any one of a range of positions in between"), but rather with the impact of the Reformation and religious persecution on his theatrical practice and "identity as a professional writer." Before turning to specific plays, Callaghan discusses the nature of theater as a new urban institution with a fixed location, the pressures of censorship on both performance and print, "the social and professional conditions that molded Shakespeare's theatrical career in London," and the "competitive environment of early modern theatre." Callaghan acknowledges that Shakespeare's life "cannot explain his works, but it can help us to understand them."

Cressy, David. *Education in Tudor and Stuart England*. London: Edward Arnold, 1975.

Cressy collects over 150 sixteenth-, seventeenth-, and early eighteenth-century documents detailing aspects of formal education that reflect "the efforts of governments, philanthropists, religious writers, social critics and other leaders of opinion, as well as schoolmasters themselves, to direct the educational enterprise" of early modern England. Cressy groups the items under eight categories: perspectives on education, control of education, the organization of schools, schoolmasters, the curriculum, educational opportunity, education of women, and the universities. The selected documents "illustrate some of the social and political pressures bearing on education in the period."

Duncan-Jones, Katherine. *Shakespeare: An Ungentle Life*. London: Arden Shakespeare, 2010.

This biography, first published in a slightly different version in 2001 under the title *Ungentle Shakespeare: Scenes from His Life*, sets out to look into the documents from Shakespeare's personal life—especially legal and financial records—and it finds there a man very different from the one portrayed in more traditional biographies. He is "ungentle" in being born to a lower social class and in being a bit ruthless and more than a bit stingy. As the author notes, "three topics were formerly taboo both in polite society and in Shakespearean biography: social class, sex and money. I have been indelicate enough to give a good deal of attention to all three." She examines "Shakespeare's

uphill struggle to achieve, or purchase, 'gentle' status."
She finds that "Shakespeare was strongly interested in
intense relationships with well-born young men." And
she shows that he was "reluctant to divert much, if any,
of his considerable wealth towards charitable, neigh-
bourly, or altruistic ends." She insists that his plays and
poems are "great, and enduring," and that it is in them
"that the best of him is to be found."

Enterline, Lynn. *Shakespeare's Schoolroom: Rhetoric,
Discipline, Emotion.* Philadelphia: University of Penn-
sylvania Press, 2012.
    Two questions inform Enterline's study of Shake-
speare's "career-long fascination" with the classical curriculum and humanist pedagogy of the early modern
grammar school: "How did [such] training influence
what counted as genteel masculinity in the period?" and
"How did early modern pedagogy affect experiences of
sexuality and desire?" Throughout the book, Enterline underscores "the significant difference between
what humanists claimed their [pedagogical] methods
would achieve [the formation of proper English gentlemen who would benefit the commonwealth] and
what the texts of at least one former schoolboy reveal
about the institution's unintended literary and social
consequences"—namely, the undercutting of the patriarchal social order that the educational system was
meant to reproduce. By assuming female roles in the
classroom, the boys learned to "identify with women
as they learned to voice the emotions needed for a persuasive oratorical performance." The introduction and
first two chapters focus on Shakespeare's grammar
school curriculum and Enterline's overall thesis con-
cerning "gender instability" in the pedagogical tradition of the time. The remaining chapters illustrate the
author's argument by way of particular poems or plays:
Chapter 3 deals with *Venus and Adonis*; chapter 4 with

The Taming of the Shrew; and chapter 5, with aspects of *Hamlet, Lucrece*, and *The Winter's Tale*.

Evans, Robert C. *Culture and Society in Shakespeare's Day*. New York: Chelsea House, 2012.
   Part of a three-part series titled *Backgrounds to Shakespeare* (the other two volumes are *Shakespeare's Life* and *Literature and the Theater in Shakespeare's Day*), Evans's illustrated overview gives historical and social-political context to the period 1564 to 1616, describing daily life as it was lived in three major centers of English existence: the countryside, London, and the royal court. Citing contemporaneous reports and comments, Evans sheds light on a diversity of topics: education; the enclosure movement and its impact on agricultural life; industries such as fishing, mining, and bricklaying; the rural poor, the rural aristocracy, and the rural parson as lawyer and doctor; courtier life, royal progresses, and the royal palaces of White-hall, Hampton Court, and Greenwich; the road system to London, English inns, and livery companies; and meals, domestic furnishings, and "sumptuary laws" specifying the proper attire for people of different ranks and occupations. Evans also includes "special features" on the rituals and customs associated with birth, marriage, and death; religious conflict in Shakespeare's England, folklore, superstition, and witchcraft; disease and medicine; and major events of the period (such as explorations of the New World, the Spanish Armada, and the Gunpowder Plot). Frequent quotation from the plays underscores connections between topics discussed by Evans and their treatment in the Shakespeare canon.

Manley, Lawrence. *Literature and Culture in Early Modern London*. Cambridge: Cambridge University Press, 1995.

Spanning the years 1475 to 1675, Manley's study of the image of London in and the city's influence on literature in the early modern period examines a variety of writings: lyrics, ballads, epics, satires, praises, plays, chronicles, treatises, sermons, official documents, pageants, and mayoral shows. Within two hundred years London was transformed from "a late medieval commune" of 35,000 inhabitants into a "rapidly changing metropolis of nearly half a million, the engine of an evolving early modern society, a capital . . . that would soon become the most populous in Europe," and a major European trading center. These changes brought "[n]ew possibilities . . . for cultural exchange and combination, social and political order, and literary expression." Among the many factors that led to making early modern London "the largest and most widely experienced human creation in Britain" were the rise of humanist learning and the impact of a print culture; "the emergence of . . . a national consciousness" that coincided with transformations of late medieval aristocracy; changes in the rural economy; the development of new class functions, "tied especially to commerce, bureaucracy, and law"; and "new types of religious . . . association." The volume's illustrations include representations of royal and civic ceremonies, emblematic images of personified early modern London, and contemporary maps of the city as a whole and of individual streets, processional routes, and areas such as Cheapside.

Manley, Lawrence, ed. *London in the Age of Shakespeare: An Anthology*. University Park: Penn State University Press, 1986.

A useful companion to Manley's later study (see above), this anthology seeks to "reflect the experience of London" during Shakespeare's time. The book's sixteen chapters excerpt writings published between 1485 and 1660; these include prose descriptions of the city, verse encomia, sermons, jestbooks, broadside ballads, satires and complaints, official records, civic myths, epigrams, poems of transit, erotica, and portrayals of London as found in stage comedy, character writing, and official pageantry. Challenges to social order—crime, disease, poor harvests, unemployment, and a growing and an increasingly diverse population—"animate the materials" gathered, underscoring how the literature of the period "amounts to a kind of city in itself, a polemical space in which competing visions and voices exert a productive influence on each other. . . . Emerging from the varied strands and forms of London life, and integrated with them, the London that was performed, imagined and sung was, in many ways, the London that was lived." As the items collected attest, Tudor-Stuart descriptions of London "reveal that a major corollary of the Renaissance discovery of man was the discovery of the city."

Potter, Lois. *The Life of William Shakespeare: A Critical Biography.* Malden, Mass.: Wiley-Blackwell, 2012.

This critical biography of Shakespeare takes the playwright from cradle to grave, paying primary attention to his literary and theatrical milieu. The chapters "follow a chronological sequence," each focusing on a handful of years in the playwright's life. In the chapters that cover his playwriting years (5–17), Potter considers events in Stratford-upon-Avon and in London (especially in the commercial theaters) while giving equal space to discussions of the plays and poems Shakespeare wrote during those years. Filled with information from Shakespeare's literary and theatrical worlds, the biography also shares frequent insights into how modern productions of a given play can shed light on the play, especially in scenes that Shakespeare's text presents ambiguously.

Schoenbaum, S. *William Shakespeare: A Compact Documentary Life*. New York: Oxford University Press, 1977.

Schoenbaum's evidence-based biography of Shakespeare is a compact version of his magisterial folio-size *Shakespeare: A Documentary Life* (New York: Oxford University Press, 1975). Schoenbaum structures his readable "compact" narrative around the documents that still exist which chronicle Shakespeare's theatrical, legal, and financial existence. These documents, along with those discovered since the 1970s, form the basis of almost all Shakespeare biographies written since Schoenbaum's books appeared. For Schoenbaum, "The story of William Shakespeare's life is a tale of two towns. Stratford bred him; London gave him, literally and figuratively, a stage for his fortune."

Shapiro, James. *Contested Will: Who Wrote Shakespeare?* New York: Simon & Schuster, 2010.

This historical investigation of the authorship controversy and its history explains "what it means, why it matters, and how it has persisted despite abundant evidence that William Shakespeare of Stratford wrote the plays attributed to him." Shapiro is able to date the onset of the controversy to the middle of the nineteenth century; he exposes as forgery documents purporting to backdate it to the eighteenth century. What gave rise to the controversy were the combination of "the presumption that Shakespeare could only write about what he had felt or done rather than heard about, read about, borrowed from other writers, or imagined" and the coincident deification of Shakespeare. So great was Shakespeare's reputation and so rich his presumed experience as it was abstracted from his writings that it became impossible for some to persist in associating him with the Stratfordian Shakespeare whose documented life consisted only of narrow legal and commercial interests. Once skepticism about Shakespeare's claim to have written his plays arose, more and more candidates for authorship began to be proposed—an activity that continues right up to the present. Shapiro acknowledges such contenders as Christopher Marlowe, Mary Sidney, the Earl of Derby, the Earl of Rutland, Sir Walter Ralegh, and Queen Elizabeth; his emphasis, however, falls on only two candidates, each of whom is the subject of a full chapter: Francis Bacon and the Earl of Oxford. For Shapiro, their candidacies are "the best documented[,] . . . most consequential [and] representative." The epilogue explains why the author thinks William Shakespeare wrote the plays and poems attributed to him.

Wolfe, Heather, curator. *Shakespeare Documented.* Digital Project. 2016. The Folger Shakespeare Library. Washington, D.C. See http://www.shakespearedocu mented.org.

Assembled by the Folger Shakespeare Library to commemorate the 400th anniversary of Shakespeare's death, this multi-institutional collaboration brings together the resources of the Folger, the Bodleian of Oxford University, the Shakespeare Birthplace Trust, the National Archives, and the British Library to provide the "largest and most authoritative" collection of primary source materials documenting the life of William Shakespeare. Materials include all known manuscripts and print references relating to the poet-playwright, his works, and family, including a letter addressed to him, manuscripts signed by him, and references to his coat of arms. Dating from his lifetime and shortly thereafter, the documents reveal a portrait of Shakespeare as a professional playwright, actor, poet, businessman, and family man who lived in both London and Stratford-upon-Avon. They trace his path "to becoming a household name," from the earliest reference to his father in Stratford (1552) through the publication of the First Folio in 1623 to the gossiping about him in the following decades. Images, descriptions, and transcriptions of 107 manuscripts that refer to Shakespeare by name, ninety-five printed books and manuscripts that mention or quote his plays or poems, and eighty-four printed editions of his plays and poems up to and including the First Folio point to "a remarkable legacy for someone of his socio-economic status and profession."

Shakespeare's Theater

Astington, John H. *Actors and Acting in Shakespeare's Time: The Art of Stage Playing.* Cambridge: Cambridge University Press, 2010.

Astington describes and analyzes the "cultural context of stage playing, the critical language used about it, and the kinds of training and professional practice employed" by actors on the early modern English stage from Richard Tarlton to Thomas Betterton. Drawing on recent discoveries "about actors and their social networks, about apprenticeship and company affiliations, and about playing [venues] outside" the theatrical center of London, this study compares "the educational tradition of playing in schools, universities, legal inns and choral communities . . . to the work of the professional players." In addition to portraying the early modern actor's versatility in playing many parts, Astington attends closely to the study of oratory in the grammar school curriculum and to the use of dramatic performance as a pedagogic tool, even at the university level, thereby underscoring the connection between "the performative arts of the stage and the select and remote realm of contemporary formal education." In the chapter "Players at Work," he uses Shakerly Marmion's *Holland's Leaguer* (1631) and Philip Massinger's *The Roman Actor* (1626) "to approach some of the pragmatics of a particular moment of theatrical production in the earlier seventeenth century." Astington concludes with commentary on changes in acting styles and the "social place" of actors: neither descendants from gentry nor university graduates, leading actors were, nevertheless, "of a social rank equal to the respectable citizens of London"; journeymen actors, however, lived "on the margins of poverty." An appendix provides a comprehensive biographical dictionary of all major professional actors in the years 1558 to 1660.

Berry, Herbert. *Shakespeare's Playhouses*. New York: AMS Press, 1987.

    With illustrations by Walter Hodges, Berry's six essays collected here discuss varying aspects of the four playhouses in which Shakespeare had a financial stake: the Theatre of 1576 in Shoreditch (the subject of two essays), the Blackfriars of 1596, the Globe of 1599, and the Globe of 1614. The final essay, "A New Lawsuit about the Globe," addresses the legal action brought by the King's Men in their efforts to seek an extension of their lease on the Globe property, which was due to expire in 1635. The four theaters at the core of Berry's study "embrace and virtually define the whole of the most remarkable period in English theatrical history."

Berry, Herbert, William Ingram, and Glynne Wickham, eds. *English Professional Theatre, 1530–1660*. Cambridge: Cambridge University Press, 2000.

This study of the English professional theater in the years designated consists of three parts: "documents of control," "players and playing," and "playhouses," each part divided into chapters with their own subdivisions. Wickham presents the government documents designed to control professional players, their plays, and playing places. Ingram handles the professional actors, giving as representative a life of the actor Augustine Phillips, and discussing among other topics patrons, acting companies, costumes, props, playbooks, provincial playing, and child actors. Berry treats the twenty-three different London playhouses from 1560 to 1660 for which there are records, including four inns. As he reminds us, "Probably nothing of the kind had happened in any other city on earth." The documents supporting the third part are primarily legal.

Cook, Ann Jennalie. *The Privileged Playgoers of Shakespeare's London.* Princeton: Princeton University Press, 1981.

Cook sets out to answer the question, "Who were the people for whom Shakespeare, Marlowe, Jonson, Webster, and their fellow dramatists wrote plays?" Were they "ignorant or intelligent, riotous or refined, libertine or law abiding, plebeian or privileged?" In contrast to Alfred Harbage (see below), Cook argues, on the basis of sociological, economic, and documentary evidence, that Shakespeare's audience—and the audience for English Renaissance drama generally—consisted mainly of the "privileged," a group that ranged "from the threadbare scholar or the prospering landholder, newly risen from the yeomanry, all the way up to nobility and royalty itself." Such an audience was ready-made, given the fact that the "privileged had long fostered the drama as schoolboys, as patrons, and even

as playwrights themselves." To claim that the "privileged" dominated the "plebeians" as playgoers is not to
say that they did so exclusively: "Ordinary people who
could afford the price of a ticket made their way to
attend a play on any given day, especially on holidays,
but not (as the economic and social pressures affecting
them demonstrate) in the numbers or frequency previ-
ously thought."

Dutton, Richard, ed. *The Oxford Handbook of Early
Modern Theatre*. Oxford: Oxford University Press, 2011.

Dutton divides his study of the theatrical industry of Shakespeare's time into the following sections:
"Theatre Companies," "London Playhouses," "Other
Playing Spaces," "Social Practices," and "Evidence of
Theatrical Practices." Each of these sections is further
subdivided, with subdivisions assigned to individual
experts. W. R. Streitberger treats the "Adult Playing
Companies to 1583"; Sally-Beth MacLean, those from
1583 to 1593; Roslyn L. Knutson, 1593–1603; Tom Rut-
ter, 1603 to 1613; James J. Marino, 1613–1625; and
Martin Butler, the "Adult and Boy Playing Companies
1625 to 1642." Michael Shapiro is responsible for the
"Early (Pre-1590) Boy Companies and Their Acting
Venues," while Mary Bly writes of "The Boy Compa-
nies 1599–1613." David Kathman handles "Inn-Yard
Playhouses"; Gabriel Egan, "The Theatre in Shoreditch
1576–1599"; Andrew Gurr, "Why the Globe Is Famous";
Ralph Alan Cohen, "The Most Convenient Place: The
Second Blackfriars Theater and Its Appeal"; Mark
Bayer, "The Red Bull Playhouse"; and Frances Teague,
"The Phoenix and the Cockpit-in-Court Playhouses."
Turning to "Other Playing Spaces," Suzanne Westfall
describes how " 'He who pays the piper calls the tune':
Household Entertainments"; Alan H. Nelson, "The
Universities and the Inns of Court"; Peter Greenfield,

"Touring"; John H. Astington, "Court Theatre"; and Anne Lancashire, "London Street Theater." For "Social Practices," Alan Somerset writes of "Not Just Sir Oliver Owlet: From Patrons to 'Patronage' of Early Modern Theatre," Dutton himself of "The Court, the Master of the Revels, and the Players," S. P. Cerasano of "Theater Entrepreneurs and Theatrical Economics," Ian W. Archer of "The City of London and the Theatre," David Kathman of "Players, Livery Companies, and Apprentices," Kathleen E. McLuskie of "Materiality and the Market: The Lady Elizabeth's Men and the Challenge of Theatre History," Heather Hirschfield of "'For the author's credit': Issues of Authorship in English Renaissance Drama," and Natasha Korda of "Women in the Theater." On "Theatrical Practices," Jacalyn Royce discusses "Early Modern Naturalistic Acting: The Role of the Globe in the Development of Personation"; Tiffany Stern, "Actors' Parts"; Alan Dessen, "Stage Directions and the Theater Historian"; R. B. Graves, "Lighting"; Lucy Munro, "Music and Sound"; Dutton himself, "Properties"; Thomas Postlewait, "Eyewitnesses to History: Visual Evidence for Theater in Early Modern England"; and Eva Griffith, "Christopher Beeston: His Property and Properties."

Greg, W. W. *Dramatic Documents from the Elizabethan Playhouses.* 2 vols. Oxford: Clarendon Press, 1931.

Greg claims that "generally speaking it may be said that for every piece in the repertory of an Elizabethan theatre company there must have existed three playhouse documents or sets of documents. First . . . was the Book, or authorized prompt copy. . . . Next there were the Parts of the several characters, written out for actors on long scrolls of paper. . . . Last there were the Plots, skeleton outlines of plays scene by scene, written on large boards for the use of actors and others in the playhouse." In the first volume, Greg itemizes and briefly describes almost all the play manuscripts that survive from the period 1590 to around 1660, including so-called prompt copies, players' parts, and plots. His second volume offers facsimiles and transcriptions of selected manuscripts associated with the playhouses. (For some other kinds of playhouse documents, see the books by Stern and by Werstine, below.)

Harbage, Alfred. *Shakespeare's Audience.* New York: Columbia University Press, 1941.

Harbage investigates the fragmentary surviving evidence to interpret the size, social composition, behavior, and aesthetic and intellectual capacity of Shakespeare's audience. He concludes that commoners, the plebeians, and not the privileged were the mainstay of Shakespeare's audience. In contrast to public theaters like the Globe, private theaters such as the Blackfriars were the domain of the upper levels of the social order. The book's seven chapters are titled "The Evidence," "How Many People," "What Kind of People," "Behaviour," "Quality: Elizabethan Appraisals," "Quality: Modern Appraisals," and "Our Shakespeares and Our Audiences." Two appendices provide, respectively, estimates of attendance and attendance charts. Harbage's view remained uncontested until Ann Jennalie Cook's argument for the privileged (see Cook, above).

Keenan, Siobhan. *Acting Companies and Their Plays in Shakespeare's London.* London: Bloomsbury Arden Shakespeare, 2014.

Keenan "explores how the needs, practices, resources and pressures on acting companies and playwrights informed not only the performance and publication of contemporary dramas but playwrights' writing practices." Each chapter focuses on one important factor that shaped Renaissance playwrights and players. The initial focus is on how "the nature and composition of the acting companies" influenced the playwrights who wrote for them. Then, using "the Diary of theatre manager Philip Henslowe and manuscript playbooks showing signs of theatrical use," Keenan examines the relations between acting companies and playwrights. Other influences include "the physical design and facilities of London's outdoor and indoor theatrical spaces" and the diverse audiences for plays, including royal and noble patrons.

Stern, Tiffany. *Documents of Performance in Early Modern England*. Cambridge: Cambridge University Press, 2009.

Stern interrogates "two competing current schools of thought on playscripts: whether surviving playbooks are ever fully representative of plays as they were performed ('performance texts') and whether playbooks are ever fully stripped of the theatre to become plays in an ideal literary form ('literary texts')." Singling out the label "play-patcher," one of several used to identify playwrights in Shakespeare's time, she argues that despite its pejorative connotation, the term accurately depicts the patchwork nature of dramatic texts "made from separate documents." Stern's extensive examination of early modern playscripts allows her to consider the many papers created by authors and theaters before the actual opening performance of a play. These documents, each treated in its own chapter, are as follows: plot scenarios; playbills and title pages; "arguments" as programs and as "paratext"; prologues and epilogues (often drawn up on pieces of paper separate from the play they flanked and not necessarily by the author(s) of the rest of the text); songs ("completed and sometimes written by composers, and disseminated to be learned separately"); scrolls (including such property documents as letters, proclamations, bills, and verses that were to be read aloud during a performance); backstage plots ("profoundly theatrical document[s]" that hung in the tiring-house and that provided detailed stage entrances, including the properties needed by actors when onstage); and, finally, actors' parts. What lies behind a theatrical production in the early modern English theater, then, was not "any single unified [and authorized] book" but rather a "patch-work" of parts "easily lost, relegated or reused," always open to continual revision and to new configurations for subsequent performances. Taken together, the performance documents explored by Stern were "the play," a conclusion that not only "redefin[es] what a play actually is" but also redefines "what a playwright is"—namely, a "play-patcher." Unlike the "whole artworks [that] poems" were considered to be, "plays had the bit, the fragment, the patch in their very natures." (For accounts of extant playhouse manuscript books and quartos used as playbooks in the theaters, see Greg, above, and Werstine, below.)

The Publication of Shakespeare's Plays

Blayney, Peter W. M. *The First Folio of Shakespeare.* Hanover, Md.: Folger, 1991.

Blayney's accessible account of the printing and later life of the First Folio—an amply illustrated catalogue to a 1991 Folger Shakespeare Library exhibition that showcased twenty-four of the Folger's First Folios—analyzes the mechanical production of the First Folio, describing how it was made, by whom and for whom, how much it cost (probably a retail price of 15s for an unbound copy), and its ups and downs (or, rather, downs and ups) since its printing in 1623. Blayney contends that probably no more than 750 copies were printed. Among the topics discussed are the order of the pages, the importance of casting off (the process of setting a Folio quire by first estimating just what text would fit in the first six pages), stop press corrections, the portrait of Shakespeare, the belated inclusion of *Troilus*, and the activities of Henry Clay and Emily Jordan Folger, the founders of the Folger Shakespeare Library, as collectors.

Hinman, Charlton. *The Norton Facsimile: The First Folio of Shakespeare.* 2nd ed. New York: W. W. Norton, 1996.
This facsimile presents a photographic reproduction of an "ideal" copy of the First Folio of Shakespeare; Hinman attempts to represent each page in its most fully corrected state. The second edition includes an important new introduction by Peter W. M. Blayney, which consists of four sections: "The First Folio and Its Publishers," "The Players and Their Manuscripts," "The Proofreading," and "The Printing" (which includes a table listing the pages of each play in the order in which they were set and the "more reliable compositorial reattributions that have been offered since 1963"). A significant feature of the Hinman facsimile is its "through line numbering" system (TLN), based on the lines printed in 1623 rather than on the acts, scenes, and lines of a modern edition.

Hinman, Charlton. *The Printing and Proof-Reading of the First Folio of Shakespeare.* 2 vols. Oxford: Clarendon Press, 1963.
Prior to the 2012 publication of Eric Rasmussen and Anthony James West's descriptive catalogue of the Shakespeare First Folios (see Rasmussen and

West, below), Hinman's attempt to reconstruct how the Shakespeare First Folio of 1623 was set into type and run off the press, sheet by sheet, was the most arduous study of a single book ever undertaken. This two-volume celebration of the 1623 collection—based on a thorough examination of many of the eighty-two copies of the First Folio in the Folger Shakespeare Library—also identifies individual compositors and provides almost all of the variations in readings from copy to copy; it was thus a seminal work for future editors and bibliographical scholars.

Murphy, Andrew. *Shakespeare in Print: A History and Chronology of Shakespeare Publishing.* Cambridge: Cambridge University Press, 2003.

Murphy's comprehensive account of Shakespeare publishing provides a discursive history of the most editorially significant texts of Shakespeare's poems and plays (both single and collected editions) published in Britain and America between the years 1593 and 2002. Focusing on the circumstances surrounding the publication and the reception of these printed texts, the eleven-chapter history begins with coverage of the early quartos and the early collected editions—Folios 1 (1623), 2 (1632), 3 (1663–64), and 4 (1685). Murphy then moves on to the "emergence of a theoretically self-conscious tradition of Shakespeare editing" in the eighteenth century (with its "market-leading 'celebrity-edited'" collected works), followed by chapters on nineteenth-century popular and scholarly editions, the New Bibliography of the early twentieth century (established by W. W. Greg, R. B. McKerrow, A. W. Pollard, and John Dover Wilson in his Cambridge New Shakespeare), and, turning to the later twentieth century, such publications as the selectively modernized *Riverside Shakespeare* and the "bold . . . and experimental" Oxford Shakespeare. The history section of the volume concludes with an examination of the electronic and hypertext editions of the twenty-first century, which reveal technology to be as important as textual theory. An annotated chronology of more than 1,700 editions constitutes the second part of the book, with five helpful indexes organizing the annotated editions by play/poem title, series title, editor, publisher, and place of publication (excluding London).

Rasmussen, Eric, and Anthony James West, eds. *The Shakespeare First Folios: A Descriptive Catalogue.* Basingstoke: Palgrave Macmillan, 2012.

While biographies of Shakespeare, performance studies of the plays, and accounts of the Folio's pre-publication history abound, "little has been offered on the relationship of the First Folio's post-publication history to Shakespeare's reception and recognition over the centuries." The editors of this catalog—the result of twenty years of research during which 232 surviving copies of the First Folio were located and carefully examined—seek to remedy this situation by providing "full bibliographic descriptions of each extant copy, including accounts of press variants, watermarks, damage or repair, leaves in facsimile, annotations, bindings, end-papers, bookplates, and provenance [including lists of ownership]." Praising the editors' meticulous description of each copy, Paul Werstine writes in the catalog's preface that Rasmussen and West take their place beside the monumental efforts of Charlton Hinman (see above). Werstine singles out as the editors' "greatest gift to Shakespeareans[:] . . . their significant expansion of our knowledge of the extent to which press corrections have interposed themselves between manuscript printer's copy . . . and the early printed texts of the plays." Because of their labors in producing a complete record of press variants in all accessible volumes, future editors "can provide Shakespeare's readers with editions of the [eighteen] Folio plays based on fully informed decisions about which printed variant has the highest probability of reflecting the manuscript from which the text was printed."

Werstine, Paul. *Early Modern Playhouse Manuscripts and the Editing of Shakespeare*. Cambridge: Cambridge University Press, 2012.

Werstine examines in detail nearly two dozen texts associated with the playhouses in and around Shakespeare's time, conducting the examination against the background of the two idealized forms of manuscript that have governed the editing of Shakespeare from the twentieth into the twenty-first century—Shakespeare's so-called foul papers and the so-called promptbooks of his plays. By comparing the two extant texts of John Fletcher's *Bonduca*, one in manuscript and the other printed in 1647, Werstine shows that the term "foul papers" that is found in a note in the *Bonduca* manuscript does not refer, as editors have believed, to a species of messy authorial manuscript but is instead simply a designation for a manuscript, whatever its features, that has served as the copy from which another manuscript has been made. By surveying twenty-one texts with theatrical markup, he demonstrates that the playhouses used a wide variety of different kinds of manuscripts and printed texts but did not use the highly regularized promptbooks of the eighteenth-century theaters and later. His presentation of the peculiarities of playhouse texts provides an empirical basis for inferring the nature of the manuscripts that lie behind printed Shakespeare plays.

Key to
Famous Lines and Phrases

He hath indeed better bettered expectation than you must expect of me to tell you how.
[*Messenger* —1.1.15–17]

How much better is it to weep at joy than to joy at weeping! [*Leonato* —1.1.27–29]

He is a very valiant trencherman . . .
[*Beatrice*—1.1.50]

. . . the gentleman is not in your books.
[*Messenger*—1.1.76–77]

". . . Benedick the married man." [*Benedick*—1.1.262]

. . . as merry as the day is long. [*Beatrice*—2.1.49]

Speak low if you speak love. [*Prince*—2.1.97]

. . . it keeps on the windy side of care.
[*Beatrice*—2.1.307–8]

I was born to speak all mirth and no matter.
[*Beatrice*—2.1.322–23]

. . . I will tell you my drift. [*Prince*—2.1.378]

He was wont to speak plain and to the purpose . . .
[*Benedick*—2.3.18–19]

He hath a heart as sound as a bell . . .
[*Prince*—3.2.11–12]

Are you good men and true?   [*Dogberry*—3.3.1]

. . . you may say they are not the men you took them
for.   [*Dogberry*—3.3.46–47]

. . . they that touch pitch will be defiled.
[*Dogberry*—3.3.56]

Not for the wide world.   [*Benedick*—4.1.304]

. . . there was never yet philosopher
That could endure the toothache patiently . . .
[*Leonato*—5.1.37–38]

. . . some of us will smart for it.
[*Leonato's Brother*—5.1.122]

What though care killed a cat? Thou hast mettle
enough in thee to kill care.   [*Claudio*—5.1.145–47]

. . . I was not born under a rhyming planet . . .
[*Benedick*—5.2.40–41]